London Gin

The Gin Craze

Thea Bennett

GGP

First published in the UK in 2013 by Golden Guides Press Ltd.

10 8 6 4 2 1 3 5 7 9

Copyright © Thea Bennett, 2013

The right of Thea Bennett to be identified as the Author of the Work has been asserted by her in accordance with the Copyright, Designs and Patent Act 1988.

A CIP catalogue record for this book is available from the British Library.

ISBN 978-1-78095-008-2 (paperback)
ISBN 978-1-78095-054-9 (Mobi)
ISBN 978-1-78095-055-6 (ePub)

Typeset in Palatino by Mac Style, Driffield, East Yorkshire.
Cover design by Mousemat Design Ltd.
Printed and bound in the UK.
Ebook produced by ePubDirect

Golden Guides Press Ltd
P.O. Box 171
Newhaven
E. Sussex
BN9 1AZ
UK
admin@goldenguidespress.com
www.goldenguidespress.com

Thea Bennett

LONDON GIN
The Gin Craze

To Robert Connor and Kate van Millingen

Contents

Introduction

GIN. SAY the word, and your palate is already tingling in anticipation of those subtle herb, spice and citrus flavours that give a shock of pleasure like nothing else. The invigorating, yet also relaxing, hit of a gin and tonic at the end of a long, hard day is a non-negotiable ritual for many of us. It's got something of the familiar and refreshing qualities of that other very British institution, the cup of tea, but the exotic blend of flavours and the fizz of the tonic offer a lift to the spirits that tea just can't quite match. No wonder that gin has been a firm favourite with the British ever since it arrived here, in the guise of 'Geneva', at the end of the Seventeenth Century.

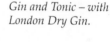

Gin and Tonic – with London Dry Gin.

Chances are that, as you pick up a bottle to pour out your measure of gin, you will see the words 'London Dry Gin' on the label. But have you ever thought what this really means?

There's been a long and sometimes stormy relationship between the quintessential English drink and the capital city, which dates back to the Gin Craze of 1720–1751, epitomised in Hogarth's iconic print, *Gin Lane*. And there's a strong connection, too, between this diverse spirit and London's once-thriving Docks, which brought into the heart of the capital the exotic ingredients so essential to the flavour of gin.

But the name 'London Gin' is also, in these days of EU red tape, a formal definition. According to the EU specification laid down in February 2008, so long as the gin is distilled according to strict guidelines, it doesn't have to be produced in London. As long as it satisfies these criteria, a gin made in Scotland, or even in California, may bear the proud title 'London Dry Gin' on its label, and it will give you the same taste and texture qualities as the gins produced in the capital.

But surely it's the long association with London's history and with its people that gives London Gin its very special allure – a little touch of magic that buys in to a mix of tradition and anarchy – of pleasure, escapism, and above all, enjoyment.

The essence of gin is embedded in the very paving stones of the capital and in the bricks and mortar of those old houses and hidden courtyards than have withstood the passage of time. Go back almost four hundred years, to the height of Gin Craze and, in some areas, you'd find one in four habitable buildings housing a still, and you'd be able to buy a cheap 'dram' not just from a public house or a corner shop, but also from the many vendors pushing their wheelbarrows through the streets. You can imagine the many instances of drunken and riotous behaviour that resulted from this. An inevitable clampdown followed – but it took five Acts of Parliament to deal with the excesses of the gin-lovers.

Once the Craze was quelled, gin slowly gained respectability. Through the Victorian era, glittering Gin Palaces replaced dowdy and disreputable dram-shops and wheelbarrows. You can still visit many of these cut-glass extravaganzas, now doing duty as Public Houses. As the British Empire expanded across the globe, our colonial soldiers and administrators came to rely upon a nightly gin and tonic or two, utilising the quinine-rich tonic to ward off the dangers of malaria.

Gin drinking wasn't just a British habit. In the late-Nineteenth Century, cocktails were being invented across the Atlantic and, as the Twentieth Century dawned, the Titanic and her sister ships boasted several different brands behind their on-board bars. Prohibition reigned between 1920 and 1930 – but it didn't stop American gin-lovers making their own version in their bathtubs. Raymond Chandler's hero, private detective Philip Marlowe, notoriously loved a Gimlet cocktail (see *Chapter Sixteen*).

Back on this side of the pond, cocktails grew in popularity, too – all through the Prohibition years, rich Americans came over on the new trans-Atlantic flights to

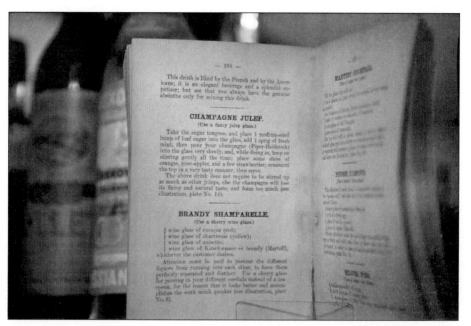

A copy of The Savoy Cocktail Book *at the Ginstitute Museum, 171 Portobello Road.*

drink at our bars and clubs. *The Savoy Cocktail Book*, published in 1930 by Harry Craddock of the American Bar at the Savoy, still inspires today with its hundreds of mouth-watering recipes.

For a while, in the 1970s and 1990s, gin suffered a decline in popularity. Vodka was the thing, especially for the younger generation. But things have changed since those days. It's great, now that the Twenty-first Century is well under way, to see younger drinkers in my local pub choosing from the different brands of gin behind the bar – and to hear them discussing the merits of Bombay Sapphire, Hendrick's, Beefeater 24 and Sipsmith.

This sudden appearance of new brands of gin in my local is just one sign of the new Gin Craze that's taking hold in the capital and beyond. Traditional distillers are creating new brands to entice younger drinkers to embrace gin. And there are new kids on the block, too. Enthusiasts are setting up new, small-scale distilleries in London to create high-quality artisan gins that bring a whole new lease of life to the traditional delights of the cocktail. There's even a brand that's been designed to taste good when mixed with coke or cranberry juice. It's Hoxton Gin. And you, too, if you like, can bring your creative powers to bear on the spirit by using ready-distilled botanicals to bespoke your very own blend of gin (see *Chapter Twenty-one*).

The London connection is as important to the new gin-makers as it has always been to the old-established names like Beefeater – named for the iconic red-clad residents of the Tower of London. One new distiller makes a regular pilgrimage several times a week to the spring where the Thames rises in Gloucestershire, to ensure that the water used in making his gin is from London's great River – going right to the very source to ensure the necessary purity.

As a Londoner born and bred, I'm proud of my heritage. And I love the fact that the history and diversity of the great city where I grew up is reflected in the culture and the origins of my favourite drink. Gin is all about people. It's about the wisdom and passion, the experience and bold innovation, of so many connected with the gin industry – from the Master Distillers whose lineage in the craft stretches back for generations to the trend-setting young 'mixologists' who are concocting the latest luscious cocktails.

The following chapters will take you right to the heart of London Gin. As you use this book to learn how it came into being, hear what the contemporary distillers are up to, explore the wonderful flavours of the spirit, and last-but-not-least meet the botanicals – the herbs, spices, seeds, fruits and barks that make their own special contribution – you'll realise the truth of the saying that gin is 'history in a glass'.

Sit back and relax, take your glass in hand, and let the story begin …

Part One

Chapter One

The Early History of Gin

Timeline

Late 700s to early 800s AD – Arab scientists invent the alembic still (*al-anbiq*) and experiment with distilling alcohol

Early 1100s – spirituous liquors are made at the medical school in Salerno, Italy, using alcohol made from grapes

1500s – the Dutch experiment with distillation of a grain 'mash'

1600s – *Genever* – grain-based alcohol flavoured with juniper berries comes on the scene

Mid-1600s – English soldiers bring *genever*, or 'Dutch Courage', home from the Thirty Years War

Late-1600s – after the Restoration of Charles II, *geneva*, also known as 'strong water flavoured with Juniper' joins other flavoured spirits which were popular as remedies and prophylactics against the plague and other ills

Dutch Courage

W E'RE in the Low Countries, in the place we now call Holland. It's the mid-Seventeenth Century. Picture a bedraggled troop of English soldiers, shivering in the icy wind that cuts like a knife as it blows in unobstructed across the flat landscape. The men have had a long, hard campaign – one of many in the Thirty Years War that dragged on from 1618 until 1648 –and now there's another battle to fight. Up ahead, their Dutch opponents are shouldering pikes and muskets, ready to attack. But before they make a move, the Dutchmen huddle together round a wooden hogshead. They pass a rough leather cup from hand to hand as they gulp down the liquid it contains. The Englishmen watch with alarm as the enemy, with a sudden surge of energy, spring forward to the attack, their faces red with battle rage.

Did you know?

Dutch grain spirit flavoured with juniper was encountered by the French when they were fighting in Holland before the Thirty Years War. They called it *eau de genièvre* – 'juniper water'. The English preferred to use the name 'Geneva'- somewhat less of a mouthful for them than the French word. 'Geneva' has no connection with the Swiss city, being an imitation of the Dutch *genever*.

What was the elixir the Dutch soldiers had just imbibed, the secret weapon that produced such an instant and galvanising effect upon them? It was a local, rough grain spirit, flavoured with juniper berries, which had been distilled in the Low Countries for around a hundred years. The Dutch word for juniper was *genever* – and they named this invigorating liquor after the berries that gave it its distinctive taste. It wasn't long before the English soldiers had got hold of some of this *genever* for themselves, and discovered its remarkable ability to inspire them with a reckless bravery in combat. They brought it back to England with them and called it 'geneva'.

Did you know?

It was during these campaigns in the Lowlands that the expression 'Dutch Courage' – still in regular use today to describe the morale boost gained from taking a quick alcoholic drink before tackling a challenging situation – was coined.

Genever – the Mother of Gin

It is impossible to put an exact date on the first appearance of *genever* in Holland, but it is likely to have been first distilled some time in the mid-1600s.

Grain spirit was a relatively new development at this time. Spirits made from wine had been around for more than five centuries, distilled mostly in southern Europe, where grapes grew in abundance. The Dutch called this grape spirit *brandewijn*, meaning 'burnt wine', from which we get the name 'brandy'.

Did you know?

Distillation of spirits was known to the Arabs, who invented the alembic still. In Europe, distillation of liquors for healing purposes began at a medical school in Salerno, Italy, in the early Twelfth Century. The clear, slightly oily liquid that dripped from the still was called *aqua vitae* – 'the water of life'. It was thought to have similar properties to the magical and mysterious 'Philosopher's Stone' that alchemists strove to create.

The name of another famous spirit – 'whisky' – comes from the Gaelic *usque beatha* also meaning 'water of life'.

The countries of northern Europe were slower to develop the distilling process than their sunnier neighbours, due to the lack of home-produced wine. Holland was one of the first countries to experiment with using a grain wash – similar to that used in brewing beer – in the 1500s. This grain spirit didn't taste as pleasant as the more mellow *brandewijn*, and needed flavouring with fruits, herbs and spices to make it palatable.

Did you know?

Gin differs from other spirits in that it's a 'compound spirit'. This means it has been distilled twice – once to make the pure grain spirit, and then one more time with the botanicals – the herbs, spices and fruits that give the distinctive flavour.

A Dr Sylvius of the University of Leyden is widely credited with the discovery that the addition of bitter juniper berries to the distilling process helped to mask the grain spirit's musty taste. The strong, spicy tang of juniper, coupled with the fiery roughness of the spirit made *genever* a wonderful antidote to the dark, cold winters of the Lowlands. From the start, it was considered to have medicinal properties, and was sold by apothecaries as a remedy for all sorts of ailments including gout, gallstones and upset stomachs.

On a more basic level, when snow lay deep on the ground, a few sips from the stone bottle that you carried with you in your deep coat pocket would help keep at bay the pain of your icy feet and your frozen face and hands.

Dɪd yoʊ knoⱳ?

There's been some confusion around the identity of the fabled Dr Sylvius. In Volume One of their recent book, *Spirituous Journey: A History of Drink*, Jared Brown and Anistatia Miller draw attention to the fact that there were two Doctors called 'Sylvius' at the University of Leyden in the mid-Seventeenth Century – Dr Franciscus de la Boe and Dr Sylvius de Bouve. Most often, you will see Franciscus de la Boe's name in texts about the early history of gin. However, it seems more likely that it was Dr de Bouve who would have experimented with adding juniper berries to spirit. He specialised in the digestive tract, and in research into remedies, while his younger contemporary Dr de la Boe focussed his studies on the brain.

Geneva Comes to England

Our soldiers brought *genever* with them when they returned from the Thirty Years War, and it joined an array of flavoured spirits that were already being produced here on a small scale, mostly for medicinal purposes. After the execution of Charles I in 1649, England was ruled by Oliver Cromwell and, under his Puritan regime, consumption of alcohol was frowned upon, along with other recreational activities such as theatre-going and Christmas.

Any distillers that were in operation were tightly controlled by The Worshipful Company of Distillers, which had been granted a monopoly by Charles I in 1638, 11 years before his death.

When the monarchy was reinstated and Charles II returned to the throne in 1660, things improved a little for the distilling industry. But, just as in Holland, the grain spirit produced in England was not pleasant to drink in its own right. It needed flavouring.

Daniel Defoe, writing at the height of the Gin Craze in 1726, harks back to some of the 'strong waters' – as these flavoured spirits were known – that were popular just after the Restoration. He lists:

Genever is still made in Holland – a modern bottle of Bols Genever *copies the shape of the old stone bottles.*

- Aniseed Water
- *Aqua Dulcis*
- *Aqua Mirabilis*

- *Aqua Solis*
- *Aqua Vitae*
- Cinnamon Water

- Clove Water
- Plague Water

Did you know?

The medicinal aura that surrounded distilled spirits – or 'strong waters' as they were often called – is reflected in the make-up of The Worshipful Company of Distillers. When Sir William Brouncker was invited to set it up by Charles I, he invited two doctors to join him. They were Sir Theodore Turquet de Mayerne, physician to the King, and Sir Thomas Cademan, the Queen's personal doctor.

Last but not least, Defore includes 'Colic Water' which, he says: 'was Geneva.' In more recent times, the term 'Colic Water' has become associated with remedies for digestive discomfort in babies and young children. The 'Colic Water' Defoe lists would have been stronger stuff. Intended primarily for soothing the troubled stomachs of adults, it was basically a strong spirit flavoured with juniper berries – hence his linking it with *genever*. And we can see from the inclusion of 'Plague Water' and such mysterious names as '*Aqua Mirabilis*' that distilled spirits with the addition of certain herbs and spices were still seen as having a medicinal effect.

For a long time, it was the aniseed flavour that was most popular, especially with Londoners, giving our home-distilled spirits a similar flavour to the rough local ouzo or raki that you might encounter on a holiday abroad.

Did you know?

During the Restoration period 'Aniseed Robin' was a well-known character who was seen wandering up and down Leadenhall Street in the City of London. He was easily recognised by the broad-brimmed hat hanging down around his ears, and the plentiful supply of his favourite aniseed-flavoured spirit, which he always carried with him.

So, it's clear that although the juniper spirit our soldiers had named Geneva was here in London by the time of the Restoration, it was merely one of many 'strong waters' available to the populace. It took another 40 years, and the deposition of Charles II's successor, King James II, before it became the Londoners' favourite drink, and the Gin Craze erupted on the streets of the capital.

Chapter Two

The Glorious Revolution

A Time of Change

B Y 1688, the Thirty Years War was long over. England was no longer at war with the Dutch. Quite the opposite. The events that came to be known as The Glorious Revolution saw the end of the Stuart dynasty when the unpopular, autocratic Catholic King James II was deposed. His nephew and son-in-law, the Stadtholder of the province of Orange in Holland, took his place, ruling jointly with Queen Mary, his wife.

It wasn't long before the fiery spirit of William's homeland was beginning its astonishing rise to popularity, due to a series of actions taken by the new King of England.

Timeline

1688 – Thirty Years War ends

1689 – Immediately after his accession, William III declares war on France, where the deposed James II has taken shelter with Louis XIV

1689 – In a manoeuvre calculated to hit the French brandy trade, William bans the importation of foreign spirits

1690 – William ends the Company of Distillers' 50-year monopoly on the distillation of spirits

Also in **1690**, an Act of Parliament is passed 'to encourage the distilling of brandy and spirits from corn'. It dramatically reduces the excise dues payable on any spirit distilled from English malted grain from 12d to 1d

Early 1700s – London's rapidly expanding population grows to 600,000 making it by far the largest city in England

1720 – South Sea Bubble bursts

Late 1720s – The Gin Craze takes off

Just as happens today with the imposition of trade sanctions between nations at war, William's 1689 ban on the import of spirits was, in effect, a boycott on French brandy. It was intended to bring economic pressure as well as military force to bear upon the England's new enemy.

This was hard-hitting, since French brandy was far more pleasant to drink than our native spirits, and was very popular in England, especially with the upper classes. The ban was rescinded in 1692 but the duties imposed on imported spirits were increased until they were prohibitively high for all but the very wealthy. War being a very costly business, William was looking for ways to finance his conflict with France.

But there were other ways to generate money from distilled spirits than raising the duty on imports. To encourage the proliferation of English distillers – and hence revenue to the Crown – William ended the 50-year monopoly of the Company of Distillers. Anyone who could afford the expense of a vat and a still was free to set up as a distiller. This was very unusual in an era when trades were, in general, very tightly controlled. Brewers of ale, for example, were still subject to very strict regulation. And, if you wanted to work as a baker, shoe-maker, carpenter or tailor, you couldn't do so without enrolling for an expensive and arduous seven-year apprenticeship. But William wasn't just being philanthropic in freeing up the distilling industry. War with France was proving expensive, and more people making spirits created more opportunities for the King to make money from the resulting duties.

As well as needing money to fund his war against France, William III was concerned about his reception as a Dutch King by his English subjects. He needed to know that they accepted him, and he was especially eager to secure support from the English landowners who formed the main power base in Parliament. The 1690 Act of Parliament that reduced tax on the distillation of British grain gained him huge popularity with the landowning classes, who now had a market for their substandard corn which wasn't of sufficient quality to be sold to bakers to make bread.

The new breed of independent distillers were quick to take advantage of the new Act, which meant that they paid just 1d per gallon of spirit distilled from malted British corn – as opposed to 12d duty per gallon on spirit distilled from any other materials.

The duty on 'low wine' – the low-proof product that resulted from a first round of distillation – was normally 12d per gallon. But now, low wine made from British corn incurred a duty of only 1d. A distiller didn't need to be a mathematician to see the way forward to making a good profit.

There were two problems. One was the quality of the grain spirit. Made from damaged and poor quality corn, it often tasted awful. The other was the lack of skill of the distillers. Historically, English distillers had used all kinds of spices to disguise this musty, unpleasant tang – but they lacked the experience and skill

---

Did you know?

The distillers of William III's time would first make a fermented wash (similar to the wash created when brewing beer). This could be made from corn, or wine, or fruit – almost anything. The distillation of this wash produced a weak spirit called 'low wine', with a low proof strength. This was put through the still again, to bring it up to proof strength, and was then sold on to a 'compound distiller' who would distill yet again, adding flavourings such as aniseed or juniper.

---

of their Dutch counterparts. And now, with any private citizen able to become a distiller – simply by posting up a notice informing the public that he was going to do so – there was even less likelihood of a pleasant-tasting result.

Despite this, the new legislation was hugely successful. It generated a tidal wave of cheap grain spirit that even poorly-paid workers and domestic servants could afford to drink. But distillers were now so numerous that it was all too easy for them to side-step even the modest legislation that applied to them. They were happy to use the very worst, rotten and foul corn that was available and they used whatever strongly-flavoured additives they could find to disgust the rank taste. Pepper, ginger, even oil of turpentine (which somewhat resembles juniper, but is much cheaper) were added to the list of spices used. Juniper, though, was still very important. So much so that these rough new spirits were known as 'Geneva' – a direct Anglicisation from the Dutch *genever*.

If you were to take a sip of this Geneva, you'd be hard put to find any resemblance to the refined, pure gin we enjoy today. Distillers strove to improve their products, but an advertisement in *The Daily Journal* of 2nd January, 1736 shows that they had made little progress over the last three decades. It offers: 'GENEVA, of the Right HOLLAND Sort, (made in *London*) the most different thing in the World from the *English* Geneva.' It was clear that, while some good quality liquor was available, there was still a lot of substandard spirit being made.

This didn't halt the rise to popularity of flavoured grain spirit with the ordinary Londoners. They revelled in this cheap new drink that was so much quicker than the traditional ale in bringing on a rush of warmth and intoxication. Soon, the folk in the slums had transformed the word 'Geneva' into an easy-to-say monosyllable – Gin.

The Streets of London

It wasn't just the availability of cheap gin that led to its huge popularity. London in the early 1700s was going through a process of rapid change – and change can generate insecurity and anxiety, creating a need for comfort in the people it affects. For many, gin brought that comfort.

With a population of 600,000, London was by far the largest city in England, and it was also growing very fast. More than 5,000 people a year came to the capital from the country, leaving behind the traditional, regimented way of life they had experienced for generations to seek new opportunities.

If you were a rural labourer life was set firmly in the same straight, muddy furrow that had bound your forefathers to the land for centuries. Long hours of back-breaking work in all kinds of weather; damp, overcrowded and insanitary accommodation; very low pay and a lack of secure employment were all you had to look forward to. And, in a small, rural community where your face was well-known to everyone you encountered, it was impossible to step out of line, or to dream of rising above your station.

In London, things were very different. You could don whatever finery you wished and, if you could afford the one-shilling entrance fee, you could take yourself to the Pleasure Gardens at Vauxhall. There, royal dukes mingled with humble merchants, and a proud aristocrat might find himself standing next to his tailor. You could meet a hundred different people in the space of just an hour and none of them would have any idea who you were. You would be taken at face value.

It must have very invigorating for a new arrival to the capital to suddenly have the freedom to reinvent him or herself, but Daniel Defoe, writing in 1725, is disapproving as he describes a young country girl arriving in London to take up a post as a servant:

> *her Neats-Leathern shoes … are transform'd into Laced-ones with light heels; her Yarn Stockings are turn'd into fine White-ones … and her high Wooden Patterns are kick'd away for Leathern Clogs. She must have a Hoop, too, as well as her Mistress; and her poor scanty Linsey-Woolsey Petticoat is chang'd into a good Silk one … In short, plain Country Joan is now turn'd into a fine London Madam, can drink Tea, take Snuff, and carry herself as high as the best.*

Not all the newcomers were lucky enough to gain employment as domestic servants – a role which, despite long hours and low pay, at least guaranteed a roof over your head. Many of these incomers had no connections in London, and no regular work. They settled in what was then Middlesex, now known as the West End of London, in the crowded and filthy slums around Holborn and St Giles. Within the walls of the long-established City of London, trades and guilds and parish regulations maintained a certain order and decorum. But, outside these walls, in the rapidly growing built-up areas of Westminster and also in the East End of London, things were very different.

Many rich aristocrats were now building luxurious neo-Classical Palladian homes for themselves in what is now the West End, on what had very recently been

---

Did you know?

Take an imaginary stroll through some of London's familiar landmarks as they were in the Eighteenth Century, and you will be astonished at the juxtaposition of extreme wealth and dire poverty. As you stand outside The Theatre Royal on Drury Lane, you'll see the rich and aristocratic theatregoers arriving in their luxurious carriages to enjoy a night's entertainment. But leave the theatre and walk down Drury Lane, and you will soon find yourself in the narrow, fetid, chaotic streets of St Giles, one of the poorest parishes in London, with soaring crime rates. Here, the houses are known as 'rookeries', for the occupants are crammed inside the rooms like birds in a nest.

You'll be very relieved to keep walking to the west, for soon, as you emerge from the stinking, noisy slums, you'll see the elegant frontage of Montague House, an imposing building on the site of the present British Museum. Walk a little further and you will breathe even more easily as you enter the elegant environs of Bloomsbury Square, built only a few years ago and now home to many wealthy aristocrats.

---

fields and farms. But these elegant buildings often found themselves cheek by jowl with a warren of twisting alleyways and crumbling courtyards, where the poor lived in conditions of incredible squalor, often renting a share of a room, or even of a bed, for as little as a penny a night.

Most people, unless they actually lived there, took good care to stay away from slums like St Giles. Quite apart from the open sewers running down the middle of the streets, filled with human waste, dead dogs, and the by-products of such noisome industries as the local slaughterhouses and the fullers, there was the risk of being killed by falling masonry. *The Gentleman's Magazine* of July 1758 reports a common incident, when an:

> *old lodging house in … St Giles … fell down … seven poor wretches were crushed to death and many more desperately maimed. There being other houses in the court in the like tottering condition, the mob assembled … and pulled them down.*

These treacherous buildings were crammed with inhabitants. In a house of four storeys, with two rooms on each floor, there might be four or five beds in each room, with two or sometimes as many as eight occupants in each. (The price of a double bed was just 3d per night.) Some had to sleep in garrets up under the roof tiles; hot in summer, freezing in winter. The most unfortunate were housed in the cellars, below street level, where they had to endure the seep of effluent from the street above.

In these dire circumstances, some turned to crime. Others struggled to get ahead by maintaining a veneer of success and respectability. An anonymous writer from 1752 describes:

> *would-be gentlemen, naked in back-garrets, boiling water in earthen chamberpots …*
> *to wash their sham necks, ruffled sleeves and worn-out roll-up stockings, that they*
> *may make a genteel appearance in the public streets and walks at noon.*

The South Sea Bubble

In return for a loan to finance the high national debt accumulated during the war against France, the House of Lords passed the South Sea Bill, which allowed the South Sea Company a monopoly in trade with South America. The Government would pay interest on the debt, while making money from the trade. Investors flocked to buy shares.

It wasn't just the poor who were seeking transformation through the early 1700s. A spirit of restlessness was abroad in London, and there were unprecedented opportunities for even the aristocracy to add to their reserves of wealth, as The South Sea Company was set up, offering investments with a very high return. For a time, London went wild. So many people swarmed to Exchange Alley to buy shares that tables had to be brought out and set up in the street. Even domestic servants flocked to buy shares, and were to be seen flaunting their new riches by driving through the streets in their own carriages.

Shares immediately rose to 10 times their value and fortunes were made. In the hope of making even more money, all sorts of companies were set up, many of them fraudulent. One such claimed to manufacture a gun to fire square cannon balls. Others simply refused to reveal what their activities might be, simply claiming them to be 'of great advantage' to the investor.

Financial speculation of this type can be addictive. The highs engendered when hopes and dreams ignite provide an escape route from the dreary reality of a life of poverty. There can be a heavy price to pay. The South Sea Bubble burst in 1720, when the price of stocks crashed, with disastrous results for those who had gambled their financial security to make a quick killing.

Soon, the tragedy was turning to farce. Respectable members of the clergy had to forfeit their life savings. Aristocrats were forced to sell their properties. Domestic servants – the footmen and ladies' maids who had given up their employment in order to ride in their new horse-drawn vehicles – found themselves destitute. Suicide was a regularly-reported occurrence, among all classes.

The Bubble Bursts

1720 saw an end to the great tide of speculation that had swept through London, engulfing rich and poor alike.

In June – Shares were worth £1,000

By August – They were valued at £750

In October – They had fallen to just £290, and were still dropping

But there was another, cheaper, far more reliable source of escape available. The abolition of controls and regulations for the distilling of English grain had led to a flood of cheap spirits onto the streets of London. The next thirty years – 1720–1730 – were to see the rise of a new hysteria. The Gin Craze had begun.

Chapter Three

The Gin Craze

Timeline

These dates and figures plot the astonishing rise and fall of the Gin Craze.

1730 – as the Craze began, records show **6,658,788** gallons of gin are being drunk – and that's the 'official' spirit. Many more gallons are being purchased from the unofficial wheelbarrows on the streets of London

1736 – there are between **6,000** and **7,000** dram-shops in London

1750 – the amount of gin being consumed has risen to **11,326,070** gallons. In the Parish of St Giles, every fourth household is selling gin. In Westminster, every eighth house sells gin, and every fifteenth in the City of London

1751 – **9,000** children die from the effects of gin

1752 – the Craze is ebbing. Just **7,500,000** gallons are drunk

1767–68 – The Craze is over. Consumption has fallen to **3,663,568** gallons

'Such simple stuff as poor souls are glad to drink ...'

AT FIRST, through the 1720s, the increase in gin production and consumption seemed like a good thing. Landowners were making profits and agricultural workers were kept in employment. The more people bought and drank gin, the more revenues went to the Exchequer.

Everyone was happy – including the gin-drinkers. British distillers might not have had the skill and expertise of their Dutch counterparts but Defoe commented that they had 'found out a way to hit the palate of the poor by their new-fashioned compound waters call'd Geneva; so that the common people seem not to value the French brandy as usual, and even not to desire it.'

However, things soon began to get out of hand. Before the reforms of William III, around 500,000 gallons of spirits – *aqua vitae* – were produced in England, and most of these were for medicinal use. Over the next 15 years, that figure had quadrupled. By 1720, just before the South Sea Bubble broke, London alone was

Did you know?

Writer Daniel Defoe was one of the literary giants of the Eighteenth Century. The huge success of his novels *Robinson Crusoe* and *Moll Flanders* (both still loved by readers and adapted many times for TV and film) brought him public acclaim, and he was the most well-known journalist in London during the years of the Gin Craze. At the start of the Craze, he was very supportive of the gin distillers. In his tract, *A Brief Case of the Distillers and the Distilling Trade in England*, published in 1726, he wrote: 'The distilling trade, considered in its present magnitude is one of the greatest improvements, and the most to the advantage of the publick, of any business now carried on in England'. Like many journalists through the ages, he was soon to be heard expressing the opposite point of view when he became one of the most vociferous opponents of gin.

producing 2,500,000 gallons of proof spirit. Some of this raw spirit would have been exported, but the vast majority went to the small compound distillers, to be made into gin.

Consumption on the streets of London crept ever higher. Life was hard for the lower classes. There were no certainties, especially for those newcomers to the city who had no settled employment. For those who did have work, it often involved long hours of back-breaking toil.

Life was particularly tough for those who had to labour out of doors. It's easy to see how a dram of gin could warm your cold limbs, raise your flagging spirits and bring cheer to your heart.

Did you know?

The hardships endured by the working people in that era were immense. A washerwoman could expect to work an 18-hour day; either at home, getting up at four and working until late at night; or at her employer's residence, where she would often arrive before the domestic servants were out of bed, and would have to wait outside, on winter days, in the cold and the dark. She would be using hard soap, or 'bucking' – a substance made from wood ash and urine. And there were no rubber gloves to protect her hands. A tailor would work a 14-hour day, crouched hunchbacked over his stitching as he sat cross-legged on a wide bench. In summer, he might sit by the window to get the benefit of the daylight. In winter, it was a case of straining his eyes by candlelight. And all that for just a couple of shillings a day.

Did you know?

The Mutiny Act of 1720 contained a provision exempting any retailer who was also a distiller from having soldiers billeted with him or her. (At this time, there were no barracks for the troops to use. They were boarded out with tradesmen such as chandlers, tobacconists or innkeepers.) The advantages of setting up a still were twofold. You could make a profit from the gin you sold, and you were released from any obligation of having to look after a group of hungry soldiers. Which, of course, meant that even more gin was available to buy.

In 1725, a market-woman spoke for many of her kind when she gave evidence to the Magistrates' Quarter Session: 'We stand all weathers and go thro' thick and thin. It's well known, that I was never the woman that spar'd my carcass; and if I spend three farthings now and then, in such simple stuff as poor souls are glad to drink, it's nothing but what's my own. I get it honestly, and I don't care who knows it; for if it were not for something to clear the spirits between whiles and keep out the wet and cold; alackaday! It would never do! We should never be able to hold it; we should never go thorow-stitch with it, so as to keep body and soul together.'

No wonder that, by 1723, the total figure for spirits production in England was hitting 3,250,000 gallons, and that four-fifths of that total was being made in London. A pint of gin – that's 16 shots – a week was being drunk by every Londoner – by men, by women, and by children, too.

A Poisonous Dram

The gin that found its way into the cups of the slum-dwellers of St Giles took many forms. It was often tinted with burnt sugar or sweet prune juice, which gave it a whisky-like colour. You'd be lucky to find juniper, coriander or cardamom, the fragrant keynotes of gin today, included in the list of additives.

A gentleman called Ambrose Cooper wrote a guide to distilling in 1757. His *Complete Distiller* gives extensive descriptions of plants, seeds and fruits that can be distilled to make medicinal remedies. He comments that apothecaries' shops used to keep a 'distilled spirituous Water of Juniper but the Vulgar being fond of it as a dram, the distillers supplanted the apothecaries and sold it under the name of Geneva. The common sort is not made from juniper berries as it ought to be but from Oil of Turpentine.'

Did you know?

Not all the health problems suffered by the poor who enjoyed a frequent dram could be attributed to the spirit itself.

As well as **oil of turpentine**, which has a pine-resin tang similar to juniper though much harsher on the palate, the gin distillers often used such additives as **oil of almonds** – a strong-tasting, cheap substitute for the more expensive coriander and other exotic spices; **sulphuric acid** – this gives an extra bite to the spirit, and makes it seem stronger when diluted; **pepper** and **ginger**, which create a burning effect in the mouth, mimicking the affect of a strong hit of alcohol and, once again, make the gin seem stronger than it actually is, and even a poisonous alkaloid – *Cocculus indicus*. Also known as '**hard maltum**' this was more commonly used as a pesticide and, when ingested caused confusion and even collapse.

The 'gin' flavoured with these noxious substances could be stirred into beer to make a drink called 'purl', but most often it was diluted with water and sold in quarter pints, also known as 'quarterns'.

Alarm bells were beginning to ring. In 1726, a committee of justices reported that gin was being sold everywhere, by landladies and street-corner vendors. Londoners couldn't go anywhere without being invited to partake of a dram. You could even get hold of gin if you were incarcerated in Newgate Prison, or if you were receiving the Eighteenth Century equivalent of Social Security, and were reduced to living in the Workhouse.

The results of this high consumption of poor quality spirit were starting to show. There were very high levels of crime and prostitution in the slums as men and women turned to whatever means they could to get money for their gin habit. Even more worrying, people were falling sick at alarming rates. Official figures show that, in 1723, the death rate in London had overtaken the birth rate. It showed no signs of falling in 1726 and stayed ahead for the next ten years. By drinking gin instead of (or often as well as) ale, London's poor were not just turning to crime, they were destroying their health.

The committee of justices found bad news everywhere. Gin drinkers were desperately poor, and yet were reluctant to work. They were often involved in vicious street fighting. They had so many health problems that they were dying faster they could reproduce.

Gin's role in the breakdown of family life was of particular concern to the committee of justices. The sight of intoxicated females receiving the immoral advances of predatory males was shocking enough, but when mothers were seen

---

Did you know?

'Madame Geneva' was a popular name for gin at this time, perhaps because women were so often seen both drinking and selling it. Madame Geneva is shown, in many engravings of the time, as a blowsy, large female, often in a state of undress.

---

to be offering gin to their young children, even to the infants they were carrying in their arms, this caused outrage.

Those children who were still at their mother's side were the lucky ones. Many youngsters were left at home while their parents roamed the streets squandering their money on 'Madame Geneva'. With neither clothes to wear, nor bread to eat, these children either ended up in the Workhouse, or lived on the streets eking out a precarious existence from begging and petty crime.

You will hear a little later of the tragic history of once such child, abandoned by her mother and taken in to the Workhouse to be cared for.

The Clampdown Begins

By 1727, Daniel Defoe was beginning to change his mind about the benefits of gin. In *The Complete English Tradesman*, he attacked the compound distillers – the small-scale operators who produced gin in their homes and shops. He described them as ne'er-do-wells who 'carry on their trade as if they were always drunk, keep no books but their slate, and no pen and ink but their chalk and tallies... They are a collection of sinners against the people, for they break almost all the known laws of Government in the Nation.'

A new monarch, George II, came to the throne in 1727. Two years later, the government passed the first Gin Act, in a disastrously ineffective attempt to curb the rise of Madame Geneva.

The Gin Act of 1729

This Act placed a duty of 2 shillings per gallon on compound spirits – which, of course, meant gin. Any retailer wishing to sell spirits had to take out a licence that cost £20.

The Act was made with the very best of intentions. It only succeeded in making the situation worse. The quality of gin – already not good in most cases – deteriorated, and its production and sale became the focus of criminal activity.

Now, if you craved a dram of cheap gin you had to turn to the back-street distillers who were guilty of producing the poorest quality spirit. Any honest and reputable trader who might have sold decent gin in the past was now unable to afford to do so. And, as with any illegal trade, a rash of touts and runners and protectors sprang up on the streets.

In spite of the 1729 Act, gin consumption in London continued to grow. Sales rose from 3,500,000 gallons in 1727 to almost 6,500,000 gallons in 1735.

The Gin Act of 1733

Following the spectacular lack of success of the 1729 Act, the Government tried again in 1733. The duties and license fees of the previous Act were repealed. However, now the sale of spirits on the streets was banned. A fine of £10 for selling spirits – *except in dwelling houses* – was introduced.

You can imagine the glee with which the slum-dwellers learned of this. If a householder wanted cheap gin, all he had to do was set up his own still at home, or invite a distiller to do so – who would thus avoid paying the £10 fine. The result was even more cheap gin for the poor – and most likely free gin, too, if you had a still in your home.

The 1733 Act was dependent on informers, who were supposed to identify illegal hawkers and bring them to the attention of the magistrates who would then convict them. But, since most of the informers came from the same underclass as those they were spying on, they were most unlikely to cause trouble for their friends, family, and next-door-neighbours who might be making a little money from selling gin. Also, though informers were entitled to a reward of £5 for each gin seller they brought to justice, they only received this if the wrong-doer paid the fine. Most of the hawkers were far too poor to do this, and were sentenced to hard labour instead. So the informer got nothing for all the risk and hard work. This scheme was doomed from the start.

The Tragic Cost of a Dram

The printed *Proceedings of the Old Bailey* tell the sad story of a young woman – Judith Defour. One Sunday evening in January 1734, Judith arrived for her night shift at a 'throwsters' (an establishment where silk was twisted and spun ready for weaving). She was drunk. Her workmates thought nothing of this. After all, girls were often still tipsy after a Sunday off.

At one o'clock in the morning, Judith sent out for a dram of gin. Her employer had an arrangement with the local dram-shop and would deduct the money from her wages at the end of the week. The fix didn't last long and, soon, Judith was desperate for another dram. Her friend Susan Jones advised her to have something to eat instead and gave her penny to buy bread and cheese. Judith came back with some bread and a ha'porth of gin.

Did you know?

A dram – often used as a general term for a small amount of spirit, as in 'a wee dram', is in fact 1/8 of a fluid ounce. In 1660, the contents of a teaspoon were considered to be 'a dram'.

Having drunk her gin, the sozzled Judith confessed that she had done something very bad – 'something that deserved Newgate.' Susan was worried her friend had done something wrong at work, and would be in trouble with the 'mistress'. But Judith confessed to something far more shocking. She had left her two-year-old child out all night in a field in Bethnal Green.

Susan knew that Judith had an illegitimate daughter, Mary, who was being kept at the Bethnal Green Parish Workhouse. She knew that Judith had been to visit the little girl on Sunday and had taken her out for the day. She believed that Judith's mother had returned Mary to the Workhouse, and was horrified to hear that this was not the case. As she told the Court, she reprimanded Judith: '*What?* says I, '*in such a dismal cold night? How can you be so cruel?*'

Judith told Susan it wasn't her fault. A woman called Sukey had made her do it. Susan Jones was very concerned for the safety of the child, and set off with Judith and another workmate, Elizabeth Scot, to try and find Mary. In the early hours of that freezing January morning, they passed the George public house in Bethnal Green, and set off across the cold fields. Judith was heading for a tumbledown shack. Suddenly, she stopped in her tracks. She seemed numb and confused, as if from the effects of the gin she had just drunk. But then Susan looked down and saw the tiny figure of a child 'strip and lying dead in a ditch, with a linen-rag tied hard about its poor neck.'

A local man, John Wolveridge, was woken by the clamour of voices shouting that a child had been murdered. A crowd was gathering in the fields now, and the parish wardens had been summoned. Later, he told the Court that he had asked Judith how she 'could be so barbarous as to murder her own infant?'

At first Judith would only reply that she had undressed the child at about seven o'clock in the evening, and then left her in the ditch but, after John Wolveridge continued to interrogate her, she suddenly burst out: 'Then, sir, I will tell you how I did it; but there was a vagabond creature, one Sukey, that persuaded me to it; and was equally concern'd with me. On Sunday night we took the child into the fields, and stripp'd it, and ty'd a linen handkerchief hard about its neck to keep it from crying and then laid it in a ditch. And after that, we went together, and sold the coat and stay for a shilling, and the petticoat and stockings for a groat. We parted the money, and joined for a quartern of gin.' John describes Judith as being 'in an agony of grief' as she said this.

The Court heard that little Mary had recently been given these clothes by the parish, and that her mother had exclaimed at how smart she looked when she went to pick her daughter up from the Workhouse on Sunday morning. Mary spent all day with Judith, while the young woman drank gin with someone called Susanna – or 'Sukey'. At about six o'clock in the evening they ran out of money. Sukey suggested selling Mary's clothes and leaving her in a field. The child would be all right. Someone would probably find her and look after her. The two women went ahead with this plan, but, as Judith explained, every time she started to walk away, Mary cried. So they 'ty'd a linen rag very hard about the child's neck, to prevent its crying out, which strangled her, and afterwards they went together, leaving the child dead.'

The two women sold the clothes for sixteen pence and spent it all on gin.

This story was fuel to the anxious Members of Parliament and also to the zealous reformers of the Society for Promoting Christian Knowledge. Here was a horrific case which highlighted all their concerns. A young woman who drank gin while at her work, who had an illegitimate child, who had cheated the welfare system, and who was guilty not only of neglect and appalling cruelty towards her daughter, but of murder. A woman, in other words, who completely turned aside from her role as a mother. And it was all because of gin.

A committee of justices set up to investigate the problems caused by gin were also concerned about its effects upon unborn children. In 1736, the committee expressed grave concern about the weak and sickly babies that were being born to mothers who habitually drank gin. These babies were described as looking shrivelled – as if they were of great age rather than extreme youth. And, once again, the practice giving of gin to young children caused outrage. Infants, even before they could walk, were getting a taste for the spirit.

Things were not looking good for Madame Geneva.

The Gin Act of 1736

There was now no doubt of the failure of the 1733 Gin Act. The magistrates reported that, since 1729, the number of retailers selling spirits had risen from 6,187 to 7,044 – though there was some doubt as to the accuracy of this figure, since the constables who came up with the figures were many of them in the business of retailing gin themselves. Along with a vast number of chandlers, weavers, tobacconists, shoemakers, barber, tailors, dyers and others.

Parliament went straight to work, drafting a Bill which would put an end to this. The Bill, shortly to become the 1736 Gin Act, laid down that:

… no person shall presume, by themselves or any others employed by them, to sell or retail any brandy, rum, arrack, usquebaugh, Geneva, aqua vitae, or any other distilled spirituous liquors, mixed or unmixed, in any less quantity than two gallons, without

first taking out a licence for that purpose within ten days at least before they sell or retail the same; for which they shall pay down £50, to be renewed ten days before the year expires, paying the like sum, and in case of neglect to forfeit £100, such licences to be taken out with the limits of the penny post at the Chief Office of Excise, London, and at the next Office of Excise for the country. And be it enacted that for all such spirituous liquors as any retailers shall be possessed of on or after September 29th, 1736, there shall be paid a duty of 20s. per gallon, and so in proportion for a greater of lesser quantity above all other duties charged on the same.

With such high licence fees and duties, the price of gin would now be pushed so high that only the very rich could afford to drink it.

Robert Walpole – a pre-eminent and highly influential member of the Cabinet, subsequently considered to be Britain's first *de facto* Prime Minister – was worried. He had opposed the Act, believing that it was impossible to enforce. He also believed that the majority of gin shops were so small and poor that it wouldn't be worth prosecuting them.

He was also afraid that the slum-dwellers would be so enraged at the loss of their gin that they might erupt into violence on the streets. He took precautions against this, as the *Daily Post* of 29th September reported:

… a double guard was mounted at Kensington; at noon the guard at James's, the Horse Guards and Whitehall were reinforced and last night about 300 life-guards and horse-grenadier guards paraded in Covent Garden, in order to suppress any tumult that might happen to arise at the going down of Gin.

All however, remained quiet – for now. The riots would come later.

Chapter Four

Madame Geneva Fights Back

S THE Government strove to limit the consumption of gin, ordinary Londoners made their opposition very clear.

Timeline

1736 – On the eve of the Gin Act of this year, public demonstrations take place in many cities. Also in **1736** – Captain Dudley Bradstreet sets up in business to sell gin 'at the Sign of the Cat'

1737 – The Government pass The Sweets Act – another blow to the gin-sellers

1737–38 – Riots take place on the streets of London

A Very Public Grief

If you were out and about on the streets of London on the eve of the implementation of the 1736 Act, you might have the bizarre sight of a funeral procession passing by, with the full-blown figure of Madame Geneva laid flat upon a bier. She was given a good send-off by her heart-broken devotees. Mock funerals were not just staged in London, but also in Plymouth, Bristol and Norwich. Geneva, dressed in voluminous, if revealing robes, was placed on a large float and ragged through the streets by her drunken entourage. All along her route, the signs hanging outside public houses and gin shops were swathed in black. The country was in deep mourning.

Emotions were so extreme that some of Madam Geneva's disciples chose to take their own lives rather than carry on without her. The *Daily Post* of 24th September reports that a bricklayer 'being too deeply affected at the approaching fate of his idol, and resolv'd not to see that unhappy day, took a rope, went upstairs, shut himself in, and hang'd himself up to a staple drove into a beam in his room.' A few days later, a man who sold spirits and wine on Leadenhall Street slashed his throat with a razor.

Poets, ballad-writers and dramatists took up the cause. One who styled himself 'Jack Juniper, a Distiller's Apprentice, just turned Poet' penned a verse drama titled *The Deposing and Death of Queen Gin, with the ruin of the Duke of Rum, Marquess de*

Nantz, and the Lord Sugarcane, etc. In it 'The Mob' declaimed this inflammatory line: 'Liberty, Property, and Gin for ever!'

Not everyone was swept along by the tide of tumultuous emotion. A black-bordered leaflet entitled *An Elegy on the Much Lamented Death of the most Excellent, the most Truly-Beloved, and Universally-admired Lady, Madam Gineva* was, in fact, a tongue-in-cheek satire on the overblown outpourings of grief and outrage.

As the hours counted down to Act becoming law on 24th September, Londoners pawned their worldly goods to buy quarts and gallons of gin for a final drink. Some distillers were giving the spirit away – since they would now longer be able to sell it.

All through the night of the 23rd, crowds marched through London, following their beloved Madam Geneva and howling curses against Prime Minister Walpole. As the fateful day dawned, hundreds of them littered the pavements, snoring in a drunken stupor. They were too incapacitated by their overindulgence to commit the violence that Walpole had dreaded.

Despite the hysteria, things soon returned to normal. It wasn't long before the familiar wheelbarrows were trundling up and down the streets again. The liquid they were selling didn't look like gin but, once sampled by the eager public, there was no doubt that's what it was. Since a wine licence cost only a few shillings, as opposed to the prohibitive £50 for a gin licence, it was all too easy to add some wine and a bit of colouring to illegally distilled gin, and pass it off as wine. And this adulterated spirit didn't cost much more than before the Act. Things were drifting back to the way they were.

Of all the thousands of distillers in London, only two approached the Excise Office to take out the £50 licences. Once again, the government's attempt to vanquish Madam Geneva had failed.

Did you know?

A recent arrival to the ranks of Twenty-first Century premium London Gins is £50 Gin – so-called after the £50 licence fee of 1736. Aimed initially at the Spanish market, though distilled and bottled in London, it has a distinctive bottle shape – similar to the old stone bottles.

The Gin Legislation of 1737

The government had to act quickly. They did so under the guise of The Sweets Act of 1737. (This Act has nothing to do with confectionery – English fruit wines of the Eighteenth Century were known as 'Sweets'.)

The Sweets Act reduced the duty on these wines, a welcome move for the West Indian sugar merchants, who could no longer rely on the rum market due to the regulations against spirits. It was hoped, too, that with cheaper wines on sale, the lower classes would forget about gin.

But there was another blow to the gin-sellers, tacked on in the form of some clauses at the end of the Act. These introduced legislation that promised informers a guaranteed financial reward for catching a gin-hawker.

It should have been a simple matter to bring the illegal gin-sellers to justice, now that the informers would be properly paid for their work. But this was not the case. The fears that Prime Minister Robert Walpole had expressed back in 1736 were now shown to be well-founded. The gin-lovers were about to start fighting back.

Riots

A couple of months before the Sweets Act, the *London Evening Post* of 17th January had reported an unpleasant incident in Hanover Square – one of the elegant residential areas that were being built in London's West End. A mob of rowdy slum-dwellers had made an effigy of an informer called Pullin, who had informed against a food-seller who sold 'spirituous liquors'.

The *Evening Post* described the scene: '… he [the effigy of Pullin] was fixed on a chair pole in Hanover Square, with a halter about his neck, and then a load of faggots placed round him, in which manner he was burnt in the sight of a vast concourse of people.' The sight must have been a terrifying one to the alarmed residents of the big houses nearby.

Did you know?

Magistrates in the Eighteenth Century had a wide range of responsibilities. Not only did they pass judgement on crimes, they also investigated them. They undertook activities that are now the province of the police, local councils, social services and highways agencies. Magistrates received no money for this, and had no training. They were supposed to be gentlemen of private means, which would make them immune to bribery. Thomas De Veil wasn't a typical magistrate. He was exceptionally hard-working and ambitious and had risen from humble origins as an apprentice and a soldier, and after winning a commission in the dragoons he returned to civilian life and took up office on the Commission of Peace for Middlesex and Westminster. He gained the attention of those in power after breaking up a gang of thieves and surviving an assassination attempt in 1735, and was working out of an office in Leicester Fields (now Leicester Square) which became a court of summary justice.

One of the Middlesex Magistrates who were responsible for the area, Thomas De Veil, spent the whole of that night collecting fines from the riotous gin-sellers, and sending them to Bridewell House of Correction. His zeal and hard work had little effect. There was much worse to come.

In the very same month that the Sweets Act was passed, the violence accelerated – and this time it was for real. An informer named Briat – a farrier by trade – bought half a pint of Geneva from a distiller called Mound, telling him that he needed the spirit to give to an ailing horse. When Briat took the gin to the Excise Office and informed against Mound, he was attacked by a mob and pelted with stones and brickbats. In July, another informer was thrown into the Thames, and almost lost an eye as he struggled to save himself from the wrath of his attackers.

The attacks against informers grew in violence. On 20th October, as reported in the *London Evening Post*, an informer suffered a savage attack outside a cook's shop, while in the process of spying on the proprietor. A crowd 'beat him with sticks, kicking him about in a terrible manner, dragged him to dunghill in Bishop's Court, St Martin's, and there buried him for time with ashes and cinders.'

The owner of the cook's shop was committed to Bridewell by Thomas De Veil for selling illegal gin, but the man who informed on him never received his due reward of £5. He died a few days later of the injuries received during the attack.

Even those who sought sanctuary at De Veil's substantial home in Thrift Street in Soho (now Frith Street) weren't safe. On 19th November the *Evening Post* reported

---

The Riot Act

The Riot Act was passed in 1714, in response to a fear that Jacobite mobs might rise up and attempt to overthrow the Hanoverian King George I. It was designed to help local magistrates gain control of mobs and stem potential riots.

It contained the words: 'Our sovereign Lord the King chargeth and commandeth all persons, being assembled, immediately to disperse themselves, and peaceably to depart to their habitations, or to their lawful business, upon the pains contained in the Act made the first year of King George, for preventing tumults and riotous assemblies. God save the King.'

Once a magistrate had read the Act, the riotous persons had one hour in which to disperse, or else be arrested.

After the Hanoverian monarchs became established, The Riot Act faded into obscurity. It was rarely called upon through the Nineteenth and Twentieth Centuries though it remained on UK statue books until it was repealed in 1973. It has now been superseded by the Public Order Act of 1986.

that an informer tried to seek sanctuary at the magistrate's house. This man was 'almost ready to expire, being terribly beat, cut and bruis'd, and all over mire, that it was impossible to guess he was a man but by his walking, he being, (as it seemed) one entire lump of dirt.'

The informer didn't arrive at De Veil's door alone. He was accompanied by his tormentors, who were so unruly that the magistrate was forced to read the Riot Act to them. Luckily, this had the desired effect and the mob dispersed.

The situation was becoming extremely volatile. Despite the efforts of the informers, spurred on by their financial incentive, and the speed with which De Veil and his fellow-magistrates dispatched the convicted gin-sellers to Bridewell, the figures for both gin-distilling and drinking were still rising.

Things came to a head early in 1738. Elizabeth Beezley and Martha Sawyer caught a gin-hawker, Elizabeth Voucher, and dragged her through the streets to De Veil's house. Before the magistrate could act, a man called Edward Arnold threatened to kill Beezley and pull her house down. De Veil ordered Arnold to be committed to Newgate.

Arnold took immediate action to prevent this happening. Within a very short while, he had gathered a crowd of around 1,000 supporters who came flocking to Thrift Street, yelling that they were ready to kill both De Veil and the two women, Beezley and Sawyer, who were hiding in his house. De Veil had no hesitation. Once again, he read the Riot Act to the mob, who were milling around in the packed street, swinging from shop signs and attempting to gain entry to the house. This had worked before, and he had every reason to believe that it would do so again.

Once the Riot Act had been read, any crowd of more than 12 people was obliged to disperse within one hour. De Veil's luck had run out. No one took any notice. Instead of dispersing, the mob grew even larger. The magistrate dodged back into the house and peered out of a chink in the shutters. As always, the *London Evening Post* gives a graphic account of events: 'Observing among the rest a profligate fellow, who was the great encourager of this tumultuous assembly, (one Roger Allen) and who encouraged them to pull down the Justice's house and kill the informers, he [De Veil] had him seized.' Despite Allen's arrest, the crowd continued to mob the magistrate's house. It took the intervention of the army to clear Thrift Street and rescue the two informers from their hiding place.

This blatant defiance of the rule of law was terrifying. In Westminster, just a short walk away from Soho, the government was growing increasingly uneasy.

Captain Dudley Bradstreet at the Sign of the Cat

Violence was not the only way that gin-sellers showed their derision for the new legislation.

Captain Dudley Bradstreet was no fool. He'd had a very successful career as an informer, brought a lot of illegal gin-sellers to justice, and earned himself a lot of £5 rewards. But it was clear from the way things were going on the streets that he was putting his life at risk. He decided to join the other side.

'The Mob being very noisy and clamorous for want of their beloved Liquor, which few or none at last dared to sell, it soon occurred to me to venture upon that Trade,' he explains in his 1754 autobiography *The Life and Uncommon Adventures of Captain Dudley Bradstreet*. Bradstreet went about establishing himself in his new trade with great caution and attention to detail. He had no intention of finding himself in the position of those he had previously entrapped:

> *I bought the Act, and read it over several times, and found no Authority by it to break open Doors, and that the Informer must know the Name of the Person who rented the House it was sold in. To evade this, I got an Acquaintance to take a House in Blue Anchor Alley in St Luke's Parish, who privately convey'd his Bargain to me; I then got it well secured, and laid out in a Bed and other Furniture five pounds, in Provision and Drink that would keep about two Pounds, and purchased in Moorfields the Sign of a Cat, and had it nailed to a Street Window; I then caused a Leaden Pipe, the small End out about an Inch, to be placed under the Paw of the Cat; the End that was within had a Funnel to it.*

Captain Bradstreet was now ready for business. He then obtained a supply of good Gin from a 'Mr. L-dale in Holbourn'. This cost him £13, the sum total of his savings. The gin was dispatched to his new house, which conveniently offered a discreet entrance at the back, rendering use of the front door superfluous, and guaranteeing anonymity. Now all Bradstreet had to do was find some customers.

> *... I got a Person to inform a few of the Mob, that Gin would be sold by the Cat at my Window next Day, provided they put the money in its Mouth, from whence there was a Hole that conveyed it to me. ... [I] got up early next Morning to be ready for Custom; it was nearly three Hours before any body called, which made me almost despair of the Project; at last I heard the Chink of Money, and a comfortable Voice say, "Puss, give me two Pennyworth of Gin". I instantly put my Mouth to the Tube, and bid them receive it from the Pipe under her Paw, and then measured and poured it into the Funnel, from whence they soon received it. Before Night I took six Shillings, the next Day above thirty Shillings and afterwards three or four Pounds a Day; from all Parts of London People used to resort to me in such Numbers, that my Neighbours could scarcely get in or out of their Houses. After this manner I went on for a Month, in which time I cleared upwards of two and twenty Pounds.*

It was hardly surprising that Captain Bradstreet's neighbours weren't too happy with the queues of gin-quaffers lining the street outside their homes. They spoke to their Landlords, insisting that the anonymous 'Cat-man' must go.

The authorities were soon knocking on Bradstreet's front door, but the astute Captain kept it firmly closed. Instead, he played his trump card and sent his mistress Mrs Winnett to speak to them out of a top-floor window. Watched by a crowd of curious onlookers, including the angry neighbours, the lady:

> ...*took Courage on this Occasion, dressed herself, and threw up the Sash. Greater Crouds [sic] were not to behold the Venetian Embassador [sic] to make his public entry, than Upon this Occasion to see Mrs. W-net, with all the Glories of Youth, Beauty, and Dress in such a Place; the Sight of her captivated the Youth and Aged, from Enemies they soon became Admirers. The Word became general among them, by swearing she was the Queen of Love, she addressed them with her harmonious Voice, saying "Gentlemen, why do you assemble in this tumultuous manner before my Door". The Effect of Beauty is surprising, when speaking to a rude ungovernable Mob; they instantly changed from Jarring and Discord, to Silence equal to the Dead: She proceeded, saying, "If you have a lawful Authority to break open my Doors, spare them not, otherwise at your Peril be it; My Manners are very inoffensive, here my Cat and I only sell the water of Life, which if drank by any Person they shall never die, while they continue using it". This Speech had a most incredible Effect upon five of the Hearers, who were, I suppose, enthusiastically mad before; for they instantly threw themselves on their Knees to worship her. The Justices and other Officers begged her Pardon and sneaked off, being hooted by the insulting Mob. She then disappeared and came down Stairs.*

Captain Bradstreet had no further confrontations with the authorities and was left in peace to dispense his illegal gin. But it wasn't long before his innovative idea was being poached by others: 'My Scheme of a Puss, now being common, was practised by many others, which greatly diminished my Business, and made me drop it, and turn my Head to something else,' he wrote.

All through the back streets of London, signs bearing the painted image of a cat could be found. You simply called out 'Puss!' and on hearing the whispered reply 'Mew!' you put your two pennies into the cat's mouth, and out would pour your measure of gin. Once again, the latest Gin Act had failed to topple Madam Geneva from her place in the hearts of Londoners. Gin was still affordable, and it was more plentiful than ever, even if you had to resort to a little subterfuge to get hold of it.

Though some might see the events following the Gin Act of 1736 as a triumph of the will of the people over an unpopular and inefficient piece of legislation, the government would not let violence, intimidation and blatant bootlegging continue. It was time to tighten things up.

Chapter Five

The End of the Craze

THROUGH the mid-1700s, the government continued to try and reduce the consumption of gin – but there was also a need to bring in revenue from excise duties to fund war efforts overseas.

Timeline

1743 – A Gin Act introduced to raise revenue from duties. **8,500,000** gallons of gin are distilled in Britain, and Londoners are now drinking two pints of gin per week. Concerns are expressed over the effects on health and morality

1747 – Another Gin Act changes the legislation on duties. Fears about the dangers of gin continue to grow

1750 – Hogarth's iconic print 'Gin Lane' embodies the worst fears of the anti-gin lobby

1751 – A Gin Act which finally limits gin consumption – in Britain as a whole, this falls to **2,000,000** gallons over the next year

1757–1760 – A series of bad harvests limit the grain available for distillation, and gin production falls dramatically

1784 – Consumption of gin in Britain has fallen to **1,000,000** gallons per year. The Craze is over

---

'This poisonous debauchery ...'

Gin consumption in London had risen to two pints a week by 1743. 8,500,000 gallons of spirit per year were being distilled in Britain. The customs officers had only managed to collect duty on 40 gallons of this. And only two distillers had taken out the £50 retail licences. It was clear that the only beneficiaries from the previous Gin Acts were the lovers of Madame Geneva.

England was at war again, this time supporting the new ruler of Austria, Maria Theresa, against France and Prussia, who claimed her succession was invalid because she was a woman. Prime Minister Walpole was now gone from Parliament, and it was Carteret, the Secretary of State, who had the difficult task of funding England's role in the Wars of the Austrian Succession.

Just as Walpole had done, he turned to Madame Geneva for help. Such a huge volume of spirits was now being distilled and consumed that it would only take a small amount of duty on these to bring in a profit. And so, the 1743 Gin Act was introduced – to bring in much needed revenue. It would also help to eliminate the illegal gin shops that had so successfully flouted the previous Acts by bringing both gin-selling and gin-drinking back into the open.

The Gin Act of 1743

This reduced the cost of a retail licence from £50 to £1. Only those who kept alehouses, taverns, inns, coffee houses or victualling houses could buy one. Distillers were no longer allowed to hold a retail licence. Duty on low wines made from corn was doubled to twopence per gallon, and to sixpence on spirits.

These duties were very modest, and, unlike those imposed by the previous Acts, kept the price of gin affordable for the lower classes. The thousands of inns, coffee houses and eating places shops in London found the new £1 licence fee well within their means – which, the government was hoping, would spoil trade for the illegal wheelbarrow women and the under-the-counter tobacconists and chandler's shops. The government could only hope that, this time, the law would be accepted and obeyed.

The Act was fiercely debated. The reformers were vehemently opposed to the abolition of the restrictions against gin. Parliamentary records from 1743 report the words of Lord Lonsdale, who walked through the parishes of Middlesex to see for himself how gin was affecting the lives of the poor. He claimed that: 'To see men enfeebled and consumed, or rioting in all the most horrid sorts of wickedness; to see women naked and prostituted; to see children emaciated, starved, or choked; and all by the use of this pernicious liquor called gin …' and believed that his heartfelt words would surely cause those debating the Bill to reject it.

'The physicians and nurses of our hospitals …' he continued, 'will inform you, that a vast multitude of diseases and accidents proceed from gin-drinking; the overseers of the poor … will tell you, what numbers of poor objects are brought upon the parish; and if any of the gin-shop-keepers themselves are honest enough, they will tell you, that when poor creatures fall once into the habit of gin-drinking, they never leave it off as long as they have a rag to wear, or a leg to crawl on.'

And there was yet more to his argument. What about the effects of gin on the next generation of the workers who would support England's economy, and of the soldiers and sailors who would fight in her wars?

Did you know?

The 1743 Act was successful in bringing in revenue. By January 1744, 1,000 licences to sell gin had been taken out. And £90,000 in duties had been paid into the Excise Office. This was a vast improvement on the old £1 per gallon duty, which achieved less than £40 per year.

'The use of distilled liquors impairs the fecundity of the human race, and hinders that increase which Providence has ordained for the support of the world. Those women who riot in this poisonous debauchery are quickly disabled from bearing children, or, what is still more destructive to general happiness, produce children diseased from birth, and who, therefore, are an additional burden, and must be supported through a miserable life by that community of which they cannot contribute to the defence.'

Lord Lonsdale's contribution to the bitter arguments that raged in Parliament was of no avail. The reformers were defeated, and the Act was passed by a substantial majority.

Production of spirits fell in 1744, by almost a fifth. With the increase in revenue as well, the Act was achieving its aims on both fronts. However, there were two powerful groups who weren't happy. The reformers were furious that gin was still being consumed at high levels, and the Company of Distillers were lobbying for their members to be able to retail spirits. Another adjustment to the legislation was called for.

The Gin Act of 1747

Responding both to the pressure from the distillers and to the continuing need for funds to finance the war effort, this new act raised the duty on gin and allowed wholesale distillers to sell it.

In the first year after this Act was passed, more than 600 distillers took out a licence to sell spirits over the counter. Revenue from spirits licences went up to over £35,000. In 1744, 1,000 licences for retail had been taken out. Five years later, the total rose to 5,297 – a huge increase.

The reformers were far from happy. Fuelled by gin, crime, prostitution, high fatality rates and infant mortality looked set to continue. But things were going to get much worse.

An Increase in Crime

In 1748, the War of Austrian Succession ended. For the servicemen who came flocking back home to England, there wasn't a great deal to look forward to. Discharged from the army and the navy, these 70,000 service men had no support from the government – not even a 'demob' suit to replace the uniforms they had been fighting in.

With such a huge influx of men onto the employment market, there was not much chance of a job either. The government set up a scheme for retired soldiers to emigrate to Nova Scotia in Canada, and, back in this country, offered sailors the chance to set up a herring fishery. Neither of these projects proved popular. The starved ex-soldiers and sailors were reduced to begging from door to door, or, much more lucrative, taking to crime.

Did you know?

More than half of the criminals hanged at Tyburn in 1749 were ex-servicemen.

The wealthy bore the brunt of the muggings and other violent crimes that were increasing rapidly in London. The streets – even in the elegant, newly-built residential areas, were not safe. People were afraid to go out after dark, and if they did, they took precautions – when travelling by sedan chair, a wise lady traveller might attempt to foil any would-be robbers by hiding her jewellery under the seat.

Horace Walpole (son of the ex-Prime Minister, Robert Walpole) was mugged twice, the first time in terrifying circumstances. As he travelled home through Hyde Park, around 10 o'clock one night, he was set upon by two highwaymen. In a letter to Horace Mann he wrote: '… the pistol of one of them going off accidentally, razed the skin under my eye, left some marks of shot on my face, and stunned me …' If he had sat a few inches to his left, the shot would have killed him. In 1752, in another letter, he stated: 'One is forced to travel, even at noon, as if one was going to battle.'

Such stories were fuel to the zeal of the reformers. Two earthquakes that shook London, one on 8th February 1750 and another exactly one month later, seemed to point to divine wrath against the wrongdoings of her citizens. The bishops in the House of Lords were quick to use this in their sermons. And there was a focus for their righteous wrath – gin.

In the poor parishes like St Giles, nothing much had changed since the start of the Gin Craze in 1720. An anonymous pamphlet describes the 24-hour culture of gin drinking. Gin shops were full all through the night and on into the next day. In the early hours of the morning the writer saw 'common whores telling their

lamentable cases to watchmen on their stands, and treating them with Geneva ...'
By six in the morning, he found servant women who had just got up, and who were
about to start work, drinking gin in public houses 'with their stockings about their
legs, caps and petticoat half off ... playing with fellows who have been drinking,
swearing, and playing at cards all the past night.' Later, the streets were filled with
'poor devils of women, with empty bellies, naked backs, and heads intoxicated with
Geneva, standing and gossiping with each other ...' And, when those who had been
lucky enough to be working through the day shut up shop, they '... retire to the
Geneva-shop.'

Did you know?

Gin still claimed many victims among children. The *Gentleman's Magazine*
reports a tragic case in 1748. At a christening in Surrey 'the nurse was so
intoxicated that after she had undressed the child, instead of laying it the
cradle she put it behind a large fire, which burnt it to death in a few minutes.'
The nurse, when examined by a magistrate, claimed to be so stupid and
senseless that 'she took the child for a log of wood'.

Gin Lane and the Demise of Madame Geneva

Another writer who observed such scenes of debauchery, misery and degradation
was Henry Fielding. Once the author of satirical plays which made fun of the
government's efforts to clamp down on Madame Geneva, (these lampoons were
soon banned from the stage by the Theatrical Licensing Act of 1737) he later became
a magistrate, and, along with his brother John, set up London's first police force – the
Bow Street Runners – in 1748.

The excesses of his younger days had created problems for Henry Fielding.
Emaciated and plagued with gout, he often had to be pushed in a wheelchair to carry
out his official duties. The heavy price he was paying for overindulgence gave an
added poignancy to his essay: *An Enquiry into the Causes of the Late Increase of Robbers.*
In this he wrote:

*Wretches are often brought before me, charged with theft and robbery, whom I am
forced to confine before they are in a condition to be examined; and when they have
afterwards become sober, I have plainly perceived ... that Gin alone was the cause of
the transgression, and have been sometimes sorry that I was obliged to commit them
to prison ...*

He also gave a brief insight into what he must have witnessed, both out on the streets and in the close, confined atmosphere of the crowded courtroom:

Gin is the principal sustenance (if it may be so called) of more than a hundred thousand people in the metropolis. Many of these wretches there are, who swallow points of this poison within the twenty-four hours; the dreadful effects of which I have the misfortune everyday to see, and smell, too.

A stunning visual image of this squalor was created in 1750 – just before Fielding wrote his *Enquiry*. So striking is William Hogarth's famous print *Gin Lane* that it appears almost everywhere whenever the Gin Craze is written about.

The print shows many different aspects of the evils of excessive gin-drinking. In the centre sprawls a blowsy, half-naked woman, her legs covered in syphilitic lesions. She's grinning woozily, and taking a pinch of snuff – completely oblivious to the fact that her terrified toddler has fallen from her lap and is tumbling to its death in the vault below. Next to her, a skeleton-like man lies in a drunken coma, while a dog waits to lick the last drops from his gin glass. Behind these two figures, there is a vista of despair and degradation. A child can be seen having gin poured down its throat, while another lies forsaken on the pavement, next to its mother's coffin. A starving man shares a bone with a dog. In a ruined building where the wall has tumbled down, a suicide hangs from a rope.

Did you know?

Hogarth's Gin Lane shows the door of the dram-shop, where a jug-shaped sign bearing the words 'Gin Royal' is hanging. Under this is written the famous saying: 'Drunk for a penny. Dead drunk for twopence. Clean straw for nothing.'

These two pieces of powerful propaganda were instrumental in bringing about new legislation.

The Gin Act of 1751

This banned the sale of gin in prisons and in Workhouses. Chandlers, the shops that sold the staples of everyday life to the poor, such as bread, cheese, beer, coal and such sundry items as mops, could now no longer offer that other staple – gin. Distillers, too, lost the right to sell gin. Publicans might still do so, but only if they paid a rent of more than £10. And, perhaps more tellingly, it was now not feasible

47

for them to offer credit to those desperate for a dram, since debts under 20 shillings were not recoverable in law. And, as a final nail in the coffin, anyone caught trying to protect or rescue an offender who went against this new Act, was liable to be transported for seven years.

This Act worked. Gin was becoming too difficult for London's poor to get hold of. And it was too expensive. A succession of disastrous harvests in 1757, 1759 and 1760 didn't help, since this meant that grain was sometimes not available for distilling. The lower classes began to revert to their old favourite – beer.

Just after the Act, the consumption of spirits in Britain fell to around 2,000,000 gallons. By 1784, due to the imposition of higher duties, it had fallen to 1,000,000 gallons.

Figures from Westminster show a sharp decline in the number of places to buy gin, over the second half of the Eighteenth Century. In 1750, there were 1,300 licensed and 900 unlicensed outlets. In 1794, there were only 957 retailers, all of which were licensed. Given the fact that the population had increased, this is a huge reduction.

Did you know?

The 1751 Act was unpopular with many. Those working in prisons and Workhouses were often almost as poor as the inmates, and it was a blow to lose the income from selling cheap gin. For the people of the slums, the memory of cheap gin died hard. In 1780, during the Gordon Riots, a mob attacked the distilleries in Holborn belonging to Thomas Langdale. Ostensibly, this was because of his Roman Catholic beliefs. Yet the distillery was said to contain 120,000 gallons of gin. Horace Walpole remarked that more people seemed to be killed by drinking than being shot or bayoneted during the riot.

It might be much harder to get hold of her, but Madam Geneva had not disappeared from London. She had simply moved up a level. Now that the small scale back-street distillers had gone, the gin that was still being made was of a much higher quality. A whole new era was about to begin.

Chapter Six

Old Tom and London Dry: Gin Becomes Big Business

I N THE hundred or so years after the Eighteenth-Century Gin Craze, many family distilling businesses established themselves in London. Most of their names and brands are still familiar today, though only one – Beefeater – is still based in the capital. These firms gradually came to dominate the industry, as smaller outfits went out of business.

Timeline

1730s – Nicholson's Gin established in Clerkenwell

1740s – Booth's Gin set up in Clerkenwell

1750s – Burnett's White Satin Gin established in Vauxhall

1786 – Gordon's established in Clerkenwell

1822 – Seager Evans set up in Pimlico

1832 – Tanqueray established in Bloomsbury

1863 – Beefeater: James Burrough bought the Chelsea Distillery

1867 – Gilbey's Gin established in Camden Town

Did you know?

The Port of London was a must-see for European tourists visiting the capital. There were so many ships moored up on the River Thames that if they so wished they could cross to the other side without getting wet by stepping from deck to deck.

By the end of the Eighteenth Century, distilling had become quite respectable, and the disreputable image of the Gin Craze was forgotten. In 1794, Sir Robert Burnett, maker of Burnett's White Satin, was made Sheriff of the City of London.

At the end of the Eighteenth Century, London was the biggest city in England, and was producing around 90% of the gin made in this country. This wasn't just because of the large population of Londoners eager to drink the spirit. Trading ships could navigate the tidal River Thames right up to the London Docks, close to the centre of the city. It's no coincidence that the distilling industry grew in size as the docks expanded ever eastward until London was the busiest port in the world.

Production could not have been sustained without a constant, reliable supply of grain from the farms of East Anglia (with no network of paved roads at this time, the cargo of grain would have been sent by sea), spices and herbs from the East India Company, citrus fruits from the Mediterranean, and sugar from the Caribbean.

An early-Twentieth Century Poster for one of the old firms – Booth Gin. Note the barrels used for storing the gin. (Image courtesy of Nella Booth)

There are two reasons why so many of the distilleries chose to base themselves in Clerkenwell – firstly, the excellent quality of the pure water from the ancient Clerk's Well spring at the location and, secondly, the ease of access to the London Docks along the River Fleet, which at the time was a large and busy river.

The distilleries made a wide range of alcoholic drinks, including liqueurs and cordials based on flavoured French brandy and fruit gins made with raspberry, orange, ginger, lovage, lemon and blackcurrant as well as the more familiar sloe. They

---

Did you know?

In the late-1800s–early-1900s, gentlemen working in the City would take themselves at lunchtime to the spa at Clerkenwell to partake of the waters there. Sadler's Wells, just up the road, also had a spring where the water was reputed to have healing qualities.

also produced bitters and 'shrubs' – a type of fruit cordial made with alcohol. The plain gin they produced was Genever or 'Hollands' Gin, and the sweetened Old Tom.

The base alcohol used to make these liqueurs, cordials and gins was produced by large malt distillers, mostly based in East London, including the Three Mills Malt Distillery and the Currie's Malt Distillery at Bromley-by-Bow.

By the 1820s, the distilling industry had a whole range of other trades and suppliers supporting it. Three quarters of the grain that passed through the London Corn Market was bought by distillers, and a large number of craftsmen and tradesmen were supplying the distillers with barrels, stills and other distilling equipment, coal, spices, sugar and building materials.

As mentioned above, gin was still only one of many spirits produced. The quality was still very variable, and would carry some malt and other flavours from the base spirit – which was masked by sugar and other additives. But all this was about to change.

An old bottle of Nicholson's Dry Gin. (Image courtesy of the Ginstitute)

The Invention of the Column Still

In 1826 Robert Stein, a distiller in Clackmannanshire, Scotland, invented a new type of still consisting of two columns. This still was able to work continuously, and was capable of producing a very pure spirit of very high ABV.

Stein's design was improved and patented by Aeneas Coffey in 1831 and so the column still is sometimes also called a 'Coffey' still.

Did you know?

In a column still, the first column, or 'analyser' has steam rising up, and the wash of beer or wine which is to be distilled descending, through several levels or plates. The second column or 'rectifier' takes the alcohol from the wash and circulates it until it condenses at the required strength. This process can continue indefinitely, unlike in a pot still, where distillation can only be done in batches, and so the column still is sometimes also called a 'continuous still'. It can produce very pure alcohol of a very high ABV e.g. a pot still charged with wine might yield 40–50% of alcohol from the vapour, but a column still can yield as much as 96%.

This ground-breaking invention – still used in many Scottish distilleries to make whisky – meant that gin distillers now had access to a very pure, flavourless spirit, which they could then redistill with botanicals to make their gin. There was no need to add sugar to mask any unwanted tastes and London Dry Gin began to make an appearance on the scene. It was some years, though, before the taste for the sweeter Old Tom was extinguished and, through the late 1800s, there was some confusion over the name – with unsweetened gin sometimes referred to as Old Tom – perhaps as this was the accustomed name, and was considered to be a mark of quality.

Did you know?

Nineteenth-Century drinkers had a very sweet tooth, both for wines and spirits. Prior to the invention of the column still in the 1820s, the spirit used to make gin had a musty quality and distillers masked this by adding sugar or sweet botanicals such as liquorice to their gin. This type of sweetened gin was widely known as Old Tom. It was stored in and sold from barrels and had an amber or pale-straw colouration.

The Rectifiers' Club

The records of the Rectifiers' Club – an organisation set up so that distillers could meet once a month at the City of London Tavern to discuss matters relating to the distilling trade (excluding whisky distillation) – make fascinating reading.

The Club was formed in the late 1780s, as distilling began to gain prominence as a respectable industry, and probably continued well into the late-1800s, although the existing minute book, held in the Guildhall Library only refers to the years between 1819–1844.

Did you know?

It's intriguing to note that many of the names we associate with our favourite gins today are to be found in the records. In 1837, Mr Gordon provided six bottles of Champagne to celebrate the engagement of his daughter to Mr Edward Tanqueray.

The distillers didn't just use their Club for social purposes. The records show that they negotiated fixed prices for their products, and took action against any who undersold. In 1825, they wrote to the Chancellor of the Exchequer asking him to speed up a proposed reduction of duty on spirits, as sales were very poor. It says much for their influence and importance in the London of that time that the Chancellor agreed to their request.

But who was buying the distillers' gin? And where were they drinking it? In the latter half of the Nineteenth Century, the picture was very different from the wheelbarrows and dram-shops of a hundred years before.

Glitter and Luxury – The Gin Palace Era

By the end of the Eighteenth Century, Madame Geneva was in no-man's land. The days of her supremacy were past and, though she was still much loved by the working poor of London, the price of gin now meant that it was beyond the reach of most of them for everyday consumption.

Through the early years of the Nineteenth Century, two new trends emerged for beverages for the working classes. The government promoted the consumption of beer at the expense of spirits and, in 1830, the Sale of Beer Act gave anybody the right to sell beer if they could pay two guineas for a license. Duty on beer was abolished, as well. Between 1830 and 1836, the number of beer shops in England and Wales rose from 24,000 to 46,000 – and that's not counting the 56,000 public houses.

At the same time, coffee shops were gaining a foothold in London. Once the limited to the privileged classes, due to its cost and relative rarity, coffee was now almost as cheap as beer. It soon became a popular breakfast drink for the working classes. Just as with alcoholic drinks, the advantage of a hot beverage made with boiled water was that there was no risk of infection from contaminated water.

But gin was far from beaten, and was soon to make a comeback. Despite the proliferation of beer shops after the Beer Act, the breweries, with their 'tied house' pubs, didn't lose out. Instead, they went on the offensive, and turned their attention to the provision of spirits. They also transformed their old and drab premises into something much more luxurious – a Gin Palace.

In 1830, Fearon's, in Holborn, was the first Gin Palace to open. By the 1850s, there were around 5,000 of these establishments.

George Dodd, in *The Food of London* which was published in 1856, some 20 years after the Beer Act, describes the evolution of these dazzling new edifices – known as the Gin Palaces:

The Public Houses of London, as distinguished from hotels, inns, chop-houses, eating-houses and coffee-rooms, have undergone great changes within the last few years. They have been transformed from dingy pot-houses into splendid gin-

palaces, from painted deal to polished mahogany, from small corked panes of glass to magnificent crystal sheets, from plain useful fittings to costly luxurious adornments. The old Boniface, with his red nose and his white apron, has made way for the smart damsels who prepare at their toilettes to shine at the bar ... Even the pot-boy is not the pot-boy of other days; there is a dash of something about him that may almost be called gentility.

Luckily for posterity, one of the greatest writers of the Nineteenth Century was an eye-witness to the birth of gin's glamorous and semi-respectable new persona. In *Sketches by Boz*, a collection of short pieces published in 1836, Charles Dickens gives a graphic description of how luxurious and inviting one of the first Gin Palaces must have appeared to the cold and weary Londoners passing by on the street:

You turn the corner. What a change. All is light and brilliancy. The hum of many voices issues from the splendid gin shop which forms the commencement of the two streets opposite; and the gay building with the fantastically ornamented parapet, the illuminated clock, the plate-glass windows surround by stucco rosettes, and its profusion of gas-lights in richly-gilt burners, is perfectly dazzling when contrasted with the darkness and dirt we have just left.

He describes the bar, and the staff who served there:

On the counter, in addition to the usual spirit apparatus, are two or three little baskets of cakes and biscuits, which are carefully secured at the top with wicker-work, to prevent their contents being unlawfully abstracted. Behind it, are two showily-dressed damsels with large necklaces, dispensing the spirits and 'compounds'. They are assisted by the ostensible proprietor of the concern, a stout, coarse fellow in a fur cap, put on very much on one side to give him a knowing air, and to display his sandy whiskers to the best advantage.

This is a far cry from the informal dram-shops of the previous century, many of which were set up in dwelling houses and corner shops. But, despite all this pomp and splendour, some things hadn't changed very much. Dickens paints a riotous picture of the Gin Palace at the end of a long night:

... the throng of men, women and children, who have been constantly going in and out, dwindles down to two or three occasional stragglers – cold, wretched-looking creatures, in the last stage of emaciation and disease. The knot of Irish labourers at the lower end of the place, who have been alternately shaking hands with, and threatening the life of each other for the last hour, become furious in their disputes, and finding it impossible to silence one man, who is particularly anxious to adjust the difference, they resort to the expedient of knocking him down and jumping on him afterwards ... a

scene of riot and confusion ensues; half the Irishmen get shut out, and the other half get shut in; the potboy is knocked among the tubs in no time; the landlord hits everybody; and everybody hits the landlord; the barmaids scream; the police come in; the rest is a confused mixtures of arms, legs, staves, torn coats, shouting and struggling. Some of the party are borne off to the station-house, and the remainder slink home to beat their wives for complaining, and kick the children for daring to be hungry.

A scene not too far removed from many of our town centres in the Twenty-first Century, on a Saturday night. But Dickens was sensitive to more than the comic overtones of this pub brawl. Ever the reformer, he concludes his piece:

Gin-drinking is a great vice in England, but wretchedness and dirt are greater; and until you improve the homes of the poor, or persuade a half-famished wretch not to seek relief in the temporary oblivion of his own misery, with the pittance which, divided among his family, would furnish a morsel of bread for each, gin-shops will increase in number and splendour.

Did you know?

Dickens lists some of the different gins available in the Gin Palaces he visited. These would have been written up large on posters, to attract the attention of would-be imbibers: "The Cream of the Valley", "The Out and Out", "The No Mistake", "The Good for Mixing"; "The Real Knock-me-down", and "The Celebrated Butter Gin". These would have been written up in large announcements, to attract the attention of customers.

For details of old Gin Palaces you can still visit in the Twenty-first Century – see *Chapter Eighteen.*

Dry Gin Comes to the Fore

As the Nineteenth Century advanced, the taste for sweetness in spirits began to decline. The gin distiller and founder of Beefeater, James Burrough, created a gin recipe in 1879 which utilised the peel of bitter Seville oranges rather than sweet orange peel – a clear indication of this trend.

Of course, the column still was an important factor in this new fashion – producing a refined, pure alcohol that didn't have flavours and impurities that needed to be masked with sweetness. However, the trend in wines was also moving from the sweeter varieties towards the dry at this time.

At the turn of the Twentieth Century, Dry Gin and old-style Old Tom were to be found together behind the bars in clubs, hotels and on cruise liners. The Titanic and her sister ships carried both – as well as genever. Slowly, though, Dry Gin was gaining ground.

By 1930, when *The Savoy Cocktail Book* was written, Dry Gin was the preference for making cocktails, and the trend continued through the 1940s and 1950s, when the discerning drinker favoured very dry cocktails like the Martini. London Dry Gin was now the must-have in every cocktail cabinet and behind every bar.

Did you know?

In the mid-Nineteenth Century, gin and gin cordials became very popular as an addition to respectable ladies' tea parties. The spirit was either passed off as wine, or labelled 'NIG' – 'GIN' spelled backwards – so the servants (and possibly also the hostess' husband) would not know what was going on!

In Chapter Fifteen, you'll find out more about the Golden Age of Cocktails, and the colourful personalities and the fabulous concoctions that brought it into being in the early decades of the Twentieth Century.

For now, though, let's take a leap in time and move to London in the Twenty-first Century, where a whole new Gin Craze is taking centre stage in the bars, hotels and pubs of the capital.

Chapter Seven

A Whole New Craze:
Twenty-first Century London Distillers

THINGS have come a long way since the days when one in four dwellings on the rowdy, filthy streets of the parish of St Giles was producing gin for sale in dram-shops or from wheelbarrows on the street corners. Now, those same streets are unrecognisable – clean, smart and full of well-dressed shoppers visiting the high-end Covent Garden retail outlets. You'll find a huge variety of wonderful gin brands in the many upmarket hotels and bars, and there are many skilled bartenders keen to mix you a fabulous cocktail, but you'd be very hard pressed indeed to find a gin distiller in the locality.

Now, London is home to just four working gin distilleries – and they couldn't be more different from each other. What all the distillers share, though, is a passion for gin: for its past traditions and its future potential. And something of the atmosphere of the old Rectifiers' Club persists. The gin distillers of today are a close, supportive community, encouraging newcomers on the scene and supportive of any developments that will help to bring gin to a wider public and enhance the growth of the current Craze.

Beefeater

Not far from the Oval Cricket Ground in Kennington, down a quiet side street behind a supermarket and right next to a group of gasometers, a tall building rises up. It's a mix of old and new; one side is built from mellowed brick, while the other gleams with wide windows of plate glass. There's nothing ostentatious about this building. It's clean, workaday, quiet on the outside. But this is the Beefeater Distillery – the last of the great London Gin Distilleries still operating in London, and there is quite a story behind the simple words over the door – 'Established 1820'.

Beefeater History

It all began in the mid-Nineteenth Century, when a young pharmacist from Devon, James Burrough, set off to make his fortune on the other side of the Atlantic. By 1855, he'd set up in partnership with a Toronto chemist. Then, in the early 1860s, he came back to England and bought a Chelsea distilling business – John Taylor – for

Beefeater Timeline

1820s – The Chelsea Distillery, later to become the home of Beefeater, is founded

1849 – Young chemist James Burrough, creator of Beefeater, writes his first recipes – at this time, mainly for household products and pharmaceuticals

1863 – James Burrough purchases the Chelsea Distillery, then owned by John Taylor, and starts to experiment with making gin and liqueurs

1873 – Burrough wins a Gold Medal at the International Exhibition in Kensington for his gin

1879 – The first recipe for gin made with Seville oranges – bought from a Mrs Isaacs of Covent Garden. The Beefeater style, with its strong citrus tones, is now established

1897 – Death of James Burrough, in the same year as Queen Victoria's Diamond Jubilee

1900 – Export to North America begins

1908 – The Distillery moves from Chelsea to Hutton Road, in Lambeth

1919 – Beefeater is now exporting to Australia, China, France, Greece, India, New Zealand, South Africa and Spain

1950 – Export markets, particularly in America, continue to grow

1958 – Beefeater moves to its current home in Kennington, on Montford Place. Production now focuses solely on gin

1963 – Beefeater is the largest export brand of spirits in the UK

1969 – The Queen's Award for Industry is awarded to Beefeater, and it's the only brand of gin on board the QEII's maiden voyage to New York

1987 – James Burrough Ltd is bought by Whitbread

1989 – Whitbread sell their spirits division to Allied Lyons which, in 1994, merges with Pedro Domecq to become Allied Domecq

1995 – Desmond Payne moves from Plymouth Gin to become Beefeater's Master Distiller

2005 – Pernod Ricard take over Allied Domecq and initiate a large investment programme to develop the brand into the Twenty-first Century

2009 – Launch of premium gin Beefeater 24, created by Master Distiller Desmond Payne

£400. To set this in context, wages for maids and clerks around 1860 were between £12–20 per year.

Burrough's new acquisition produced mainly liqueurs, such as Curaçao, maraschino, cherry brandy and orange bitters – and also made fruit gins. He renamed the company 'James Burrough, Distiller and Importer of Foreign Liqueurs' and continued to produce the existing range. But Burrough the chemist had an inquisitive and creative approach towards his new profession. Like the monks in Italy who first experimented with distilled spirits, he was an innovator.

Burrough's notebooks from the time, still extant in the Beefeater archive, are packed with notes and drawings on ways to improve the distilling process – and also with recipes. Not content with sitting at his desk, he took an active interest in the sourcing of ingredients – the fruits, herbs and spices that were vital to the business.

Master Distiller Desmond Payne at the Beefeater Distillery, with some of the stills in the background.

James Burrough's new recipe for gin was a tribute to his skills as a chemist. He well understood how natural flavours worked with alcohol, and he knew how to create a perfect balance with those flavours. His gin was well-liked, and the enterprising young distiller wanted to make the most of its favourable reception. Ahead of his time in understanding the importance of a strong, recognisable brand image, he was keen that his gin should have a clear identity as a *London* Gin. He wanted its name to have close associations with the city, and to gain a vital resonance with an image of tradition and strength.

Did you know?

Among the archives from this time, there are some invoices that relate to the purchase of bitter Seville oranges from a Mrs Isaacs at the Covent Garden market. These would have been needed for the orange bitters and also for the orange-based Curaçao liqueur. Burrough's dry gin recipes from the 1870s include a high proportion of orange too, much more than was usual at the time. It's clear that the importance of the citrus flavours in Beefeater gin has links both with the other spirits, and with the security of provenance offered by the reliable Mrs Isaacs.

Beefeater London Dry Gin today.

He chose to call his gin Beefeater, after the iconic Yeomen Wardens – the blue and red-uniformed Beefeaters so beloved of visitors to the Tower of London. The brand image has worked well over the last 150 years. All the other gin distillers which started out in London are either relocated elsewhere in the UK, or sold off and moved to sites abroad.

The Beefeater on the label is recognisable the world over. He's changed little over the years, though he looks to have got a little younger, and he seems to stride forward with more confidence – which is hardly surprising, given the success and the phenomenal growth of the brand since it first came on the market.

The connection with the real Beefeaters remains strong. They visit the Distillery every year for a special Christmas lunch, and they all go home with a bottle of gin. How did the original Beefeaters who patrolled the Tower of London get their name? It's likely that they earned the nickname from the fact that, as important guards, they were given extra rations of beef to keep up their strength.

By the mid-Twentieth Century, James Burrough Ltd was still very much a family firm, with Eric Burrough focussing on export markets, especially in the US. A picture in the Beefeater archive shows a Rolls Royce being winched onto a ship, for despatch across the Atlantic – a thank you gift from the company to one of the US distributors.

The success of the brand grew through steeply through the lean, post-war years. In the 1950s, around 30,000 cases per year of Beefeater were being sold and, by 1970, the number rose to 2,000,000.

In 1958, the current Distillery at Montford Place (once the site of Haywards Military Pickle Factory) was purchased and developed to accommodate the growing demand for the gin.

In 1969, Beefeater received two great accolades – the Queen's Award for Industry, and the privilege of being the only gin brand carried on the maiden voyage of luxury liner QEII.

Did you know?

You may still be lucky enough to find for sale online some bottles of Beefeater Crown Jewel, a premium brand aimed mainly at the export market. Its name is a clear reference to the Tower of London connection.

By the latter end of the Twentieth Century, big changes were afoot in the drinks industry. Whitbread, soon to be acquired itself by Allied Domecq Spirits and Wines, bought James Burrough Ltd. It was a tricky time for the company. With a huge market in America, concerns were raised when the US Government tried to halt EU grain subsidies by threatening to double the import duty on certain goods – English gin being one of them. Although this threat was never actually carried out, the Burrough company realised they were in a vulnerable position, and took the option of becoming part of a larger organisation.

Other developments were taking place on the consumer front. The advent of Bombay Sapphire reawakened an interest in gin and, through the 1990s, there was a huge revival of cocktails on the London scene. The stage was set for the arrival of a new Master Distiller, Desmond Payne, then working at Plymouth Gin, which was also owned by Allied Domecq.

Did you know?

Desmond Payne is one of the most respected figures in the world of gin. He started out his long career in the industry at Harrods, working in the wine cellars, but soon moved to the firm of Seager Evans and Co, Gin Distillers and Wine Merchants. (It's interesting to note that their cellars were situated very close to the Tower of London, on Tower Hill, in what is now the Tower Hill Heritage Centre.) The company is no longer in existence, though a brand named 'Seagers Gin' is manufactured in New Zealand.

The gin distilling side of the business soon claimed all of Desmond's time and attention, as he learned the trade under Master Distiller Philip Milner. The next move, when the Seager Evans distillery closed down, was to Plymouth Gin, where Desmond stayed for 25 years. His long experience there made him an ideal candidate to take over as Master Distiller at Beefeater. He's not only a great ambassador for the brand, but his long experience and knowledge of distilling also ensure the continuity of quality. And, in the great tradition of James Burrough, he has also proved himself an innovator – with the creation of the new premium gin Beefeater 24.

By 2012, sales reached around 2,400,000 million cases per year, and around one million of those go to Spain, where the demand for good quality London Dry Gin is now insatiable.

Inside the Distillery

Every one of the 2,400,000 million cases of Beefeater sold annually is made at the Kennington distillery. It's a huge operation. Stepping inside the working area is a bit like descending into the engine room of a very large ship. There are metal stairways to climb as you move between the different areas where the huge tanks and the giant pot stills tower over you. The stills that are in operation hum quietly, and as you near the stores where the botanicals are kept, you sense a hint of an exotic, spicy cargo.

The high-quality neutral spirit for the gin is bought in from Greenwich Distillers Ltd, a specialist producer in South-East London. We're talking huge amounts here – just one of the two storage tanks can hold around 52,000 litres of spirit.

One of the pot stills at Beefeater.

Beefeater Gin is distilled in five traditional pot stills (made in London in 1959 by John Dore and Co). The stills are heated by steam from a boiler situated at the opposite end of the distillery. This ensures that no naked flames are in the vicinity – an important consideration, with so much flammable liquid around. The distillation process is completely traditional, with one or two modern technological tweaks – the stills are opened and closed by computer.

Beefeater is made five days a week, year in year out – and the routine is always consistent. The process begins when the stills are charged with alcohol and botanicals, and left to steep for 24 hours. Distillation begins early in the morning when steam comes through from the boiler to heat up the stills.

As the process gets under way, clear spirit starts to flood through into the glass boxes of the spirit safe. At various times, the different botanicals will start to come through. At 10am, fairly early in the process, there will be strong citrus, as the volatile oils from the orange and lemon need less heat for their flavours to be released than juniper and spices.

The Master Distiller and his team monitor the spirit safes carefully to check how each distillation is going. There's a certain regularity to the timing of when each botanical comes in, but the 'nose' of the spirit always has to be checked to ensure that the heart cut – from the centre of the distilling run – is taken at the right place. And that's something that is only possible with a great deal of experience.

Only the heart cut – the best and most balanced part of the distillation – is taken.

Did You Know?

The 'heart cut' is the spirit which is extracted during the middle period or 'heart' of the distillation process. This 'heart cut' is the key to a high-quality gin, with a good balance of flavours.

Citrus peels – orange, lemon, grapefruit – need less heat to release their essential oils than the juniper and spices. Their flavour comes through first from the still. The spirit that's produced in the first couple of hours of distillation will have a strong aroma and flavour of citrus. Juniper and spices take longer to release their oils. By the end of a seven-hour distillation process, the citrus oils will have been used up and only the heavier, stronger flavours and aromas will be coming through. So, the best balance of flavours occurs during the hours in the middle of the distillation. This is when the Master Distiller will take the 'heart cut' to make his gin – a judgement that requires considerable experience and a high level of skill.

Beefeater is made five days a week, Monday to Friday. The routine is always consistent:

- The day before distillation, the stills are charged with alcohol and botanicals. The botanicals are left to steep in the alcohol for 24 hours
- The next morning, the boiler is lit and, as the steam comes through, the stills start to heat up
- Once the stills are boiling, the seven-hour distillation begins. The neutral spirit, now infused with botanicals, is heated to a vapour before condensing once more to form a clear, aromatic spirit – gin
- The Master Distiller and his team monitor the distilled gin as it passes through a glass box called a spirit safe – they are waiting for the aromas of all the botanicals to come together. Citrus aromas will come through at first, followed by the heavier juniper and spices – and only through the middle period of the seven-hour distillation will all the flavours combine to give the distinctive Beefeater quality and balance. This is the 'heart' of the distillation
- When the 'nose' of the spirit is to the Master Distiller's satisfaction he will start to draw off the 'heart cut' of the gin
- When the citrus aromas start to fade, towards the end of the seven-hour distillation, the 'heart cut' is stopped

At the end of the week, the heart cuts taken from the five days of distillations are blended together to iron out any slight irregularities. These may arise from the fact

Juniper berries.

that the botanicals for Monday are steeped over the weekend, rather than for the standard 24 hours, which may give a slightly stronger flavour to Monday's gin. Consistency is vital throughout the huge output of Beefeater Gin.

Finally, the gin is sent up to Scotland where it is blended with pure Scottish spring water to bring the ABV down to the bottling strength of 40%. (For more details on the process of distillation, and the meaning of ABV, see *Chapter Eight*.)

On my visit to the Beefeater Distillery, I was really struck by the size of the stills – they're giants. That's when I began to appreciate the scale of the Beefeater operation. A tour of the vast rooms where the botanicals are stored brought home to me even more vividly just how much gin is made here on a weekly basis.

In the vast room where the juniper is kept, row upon row of hessian sacks containing the berries stretch before your eyes. And these are only waiting to serve the immediate requirements of the distillery. Far more berries are kept off site. The quality and consistency of the juniper flavour to Beefeater gin is so vital that, at any one time, the Master Distiller will have two-years' requirement in stock, just in case the juniper harvest should fail.

It's hugely enjoyable to view – and smell – all the fresh botanicals. None of them are treated or adulterated in any way before distillation. There's a fresh, delicate, piny aroma in the juniper store – and then the coriander in the next area is warm and spicy. Further on, the intense, fragrant, dried citrus peels catch the attention. It was wonderful to experience in such quantity and quality the separate ingredients

Did you know?

Sourcing such a large quantity of juniper berries and ensuring they are of consistent quality is a top priority. It's not always easy. Nearly all Beefeater's juniper comes from Northern Italy. In a good year, a producer in Tuscany may harvest 50 kilos of berries, as he walks the hillsides beating the bushes with a stick. He might feel proud of his achievement – it's a long, slow, very labour-intensive task – but the results of his labour won't go far towards filling the Beefeater requirement of around 50 tonnes per year.

that come together in the beautifully balanced aroma and flavour of Beefeater Gin.

Away from the production areas, there are exhibitions about the botanicals and the two gins currently made. Sadly, these are not for the public to see, but are used to educate and entertain corporate visitors. Beefeater can also play host to important guests in a very contemporary bar, rather in the style of a state-of-the-art London loft. With its exposed brickwork and huge plasma TV screen, it pays homage both to the past and the future of the brand, and it's a perfect place to relax and sample some of the iconic spirit in a gin and tonic.

It's a shame that the stunning Beefeater distillery is not currently open to the public. However, a visit to the website, and to the great Gin and Tales link, will help to give you some idea of what the experience is like.

James Burrough would have been delighted at the success of the venture he started in the mid-1800s. He'd have heartily approved of the faithful adherence to his excellent, balanced recipe – but he'd also have appreciated Beefeater's ability to focus on the future, while losing nothing of its vital tradition.

Sipsmith

Head a few miles west from Beefeater in Kennington, and take yourself to Hammersmith on the other side of the River Thames. Walk through the quiet residential streets and chances are that, as you wander past the unassuming garage

---

Did you know?

'Prudence' as the 300-litre swan-necked Sipsmith still is lovingly named, was made for the company in Bavaria by Carl Distilleries, a company which has been making stills since the mid-1800s. She's unusual in that she combines the traditional copper pot with a column still, which Sipsmith use to make their vodka. Prudence can also be adjusted for infusing botanicals, in a process similar to the Carterhead method. But finding the right company to make this innovative and versatile still was just the start of the story for Sipsmith.

It took Fairfax Hall and Sam Galsworthy, the two friends who founded Sipsmith, over two years to gain a licence to operate Prudence. The authorities hadn't issued a new licence for a still for almost 200 years, and it took them a while – and lot of communication with Glasgow, with its close connections with the Scottish whisky industry – before they were confident to go ahead.

One problem with the authorities was that a still must have a capacity of at least 1,800 litres (six times the size of Prudence) to gain a licence. This is an anachronism from the days of the Gin Acts, and was intended to prevent illegal distillers simply decamping, with their still, to a new location.

At the Sipsmith Distillery. Prudence gleams in the background as Sam sorts out the pipes before a trip down to Lydwell Spring to fetch water.

that houses the Sipsmith Distillery, you'll be completely unaware of the hard-working copper pot still on the other side of the garage door.

In fact, the garage has quite a history. Michael Jackson, (not the pop star, but the renowned beer and whisky writer) used to live on the site – which was once used as a brewery. So, it's a fitting home for London's first new distillery in almost two centuries.

Fairfax Hall and Sam Galsworthy, founders of Sipsmith, are long-standing friends. They've had experience of working for large companies in the drinks industry but, while over in the US, they encountered some of the new wave, small-batch artisan distilleries, and they came back inspired to set up something similar over here. With London's long and passionate relationship with gin, it seemed a 'must' to bring the art and craft of handmade gin back to its roots.

Sip-smiths

Sam Galsworthy and Fairfax Hall call themselves 'sip-smiths' in celebration of the craft and the passionate attention to detail that go into the production of their high-quality handmade spirits.

In 2007, Sam and Fairfax left their jobs and began the battle to get the distillery up and running. Another challenge was to get the gin just right. 'Sip-smiths' Sam and Fairfax were very clear what the aim was – to craft a quintessential London Dry Gin. Nothing modern or quirky about it – just a really good product of the distiller's craft. They worked on the recipe with Master Distiller and author Jared Brown, and it was several months before they were happy with the result.

Jared Brown

Jared Brown, together with his partner Anistatia Miller, has written more than 30 books on spirits and cocktails – the latest being the two-volume *Spirituous Journey: A History of Drink*. The couple have won many awards both for their writing and also for their work as distillery consultants creating new spirits. Their website, www.mixellany.com, offers a wealth of information on spirits and cocktails past and present – and includes a free online library of drinks books and videos. (See Chapter Twenty-two).

The process for making the award-winning Sipsmith Gin is now firmly in place:

- It all starts with the vodka. Sipsmith make and sell their own brand of vodka, buying in neutral barley spirit and running it through their column still, to create a very pure, smooth product which has a delicious, soft sweetness. Nothing is added, and the vodka isn't filtered – as is the norm with most brands. The copper in the still acts as a purifier, but still leaves some character in the spirit
- Some of the vodka gets bottled and sold; the rest goes back into Prudence's copper pot with the 10 Sipsmith botanicals
- Prudence's steam jacket is activated, heating her contents up to around 60°. She's then left to cool down overnight to allow the botanicals to steep gently in the warm spirit
- Next morning, distillation begins – steadily and slowly
- After the first burst of citrus, the 'heads', has come through – the heart of the cut is collected, until, after around eight hours, the flavours begin to acquire a slightly 'stewed' quality, and the cut stops. These 'tails' are discarded. Sipsmith are ruthless where quality is concerned, and lose around 20% of each distillation
- Each small-batch distillation is numbered. If you buy a bottle of Sipsmith Gin, you'll be able to cross-reference the batch number with the 'Your Batch' page of the website, to find out what was happening at the distillery on the day your gin was made

Sam testing some raw spirit at Sipsmith.

This small distillery is immaculate, pristine and efficient. Shelves laden with glass jars of botanicals catch your eye, and everywhere you'll see bottles of different hues – with Sipsmith **Sloe Gin**, **Damson Vodka** and **Summer Fruit Cup** glowing most vividly. There's a good-humoured atmosphere of creativity and experimentation in the air.

Did you know?

The London connection is very important to Sipsmith's founders. So much so that they insist on using Thames Water to dilute their gin. But, before you shudder at the thought, be advised that they aren't just popping down to the river bank in Hammersmith to fill a bucket with muddy liquid. Every few days, Sam gets up at 4am and makes the long drive to Gloucestershire, to the source of the Thames at Lydwell Spring. There, in a peaceful rural location, pure water bubbles up from the ground with incredible energy. Thames Head, the official source of the capital's great river, is a few hundred yards away, but just a stone marks the spot where a dry well stands. The real source is now at Lydwell Spring. Sam loads up the van with 1,000 litres and brings it back to the distillery, where it's filtered before being used.

The Sipsmith Distillery is tiny compared to the giant Beefeater operation. It would fit comfortably into one of the rooms that Beefeater use to store their botanicals. But James Burrough – innovative and fanatical about detail as he was – would no doubt heartily approve of the venture.

Sipsmith run regular distillery tours so, if you are interested in the distilling process, these offer a perfect opportunity to see how it all works. You will also get the chance to sample some of their delicious spirits.

Distillery Tour

Sipsmith run tours on the first and third Wednesday of every month between 6.30pm–8pm. They must be pre-booked.

On arrival, you'll be greeted with a drink, followed by an introduction to Prudence, the swan-necked copper pot still. A tutored tasting of Sipsmith's award-winning spirits winds up the visit.

To Book: Email lucy@sipsmith.com or call 020 8741 2034. You can also book a tour via their website, www.sipsmith.com/tours.

Gin Palace evenings at the Langham Hotel in London. (Image courtesy of Sipsmith Gin Palace at The Langham, London)

Sipsmith have recently begun exporting their excellent gin to Australia, China and Hong Kong. Fans of their gin who are concerned that there may not be enough left over to satisfy the home market will be pleased to know that there are plans to install a sister-still – possibly named 'Patience' – to work alongside Prudence.

In September 2012, Sipsmith launched a season of atmospheric Gin Palace evenings at the Langham Hotel, Portland Place, London W1, in the Palm Court, a venue traditionally associated with afternoon tea.

Master Distiller Jared collaborated with the Langham's cocktail guru, Alex Kratena, to create a menu of gin-infusions and cocktails to represent the different stages of the evolution of gin. Beginning with the 'Gineveristic Punchbowl', containing genever, Sipsmith gin, lime juice, lemon juice, syrup and Champagne, and ending with the very modern 'Spontaneity', featuring sesame, shiso leaf, Sipsmith gin and Falernum, the menu brought the tastes of history to scintillating life in every glass.

The Gin Palace evenings took place on Thursdays, Fridays and Saturdays from 7pm until midnight – and look set to return to the Langham in the future. For more information, contact Sipmith (details above) or the Langham Hotel (020 7636 1000).

Sacred Spirits Company

The Sacred Spirits micro-distillery in Highgate may be small in scale, but its impact on the current Gin Craze has been huge. The story behind Sacred Spirits is extraordinary – and brings together some of the most exotic and magical elements of the history of gin itself.

Ian Hart, the founder of Sacred Spirits Company, has always been an aficionado of gin. Working as a head-hunter in the financial sector, his career suffered a downturn when Lehman Brothers collapsed in 2008. Resourceful Ian saw this setback as an opportunity to focus on his favourite spirit, and he set up a distillery in his sitting room.

Did you know?

Before creating his Sacred Gin, Ian's research was meticulous. He spent a year studying the 12 volumes of a Seventeenth-Century botanical encyclopaedia, *'Hortus Indicus Malabaricus'*, which documented the new spices discovered by the Dutch East India Company, many of which were integral to the early development of gin.

On paper, the set-up at Sacred Spirits sounds like something from the Eighteenth Century – when home distilling was happening in many domestic environments. And it is very small-scale and domestic indeed – Ian's sitting room is still used as such by the family when he's not distilling. Apart from the *Hortus Indicus Malabaricus*, though, there's nothing old-world about it at all. The comfy chairs are overshadowed by the high-tech mass of coiling tubes and multiple glass vessels that make up the distillery equipment. The Beefeater Distillery is on an industrial scale – it's factory-like. Ian's operation is efficient and hugely productive, but there is something about it which resembles an eccentric professor's laboratory.

Ian uses the vacuum method of distillation – the lower temperatures involved

Ian Hart, the founder of Sacred Spirits.

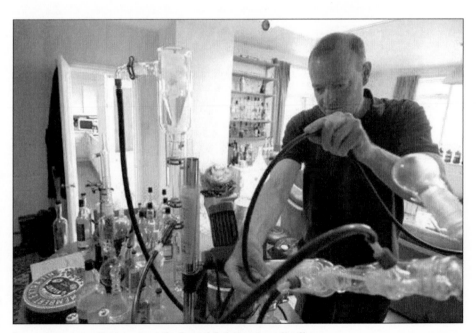

Ian makes some adjustments at the Sacred Spirits micro-distillery.

give improved flavour, and are also safer in a domestic environment – if you step out into the garden, you'll see the vacuum pump sheltering in the family's Wendy House. (You'll also notice layers of spent botanicals – cassia bark among them – spread neatly over the flowerbeds as a mulch!)

Ian's constantly experimenting with distillates – anything from delicate lemon verbena to apricot stones; from green tomato stalks to RAF Tea – a classic, strong-cup-of-tea flavour. There's a whole library of taste experiences to play with.

Ian chose 12 botanicals for his Sacred Gin – including fresh citrus fruits, and the unusual frankincense or *Boswellia Sacra* from which the gin gets its name. All these are distilled separately, and then blended together in a secret recipe.

The distillation process is highly technical, and very detailed:

- A large rotavap (as seen in Heston Blumenthal's molecular gastronomy experiments) is used to distil the botanicals, under a low-pressure vacuum
- Each botanical is distilled using English grain spirit. The process is done over two or three 'fractions' or stages
- The vapour from the first fraction is collected under glass coils cooled with ice water to about 0°C
- The vapour from the second is collected under a 'cold finger' chilled to -89° with dry ice (solid CO_2)
- The vapour from the third is collected under a cold finger cooled to -196° with liquid nitrogen
- All the fractions are then blended together

For those of you who are less technically inclined – the combination of the low temperature and the three stages of distillation ensure that each botanical has as much complexity and freshness of flavour as can possibly be extracted from it.

Ian studied natural sciences and chemistry as a young man – and it's clear that the knowledge gained then is contributing greatly to his skill as a distiller. For him, it's a given that natural substances will lose their integrity if heated above a certain temperature – citrus, for example, may sometimes come across with a marmalade quality, if traditionally heated in a pot still.

This attention to detail has paid off. From small beginnings in 2009 – Ian and his partner Hilary Whitney started out by delivering Sacred Gin by hand, carrying it on the Underground to their first customers, Gerry's of Old Compton Street and Fortnum & Mason – the Sacred Distillery has become very successful and influential, with Sacred Gin picking up awards almost as soon as it went on sale.

Sacred Open Sauce Distillates

Ian Hart has boundless enthusiasm for gin, and hopes that his own success and the resulting publicity will lead to a whole new wave of small distilleries opening up in the coming years.

More than that, he's keen that even the most amateur of gin enthusiasts should have the experience of blending their own gin, and he's created a range of his own high-quality distillates, which are available singly or in themed packs. You can use these distillates to blend together in your own unique gin – or add to cocktails for an additional hit of flavour. (See *Chapter Twenty-one: Blend your Own Gin*)

Thames Distillers

There's another place in London where distilling under vacuum takes place – and that's at Thames Distillers, which is to be found along a quiet, leafy road on an industrial estate in Clapham, not too far from the Beefeater Distillery.

Thames Distillers have developed an innovative technology to make a very low-temperature distilled gin for Oxley – but this is a specialist sideline for the busy distillery, which currently has almost 40 different brands of gin in production and development.

The man at the helm of Thames Distillers is Charles Maxwell, an eighth-generation distiller whose family have been in the business since the late 1600s.

While he was Master of Worshipful Company of Distillers in 2008–09, Charles discovered in the Company's archives the apprenticeship records of his eight times great-grandfather, dating back to the 1680s.

Did you know?

Charles Maxwell's family were connected with the old Finsbury Distillery, which was situated on Ropemaker Street, off Finsbury Square, London EC2, which was well-known for making Stone's Ginger Wine. Finsbury Gin, also made by the Finsbury Distillery, is no longer distilled in the UK. The brand was sold to Germany, where it's still made to the same recipe and is very popular there.

Thames Distillers produces high volumes of gin, but it's a very different set-up from that at Beefeater. Here, it's all about diversity. The two hard-working stills, Tom Thumb and Thumbelina, are much smaller than the vast copper pots at Montford

Tom Thumb and Thumbelina at the Thames Distillery.

Place. Some small-batch gin is made here, especially for the American market, but most of what is distilled is concentrate, with a very high ration of botanicals to alcohol. This is then rested for a couple of weeks, to allow the flavours to 'marry' together, before being diluted with neutral alcohol.

There is a lot of call for Charles' extensive experience and skill as a Master Distiller. If you would like to have your own gin brand with 'Distilled and bottled in London' on the label, Thames Distillers can offer the whole process from start to finish – or any part of it – whichever you require. As Charles says, 'We are very much like a traditional London tailor – we do as little or as much as our customers want.' There is a bottling plant, and extensive storage facilities on site, as well as the two stills. But, most important of all, there is Charles.

Charles can build you a recipe from scratch – some clients have been known to turn up and simply say: 'I want to launch a brand of gin – can you help?' but he can also help to recreate the recipes of the past – as he did for a client, Christian Jensen, who wanted to produce an old-style London Dry Gin a few years ago. Jensen's Bermondsey London Dry Gin and also Jensen's Old Tom Gin are now selling well. (For details of Jensen's gins, see *Chapters Ten* and *Twelve*.)

> ## *Did you know?*
>
> There are several different routes to re-creating an old-style gin. Notes and recipes are can sometimes be found in the record books of distilleries – such as Nicholson's, which was founded at the height of the Gin Craze in the 1730's, and which finally closed its distillery at Three Mills in 1966. When it comes to tasting brands of gin that have long been out of production – such as Nicholson's Lamplighter – *aficionados* can sometimes strike lucky and find a bottle of the old brand in Japan. The shelves in some of the specialist bars there contain treasure-troves of discontinued gins.

Almost a quarter of the brands produced at Thames Distillers are made for the Spanish market, including £50 Gin, in its dark, old-style bottle. The current vogue for London Dry Gin in Spain has created a huge market there.

As well as producing high quality dry gins like Bramley and Gage 6 O'clock Gin and many others, Charles Maxwell isn't afraid to take on a challenge – such as the long-established organic brand Juniper Green, the bright-blue London No 1 and also Oxley Gin, which is distilled at –5°C in a top-secret technology.

> ## *Did you know?*
>
> The Spanish love affair with premium gin – especially London Dry Gin – has brought many Spanish wine and spirit companies to Thames Distillers. In many bars in Spain, you'll find more gins than whiskies behind the counter – and there are some bars which boast over 100 different brands of gin.

Charles Maxwell is delighted by the gin renaissance in London – by the fact that young people like those in his own family are able to go out for a drink and choose between different brands of gin, appreciating the difference between them – and his contribution to the current Craze is no small one. If it isn't Beefeater, Sipsmith or Sacred, and you see 'Distilled in London' on the label – the gin you're drinking was probably made at Thames Distillers.

Part Two

Chapter Eight

How Gin is Made: London Gin, Distilled Gin and Compound Gin Definitions

IRST OF all, let's look at the regulations. Under EU law, there are three types of gin – described as 'Gin', 'Distilled Gin' and 'London Gin'. All are made with ethyl alcohol, which must be distilled to the minimum standard as stated in the EU Spirit Drink Regulations. All are flavoured with juniper berries (*Juniperus communis*) and other flavourings. All types of gin must have a predominant flavour of juniper, and a minimum strength of 37.5% ABV.

Compound Gin is pretty basic, and tends to be found only at the lower end of the market, so you will find only London Gins and Distilled Gins listed in *Chapters Ten* and *Eleven*.

London Gin

What characterises London Gin is that all the flavourings must be distilled with the alcohol, rather than simply added after distillation. It may not have any colouring added to it, and it must be made from a higher quality ethyl alcohol than the standard. It does not have to be made in London. There are many brands with London Dry Gin on the label which are made in other parts of the UK, and even in the US and Europe. The name refers to the style of distillation, and not the location. However, if you see 'Distilled in London' on the label, then you will know that your gin has been made at one of the four London Distilleries (See *Chapter Seven*).

An advert for London Hill Gin – made in Scotland, but definitely a London Dry Gin.

The specification is as follows:

London Gin

London Gin is made in a traditional still by **redistilling ethyl alcohol in the presence of <u>all</u> natural flavourings used.**

- The ethyl alcohol used to distil London Gin must be of a higher quality than the standard
- The methanol level must not exceed a maximum of 5g per hectolitre of 100% volume alcohol
- The flavourings used must all be approved natural flavourings and they must impart the flavour during the distillation process
- The use of artificial flavourings is not permitted
- The distillate must have a minimum strength of 70% ABV
- No flavourings can be added after distillation
- Further ethyl alcohol may be added after distillation, provided it is of the same standard
- A small amount of sweetening may be added after distillation, provided the sugars do not exceed 0.5g per litre of finished product. (This sugar is not discernible and is added to some products purely for brand protection purposes.)
- No sugar will be added in a London Dry Gin
- **The only other substance that may be added is water**
- London Gin cannot be coloured

Distilled Gin

There are fewer controls on Distilled Gin, but it is still a high-quality product, made by redistilling neutral spirit with botanicals in a traditional still.

Distilled Gin must be made by:

- Redistilling neutral ethyl alcohol in the presence of natural flavourings
- No minimum strength is laid down for this distillate
- After distillation, further ethyl alcohol of the same composition may be added
- **Additional flavourings may be added after distillation and these can be either natural or artificial**

Sloane's Gin – London Dry in style, but the botanicals are distilled separately and not all at once, so this qualifies as a Distilled Gin, not a London Gin.

- The distillate can further be changed by the addition of other approved additives and there is no prohibition on their use in the definition
- Water may be added to reduce the strength
- There are no restrictions on the addition of approved colourings

Gin

The most basic EU specification – simply described as 'Gin' – lays down the criteria as follows:

- The gin must be made from ethyl alcohol and flavourings – and the ethyl alcohol does not need to redistilled
- Flavouring may be either approved natural or artificial, and may simply be mixed together with ethyl alcohol to form gin. **In other words, the spirit and the botanicals do NOT have to be distilled together**
- There's no restriction on other approved additives, such as sweetening, and no restriction of on the colouring of the gin, if the colouring substance is an approved one
- Water is added to reduce the strength to a suitable level for retail, but not below 37.5% ABV

Gins made in this way are known as compound gins – and have a rather muted quality to the flavour. The traditional notes of juniper and other botanicals are there, but not as closely married to the neutral spirit as with London Gin and other distilled gins. Compound Gins are often found as 'own brands' in supermarkets, though many good quality Distilled and London Dry Gins can be found as 'own brands' too – it's worth checking the label.

The Pot Still

Distilled Gin and London Gin are made in traditional pot stills. Usually, these stills are copper, though they can also be made from steel. Many of these copper pot stills

---

Did you know?

Depending on the recipe, botanicals are often put into the still with the alcohol and left to macerate or steep for some hours before distillation. At Beefeater, the stills are 'charged' or loaded 24 hours before the distillation takes place to ensure the best extraction of flavour. At Sipsmith, Prudence is charged the evening before distillation and then heated up to 60°. She is then left to cool down overnight before being heated up again next morning for the eight-hour distillation process.

A new but very traditional set-up at No. 209 Distillery in San Francisco.

The loading hatch on an old copper pot still at the Xoriguer Distillery in Menorca.

are more than a hundred years old. 'Angela' at the Langley Distillery near Birmingham, where Martin Miller's Gin is made, as well as many other premium brands, is one such. The hard-working stills at Beefeater, made by John Dore, date back to 1959. Not all copper stills are vintage, though. 'Prudence', responsible for Sipsmith Gin in Hammersmith, was made to order for the distillery and started working in 2009. She was the first still to be licensed in London for almost 200 years.

In the old days, a fire might be lit under a still to get it going but, in these health-and-safety-conscious times, stills are heated by steam – which is usually produced in a boiler some distance away and piped to a jacket which fits around the bottom of the still.

Pot Still Distillation

Enough heat is applied to the still to make the alcohol boil. As the vapourised spirit starts to rise, steam pressure is adjusted to ensure that the whole distillation doesn't rush through too soon – this is called 'entrainment'.

The vapours pass up into and through the swan neck of the still and, when they reach a water-cooled condenser, become liquid again. This liquid passes into a glass box or spirit safe where it can be drawn off and the quality monitored. This is where the 'nose' of the experienced distiller is crucial.

Made in Scotland – the new copper pot still at the No. 209 Distillery in San Francisco.

The first part of the distillation, known as 'heads', is of low quality and is run off into 'feints' vats.

The distiller will assess when the botanicals are coming through steadily, in a balanced way, and will then start to take the 'heart' cut to make the gin which will have a 'still strength' of around 80% ABV.

After around seven-eight hours, the strength of the alcohol starts to fall, and the low quality, impure 'tails' containing turpenes and campenes will start to come through. The 'tails', like the 'heads', are discarded and sent to the feints vats.

When the gin cut has been taken, the still is heated again so that the remainder of the distillate comes through, leaving only water and spent botanicals in the still. The feints are either discarded, or redistilled in a rectifying still to be used as neutral alcohol again – often in other products for industry or for cleaning purposes.

Depending on the process, the still-strength gin will either be blended with other alcohols to create the flavour required, and then diluted; or, in a single-batch distillation, will be simply diluted with water – often pure spring water – before bottling.

Did you know?

Pot stills are very idiosyncratic and any slight variation in their shape may affect the flavour of the gin. A recipe that works perfectly in one particular still may not turn out the same if made in another still. Many gin producers work with concentrate – which means that they add several times the amount of botanicals needed to flavour the spirit to the pot still. The resulting concentrate is then blended with more alcohol until the flavour is right. A process which doesn't use concentrate, where the gin is brought to the right flavour in the still, is known as 'one-shot' distillation.

Carterhead Stills

These stills were developed in the Nineteenth Century by the Carter brothers, who initially worked with Aeneas Coffey (of Coffey still fame) before developing their own system. In a Carterhead still, the botanicals are held in a perforated copper basket above the still, which has a pot at the bottom and a column above. As the vapour rises up from the pot and the column, it passes through the basket and is infused with the flavour before reaching the condenser. Bombay Sapphire and Hendrick's are made in this way – by 'vapour infusion'.

Berry Tray Stills

This type of still works in a similar way to a Carterhead still, but the infusion process is slightly different. The still incorporates a frame holding a large, horizontal tray on which the botanicals are spread. As the vapour rises, it passes through the tray, making maximum contact with the surfaces of the juniper berries and other herbs, fruits and spices. The still where Caorunn Gin is made has a berry tray with four large chambers.

Low-temperature Vacuum Distillation

This is a method of distillation where the pressure around the liquid to be distilled is reduced, so that that the liquid will boil at a much lower pressure than the atmospheric pressure. Using this method means that flavour can be extracted from botanicals without 'cooking' them or changing their natural structure.

Ian Hart of Sacred Spirits uses this technology in his micro-distillery in Highgate, setting up the small glass stills in his sitting room, and housing the vacuum pump in his children's Wendy House in the garden. The intense, pure flavours of his distillates and of Sacred Gin are the result.

Oxley Gin is also made by low-temperature vacuum distillation, using a top-secret process developed at Thames Distillers in London.

One of the stills at the Sacred Spirits micro-distillery.

Did you know?

Chef Heston Blumenthal experimented with this technology to extract flavours for use in his cooking. He used a device called a rotovap, which rotates a glass distillation flask to enhance the distillation. Rotating the flask spreads liquid onto the walls of the flask which increases the surface area for evaporation.

Column Stills

These stills, also known as Coffey or Continuous stills, are used to produced the neutral alcohol, or vodka, which is then redistilled with botanicals to make London Dry Gin or Distilled Gin.

Column stills are tall and chimney-like, and work in two parts. In the first column, or 'analyser', the wash of beer or wine which is to be distilled, descends from the top and steam rises up through several levels or plates. The second column, or 'rectifier', takes the alcohol produced from the wash and circulates it until it condenses at the required strength. This process can continue indefinitely, unlike in a pot still, where distillation can only be done in batches. A column still can produce very pure alcohol of a very high ABV. (For example, a pot still charged with wine

Inside the Adnams Distillery in Southwold. (Image courtesy of Anthony Cullen)

might yield 40–50% of alcohol from the vapour, but a column still can yield as much as 96%.)

Did you know?

The neutral alcohol used for redistilling to make gin is usually made from grain – wheat or barley. A few gins from Europe, though, use grape-based alcohol. G'Vine and Xoriguer are examples of this type of gin. Williams Chase Gin, made in Herefordshire, uses an apple-based alcohol.

The Meaning of ABV

When you buy a bottle of gin, you will notice that the label carries information about the alcohol content. It will look like this: **ABV 40%**.

Alcohol by volume (usually shown as the abbreviation ABV) is the standard way that the alcohol content of an alcoholic drink is measured. The alcohol is shown as a percentage of the total volume of the liquid.

Most gins have an ABV of 40%, though the range can extend from 37.5% up to 60%. This information is always clearly shown on the label.

For comparison, here are some typical ABVs for different beverages, in order of strength:

Low-alcohol beer	0–1.2%
Beer	2–12% (usually around 4–6%)
Cider	2–8.5%
Alcopops	4–17.5%
Wine	9–18%
Bitters	28–45%
Tequila	32–60% (usually around 40%)
Vodka	35–50% (usually around 40%)
Brandy	35–60% (usually around 40%)
Rum	37.5–80%
Whisky	40–55% (usually around 40% or 43%)
Absinthe	45–89.9%

Industrial alcohols, and the pure spirit which is used to make gin, come with a much higher ABV:

Rectified spirit	95%
Absolute alcohol (ethanol)	99–100%

Did you know?

In some countries the ABV calculation is referred to as 'Degrees Guy-Lussac' after the French Chemist Joseph Luis Gay-Lussac (1778–1850) who carried out pioneering work in the measurement of alcohol and water.

The ABV of gin can vary, due to the fact that the alcohol content affects the flavour of the botanicals. This is why a Master Distiller will dilute the samples drawn off during the distillation process, so that they can get a clear picture of how the botanicals are behaving. You may have noticed when enjoying a gin and tonic, that you can taste more of the juniper or the citrus in the gin after the addition of the tonic. The flavours are coming through more strongly due to the effect of the dilution.

Did you know?

The ABV information helps you to know exactly how much alcohol you are imbibing. But, if you are wondering why the ABV varies between different brands, the answer is that it plays an important role in how the gin tastes when mixers are added. When Gerry Calabrese was developing his Hoxton Gin with coconut and grapefruit botanicals, he wanted to create something that would mix with cranberry juice and coke, as well as the conventional tonic. After working with his distiller, Gabriel Boudier, to develop the flavour of the neat gin, it took many months of adjusting the ABV before the controversial Hoxton Gin would blend well with the wide range of mixers Gerry proposed.

An old friend of my family – a retired seafarer who lives by the coast in Cornwall – is a long-standing imbiber of the 57% ABV Plymouth Navy Strength Gin. He claims that the increased alcohol content gives a much better flavour in his gin and tonic than the regular 41.2% Plymouth English Gin. In the past, we often joked that it's just the hit of the extra alcohol that gives him so much pleasure – but there's no doubt that the higher alcohol content will be affecting the flavour.

US

If you buy gin produced in the US, you will see that the ABV information on the label is presented in a slightly different way. It will look like this: **40% ALC/VOL (80%) PROOF** or **47% ALC/VOL 94% PROOF**.

Until 1980, the 'alcohol proof' definition was also found in the UK. It was exactly 1.75 or 1¾ the amount of ABV. So, 40% ABV had an equivalent of 70% alcohol proof.
In the US, alcohol proof is exactly twice the amount of ABV. So, 40% ABV is 80% proof.

ABW

Some states in the US regulate and tax alcoholic beverages according to alcohol by weight, or ABW. This can be confusing if you're used to reading the percentages as ABV, as the conversion is complicated. When the ABV is low, the ABW will be around four-fifths. So, 4% ABV is equivalent to 3.2 ABW. But, as the alcohol content rises, the conversion rate varies. 40% ABV is 3.15 ABW.

Specific Gravity

The ABV of a liquid such as gin is calculated by measuring the specific gravity with a hydrometer. This is a glass instrument with a long stem and a bulb weighted with mercury or some other heavy substance, so that the hydrometer floats upright in a vial of liquid. The point at which the surface of the liquid touches the hydrometer is used to determine the ABV.

Chapter Nine

The Botanicals

THESE are the stars of the show – the berries, fruits, seeds, peels, spices, barks and roots that give gin its wonderful flavours. Today, a very wide range of botanicals is used, ranging from the essential juniper berries – which are the predominant flavour of gin – to unusual newcomers like coconut and frankincense that feature in some of the latest London Gins.

It's no coincidence that both Holland and Britain, where gin and genever were developed, were both countries with wide colonial interests. Into the great harbours like the Port of London and the Damrak, near Amsterdam, flowed a steady supply of exotic botanicals for the early distillers to experiment with.

The art of a gin distiller is, to a large degree, dependent on their skill in selecting botanicals. Some of these are tried and tested in the production of traditional London Dry Gin but, even though the recipes may be consistent over many years, the Master Distiller must keep a vigilant eye (and nose!) on the quality of the botanicals. As they source juniper, angelica, coriander, citrus and cardamom, a wealth of experience – and a memory bank of the smells and flavours accrued over a lifetime of distilling – will seek out the products which will ensure quality and continuity.

Many of the botanicals – as well as bestowing flavour and fragrance – have a long history as remedies and medicines. Nicholas Culpepper mentions many of them in his *Complete Herbal*, published in 1653. You'll find in this section some quotes from this work – and it's interesting to look at how these plants were viewed in the years leading up to the birth of gin. Culpepper has plenty of suggestions for using herbs and fruits as remedies – but, if you're tempted to try any of these out, please remember that scientific and medical knowledge has advanced considerably since his day, and do consult your doctor or medical herbalist first!

Nine London Dry Gin Botanicals

These are the botanicals most often used in the distillation of classic London Dry Gin:

Almond

The fruits of the bitter almond tree (*Amygdalus amara*) are commonly used in gin distillation. The almond is a native of the Middle East. It's a small tree, between 12 and 30 feet in height, and can be found growing throughout Southern Europe and also in the US. California produces a large crop of the fruits (technically, an almond is not a nut, but a fruit).

Before distillation, the almonds are ground into a powder, so that the oil is easily released. Distillers can use almonds to create different flavours, depending on the quality of the oil. This can add a soft, almost marzipan-like note to the gin, or a sharp and slightly bitter tang. Almond features as a botanical in Bombay Sapphire, where the light touch of bitterness marries well with the other botanicals. If a sweeter almond is used, it will bring a nutty, soft quality to the mouthfeel and flavour of the gin.

Mouthfeel

'Mouthfeel' is the term used by gin experts to describe how the texture and the body of the gin are experienced in the mouth. Some gins, like Hendrick's, are very smooth, soft and almost oily in texture. Others, like No. 3, are crisp and sharp. Plymouth Gin is a little lighter and less intense than Beefeater. Each and every gin will be experienced in a slightly different way by the mouth and tongue. This is the result of several things: the botanicals and the way they have been treated to extract the flavour; the length of the distillation and, finally, the alcohol content.

Angelica

Some called this an herb of the Holy Ghost; others, more moderate, called it Angelica, because of its angelical virtues, and that name it retains still and all nations follow it as their dialect will permit … It is a herb of the Sun in Leo; let it be gathered when he is there … and you may happen to do wonders.

The Complete Herbal

Wild Angelica (*Angelica sylvestris)* is to be found by streams and in damp areas throughout Britain. It's an umbellifer (a member of the carrot or parsley family), with creamy white clouds of flower-heads, tinged with purple as if they'd been dipped in wine. It has a distinctive scent, similar to Garden Angelica (*Angelica arcangelica*) – the stems of which are candied and used as decoration for cakes.

In gin distillation, angelica plays a very important role – it's the botanical that gives London Dry Gin its characteristic dryness. The shredded root of angelica is

Dried Angelica Root. (Image courtesy of Sandrine Tyrbas, BB&R)

Angelica Flowers. (Image courtesy of Blackwood's)

used. Crumble some of this in your palm, and you will pick up a subtle, earthy aroma – rather like you might notice when walking through a woodland where there are fallen logs. Angelica brings this deep note to the gin profile – a perfect counterpoint to the high, piny quality of juniper. It has another very important role to play. As well as bringing a wonderful dryness to the flavour of gin, angelica also helps to marry the other botanicals together in a balanced whole.

Angelica is a plant of colder climates, and is cultivated commercially in France, Belgium and Germany. It's been used in other spirits apart from gin, including absinthe (where both roots and seeds are included), Benedictine and Chartreuse. It's also found in aromatised wines such as Dubonnet and vermouth.

Did you know?

Country folk in past centuries believed that angelica would protect them against the effects of witchcraft.

Both roots and seeds have a long history as a folk remedy for many ailments – especially against the plague. Culpepper advises: 'The stalks and roots candied and eaten fasting are good preservatives in times of infection; and at other times to warm and comfort a cold stomach.'

Angelica seed can be used in gin sometimes, too. The scent is very reminiscent of hops, and brings a lighter, floral note which complements the juniper berries perfectly. In past centuries, when juniper was not available, distillers would sometimes substitute angelica seeds, which grow freely in the British countryside.

Cardamom

Cardamom (*Elettaria cardamomum*) has rugby-ball shaped seed-pods, with a thin papery skin containing small black seeds. (Technically, the capsule containing the seeds is a 'fruit' – and you may sometimes find this term used instead of the more common 'pod'.) The scent is very distinctive – evoking, for lovers of Indian cookery, the delicate, steamy fragrance of pilau rice. Cardamom is grown mostly in Southern India, and it doesn't come cheap – after saffron and vanilla, it's the third most expensive spice on the market.

Cardamom Pods. (Image courtesy of No. 209 Distillery)

The seed-pods are crushed before distillation, as it's the seeds inside that contain the pungent, spicy flavour. Cardamom brings a very warm, aromatic flavour to gin, but must be used sparingly, as it can easily become dominant in the flavour profile.

Did you know?

Cardamom is used in traditional Chinese medicine, where it is considered warm and pungent. It is used to promote the flow of *chi*, remove dampness, warm the spleen and stomach, and help with many abdominal and digestive complaints.

Cassia

Also known as Chinese Cinnamon, cassia (*Cinnamomum aromaticum*) is grown in China, Indonesia and Vietnam. Vietnamese, or 'Saigon', cassia is considered to have the highest oil content and the best flavour.

Cassia quills are darker and much thicker and harder than the quills of cinnamon, cassia's close cousin. Unlike cinnamon quills, which are taken from

Cassia bark. (Image courtesy of No. 209 Distillery)

Did you know?

In traditional Chinese medicine, cassia is considered to be one of the 50 'fundamental herbs'. It's used to treat impotence and frigidity.

---

twigs, they are harvested from branches and whole small trees. Cassia has a harsh, bitter flavour, almost medicinal. It's similar to cinnamon, but without cinnamon's sweetness, and brings a bright, spicy note to the gin profile.

Citrus Fruits and Peels

In traditional pot still gin distillation, the dried citrus rind is used. All the highly aromatic oils – known as the 'zest' of the citrus fruit – are concentrated in the outer layer of the peel, which is taken from carefully selected oranges, lemons, grapefruits and limes.

For Dry London Gins, such as Beefeater, the peel of Seville oranges and lemons is used. Lemon peel adds a sharper bite to the profile of dry gins, and helps to bring out the juniper; while Seville orange peel has a robust, colourful, slightly bitter tone. Lighter, more floral gins will use sweet oranges instead. The Plymouth Gin Distillery prefers to use these, which contribute to the delicate flavour of Plymouth Gin.

Did you know?

Beefeater has been using Seville oranges since the mid-1800s. James Burrough's receipts for the purchase of these fruits from Covent Garden are preserved in the archives there. Now, the oranges for Beefeater Gin are specially grown in Murcia. They are hand-peeled, and the peel is then hung out to dry for a few days in the Spanish sunshine before being shipped to London.

There is another reason why whole, fresh citrus fruits are not used in traditional gin distillation. If they were boiled in a copper pot still, the fruit sugars would caramelise, forming a thick, jam-like substance and imparting a marmalady flavour. Low-temperature vacuum distillation – such as is used to produce Oxley Gin and Sacred Gin – avoids this problem. Because there is no heat to break down and cook the flesh and juice, the fresh natural flavour will be preserved in the gin. This leads to a clean, pure flavour and soft mouthfeel.

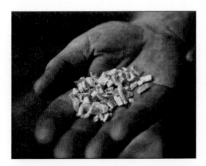

Dried Citrus Peel. (Image courtesy of Sandrine Tyrbas, BB&R)

Grapefruit is currently much in vogue as a botanical for some of modern light-and-spicy gins, and there are other, more unusual citrus fruits being using in gin distillation. Tanqueray Rangpur Gin employs Rangpur limes (a hybrid between a tangerine and a lemon) to give the gin its distinctive, exotic flavour. Tangerine is used in Rogue Spruce Gin, and the floral, summery Bloom Gin uses the dried peel of the pomelo, which is the largest of the citrus fruits, with a similar, though milder and sweeter, flavour to the grapefruit.

Coriander

It is the seeds (or fruits, as they should more correctly be called) of *Coriandrum sativum* which are used as a gin botanical. They have an intense flavour of lemon and spice and are very important in the dry gin flavour spectrum, bringing a lighter note to complement the robust flavour of juniper.

Coriander will grow in many parts of the world. The coriander seed which is sold in spice jars is often grown in India, and the seeds are quite large and have a peppery flavour. Coriander from Europe and North Africa is smaller and has a more delicate flavour than that grown in Asia and, for this reason, is often the choice of Master Distillers. At Beefeater, it's often sourced from Russia and Bulgaria – wherever the flavour is just right.

Coriander in flower. (Image courtesy of Blackwood's)

Juniper

Juniperus communis is a small conifer that grows wild throughout the Northern Hemisphere. The puckered purple berries that impart such a fresh, piny taste to gin are actually not a berry at all, but a type of small pine cone.

Juniper grows wild throughout Britain, preferring upland areas. It can even be found within a stone's throw of London, in the picturesque Surrey Downs. There's an area in Surrey called Juniper Hill – as well

Juniper growing wild. (Image courtesy of Blackwood's)

> *This admirable solar shrub is scarce to be paralleled for its virtues. The berries are hot in the third degree and dry but in the first, being a most admirable counter-poison, and as great a resister of the pestilence, as any growing...*
>
> The Complete Herbal

as a Juniper Hall and a Juniper Bottom. Juniper shrubs like to grow where the land use has changed over the years – which is why they thrive on the slopes of the South Downs where sheep once grazed, but which are now deserted.

Did you know?

Culpepper spotted plenty of juniper bushes in the London area:

> *They grow plentifully in divers woods in Kent, Warney Common near Brentwood in Essex, upon Finchley Common without Highgate; hard by the New-found Wells near Dulwich, upon a common between Mitcham and Croydon ... and many other places.*

Despite this convenient source of supply, British juniper doesn't feature in the manufacture of London Gin. The climate in the UK isn't sunny enough to produce berries of a sufficient quality or quantity, and so they're sourced mainly from the Apennines – the mountain ranges of Italy which stretch across from Umbria and Tuscany into Macedonia, part of former Yugoslavia. Altitude, as well as climate, has an effect on the flavour of the oils.

Harvesting juniper is a labour-intensive activity. Since the berries take three years to mature, and at any given time, the juniper branches will be carrying both ripe

> *The berries are not ripe the first year, but take two Summers and one Winter before they are ripe; at which time they are all of a black colour, and therefore you shall always find upon the bush green berries; the berries are ripe about the fall of the leaf.*
>
> The Complete Herbal

and unripe berries, it requires a degree of skill to gather those which are ready. The local farmers climb the hillsides, where they then have to beat the branches with sticks until the ripe berries fall onto the sacks beneath, leaving the unripe ones for next year and the year after. As each branch carries only a few berries, this can take some time.

The berries are then spread out to dry and bagged up for export. Collections of berries from each area are kept separate. Different soils and microclimates can have a dramatic effect on the oils, and the Master Distillers pay very close attention to this, to ensure that they get just the right aromatics for their gin. For a big producer like Beefeater, where many tonnes of juniper berries are needed year on year, sourcing such a large amount while keeping consistent quality and flavour is quite a task.

Did you know?

Some small-batch, handcrafted gins pride themselves on using juniper which grows in the vicinity of the distillery – The Botanist, from Islay in the Hebrides, includes, among its many local botanicals, wild juniper berries from the island, and the juniper for Cascade Mountain gin is sourced from the high desert country of Oregon.

Juniper has many other uses, besides adding flavour to gin. In the kitchen, it works well in sauces with venison and game. In Europe, it's used to flavour smoked hams and cheeses, and also beer.

Juniper's had a very long history as a medicinal remedy, too. It's been used as a diuretic for centuries and, in the Middle Ages, was believed to provide protection against the plague and leprosy. You will find more information about the use of juniper as a remedy in *Chapter Seventeen*.

Liquorice

Extract of the woody liquorice root – *Glycyrrhiza glabra* – is 50 times sweeter than sucrose, hence its popularity as sweets such as Liquorice Allsorts. It also has many medicinal uses, both as a cough remedy, and a laxative, and is used in many pharmaceutical drugs, as well as in traditional Chinese medicine.

Liquorice powder from the ground-up roots is added to gin – where it brings a distinctive woody, sweet flavour. Liquorice, without being overly sweet, can add a distinctive softness and roundness to London Dry Gin. Beefeater contains a small amount of liquorice, which helps to soften the feel of the gin when you taste it. Liquorice features more strongly in Jensen's Old Tom Gin, which uses the

> *Our English Liquorice rises up with divers woody stalks ... very well resembling a young ash tree sprung up from the seed ... boiled in fair water with some Maiden-hair and figs [it] makes a good drink for those that have a dry cough or hoarseness, wheezing or shortness of breath...*
>
> The Complete Herbal

ground root instead of added sugar to create the sweet flavour characteristic of Old Tom Gins.

Orris

The finest orris root is sourced from Northern Italy, though it can also be supplied from North Africa. The powdered orris used in gin distillation is made from the rhizomes of three different varieties of iris – *Iris pallida, germanica* and *florentina*.

The rhizomes grow like a bunch of 'fingers' underground, and are harvested, trimmed and dried for three years. At the start of the drying process, the 'fingers' smell acrid and unpleasant but, after two years, a delicate scent that closely resembles violets starts to come through, and grows in intensity.

Orris root is famous for its role as a 'fixative' in high quality perfumes – ensuring that the scent remains with the wearer and doesn't dissipate after a short time. It plays a similar role in gin distillation, acting as a fixing agent to bind the volatile elements of the other botanicals.

Other Gin Botanicals

The classic palate of botanicals listed above can be varied in many ways – even within an EU-specification London Dry Gin. Some of the herbs, fruits, spices and flowers listed below have been used for many years in gin distillation, some were used in the early years of gin and have been rediscovered, and others are completely new to the scene. You will notice that some of these botanicals are relatively commonly used, while others are so unusual that they may be found in only one brand of gin.

Aniseed

Aniseed (*Pimpinella anisum*) with its strong, liquorice-like flavour, has long been a favourite ingredient of distillers. It's used to make absinthe, Greek ouzo, Turkish raki and Italian sambuca, to name a few. It was a very popular flavouring in the early years of gin in London.

Now, aniseed is used as a botanical in both Damrak Amsterdam Original and Zuidam Genever Gin.

Basil

Basil (*Ocimum basilicum*) is best known as a herb of Italian cuisine. Its leaves have a fresh, pungent, almost aniseedy scent.

Did you know?

Culpepper had some reservations about 'Sweet Bazil', believing it to have a virulent, poisonous quality: 'Being applied to the place bitten by venomous beasts, or stung by a wasp or hornet, it speedily draws the poison to it, *Every like draws his like.'*

The Complete Herbal

Used as a gin botanical, basil adds a fresh, green zing to Gin Mare, and a note of herbal depth to Berkeley Square.

Bergamot

Bergamot (*Citrus bergamia*) is the fruit of a small tree which blossoms in winter. It's a hybrid citrus, about the size of an orange, with a lemon-yellow rind, and is grown commercially in Southern Italy.

To taste, the flesh and juice of a bergamot is quite bitter, although not so sour as a lemon. It has a very distinctive fragrance, which lovers of Earl Grey tea will instantly recognise, as it is used to give the tea its sweet aroma. It was used in the Eighteenth Century to perfume snuff – and as a gin botanical.

Dried Bergamot peels. (Image courtesy of No. 209 Distillery)

Bergamot has returned to list of botanicals in recent years, as some of the distillers of the new brands look for an addition to the citrus-flavour palate. Bergamot is found in Right Gin, The London Gin No. 1 and also in No. 209 from America.

Dⁱd you know?

Bergamot juice was once a Southern Italian folk remedy for malaria, and the essential oil of bergamot is used in aromatherapy as an antiseptic, antibacterial and antidepressant. The oil is very strong – only a tiny amount is used to give the strong scent to Earl Grey tea – and, if applied to the skin, can cause an adverse reaction in strong sunlight – so always use with caution.

Caraway

Carraway comfits, once only dipped in sugar, and half a spoonful of them eaten in the morning fasting, and as many after each meal, is a most admirable remedy, for those that are troubled with wind.

The Complete Herbal

Adnam's Copperhouse Gin, Hendrick's and Boodles all use caraway seeds (or fruits, to use the correct term) as a botanical. The aniseed-like flavour of the tiny crescent-shaped fruits is very popular in Scandinavia and Eastern Europe, where it has many applications, in bread-making, cheeses, and also in liqueurs such as aquavit and Kummel. Caraway (*Carum carvi*), which is an umbellifer (related to the carrot) and is also known as Persian cumin and meridian fennel, has long been utilised as a remedy for trapped wind.

Chamomile

A decoction made of Camomile, and drank, takes away all pains and stitches in the side.

The Complete Herbal

Matricaria recutita, or wild chamomile, is most commonly used as an infusion – chamomile tea – which is well-known for its relaxing properties. The flowers of this daisy-like plant have a strong, sweet aroma rather like apples and are found as a botanical in Hendrick's, The Botanist and Tanqueray 10.

Roman Chamomile, or *Anthemis nobilis,* is used in Bloom Gin, where it adds a summery, relaxing floweriness to the flavour.

Cinnamon

Cinnamon is harvested from the inner bark layers of trees of the *Cinnamonum* family, which are native to South India and Sri Lanka. It has many uses in cookery, both for sweet and savoury dishes, and is sometimes used in gin distillation – often alongside its less-sweet cousin, cassia. Before distillation, the cinnamon quills are finely ground, and very little of the powder is used as its warm, sweet flavour can easily dominate the other botanicals.

Did you know?

Cinnamon has long history on the trade routes from East to West. It traces its name back to a Phoenician word translated into Ancient Greek – *kinnamonon.*

A cinnamon tree grows for two years before being cut back, or coppiced. Next year, new shoots grow up from the stump, and it's these that are stripped of their bark to make the cinnamon spice. The inner bark is laid out in thin sheets which curl up into red-brown rolls or quills as they dry. These are then cut into short pieces and packed up for sale.

Broker's, Hayman's, Martin Miller's and Sipsmith are all classic London Dry Gins which list cinnamon as a botanical.

Cloves

Cloves (*Syzygium aromaticum*) are aromatic dried flower buds from a tree which is native to the Maluku Islands of Indonesia. Their unique, spicy flavour has made them an essential part of many cuisines throughout the world, and they are used in both sweet and savoury recipes. The powerful, aromatic quality of cloves is only found in Magellan Gin – where they are included as a tribute to the intrepid

---

Did you know?

During the Seventeenth and Eighteenth Centuries, cloves were worth at least their weight in gold, so expensive and difficult were they to import.

Sixteenth Century explorer. They impart a deep, aromatic note of spice to the flavour profile.

Coconut

The coconut palm, *Cocos nucifera*, grows in most tropical and sub-tropical regions. The coconut is incredibly versatile – young fruits can be eaten like melons, and the fresh 'water' is a daily drink for many people in the tropics. Its dried flesh can also be eaten, and the oil and 'milk' are widely used in cooking and in cosmetics.

There is only one gin, however, in which you will currently find coconut, and that's Hoxton Gin – where the inclusion of this very unusual botanical has caused a fair amount of controversy among gin aficionados.

Cubeb

Piper cubeb is sometimes known as the 'Java Pepper', as it is mainly grown in Indonesia. It's a spice from the pepper family, and has a strong, pungent flavour which is somewhere between black pepper and all-spice. The berries are picked before they are ripe, together with their stalks, so that, after being dried, they look like black peppercorns with tails.

Bombay Sapphire, Berkeley Square and Hendrick's all include cubeb among their botanicals.

Did you know?

Cubeb was used in ancient Chinese remedies to ward off demons, and was employed similarly in Europe in the late 1600s, where it was made into an incense to exorcise an *incubus* – a type of evil spirit that was thought to come into the bedroom at night and lie on top of a sleeping person in an attempt to ravish them.

Cucumber

Originating from the Indian sub-continent, and much loved through the summer months as a garnish in a long, cool glass of Pimm's No. 1, the cucumber (*Cucumus sativus*) has now joined the list of botanicals for a few very select gins.

Cucumber brings a soft mouthfeel and a distinct flavour of summer to Hendrick's – where it is added as a separate distillate – and it can also be found in Rogue Spruce Gin from the US.

> *When their season of the year is, take the Cucumbers and bruise them well, and distil the water from them, and let such as are troubled with ulcers in the bladder drink no other drink. The face being washed with the same water cures the reddest face that is; it is also excellent for sunburning, freckles and morphew.*
>
> The Complete Herbal
>
> It's clear from Culpepper's words that the soothing and softening qualities of cucumber are not confined to Hendrick's! (And a 'morphew' is an 'eruption of scurf'.)

Damiana

Damiana (*Turnera diffusa*) is a small shrub native to Central and South America and the Caribbean. It has a strong, spicy smell rather like chamomile, and is used to make a native Mexican liqueur.

As a botanical in Edgerton's Pink Gin, damiana adds an unusual hint of smoky mintiness.

Did you know?

Damiana is valued by native peoples in Central and South America for its relaxing effects, when drunk as a tea. It's also reputed to have an aphrodisiac effect. Spanish missionaries recorded the Mexican indigenous people drinking the tea mixed with sugar for this purpose.

Dragon's Eye

Dragon's Eye (*Dimocarpus longan*) also known as the 'longan' is a relative of the lychee, and it's so-called because the black seed is visible through the flesh of the fruit, and looks rather like the pupil of an eye. In Chinese medicine, it's reputed to generate 'internal heat' – creating vitality and sexual energy.

Dragon's eye is a newcomer to the world of gin distilling, and is used as one of the botanicals for Broker's Gin.

Elderflower

The blossom of the elder tree (*Sambucus niger*) is a recent addition to the list of gin botanicals. Its curd-white, flat flowerheads and heady scent are a feature of hedgerows in May and June, and the sweet flavour will be familiar to many from Elderflower cordial.

Elderflower in bloom. (Image courtesy of Blackwood's)

Elderflower is used in several Scottish gins, Darnley's View and Blackwood's among them, and also appears in Beefeater Summer Gin, Hendrick's and Williams Chase Gin. It brings a summery, flowery, fruitiness to the mix.

Despite its floral sweetness, elderflower can pack quite a punch when added to the botanicals, and will mask other flavours if not used sparingly.

Fennel

This herb was probably introduced to Britain by the Romans, and now its plumes of silky, hair-like leaves are to be seen growing wild on many roadsides, especially in coastal areas. These leaves smell of aniseed, and are often cooked with oily fish. The seeds, like caraway, may be eaten as a digestive. Fennel (*Foenicularum vulgare*) is the principal herb used in absinthe, and is found as a gin botanical in Adnam's First Rate, Boudier Saffron and Death's Door.

Fennel has a similar flavour to star anise, but it is lighter, and brings a gentle, lingering note of aniseed to the gin taste profile.

Frankincense

Frankincense, which is the aromatic resin of the *Boswellia sacra* tree, was one of the precious substances brought to Bethlehem by the three wise men.

You won't find frankincense listed among gin botanicals anywhere except on a Sacred Gin bottle. Micro-distiller Ian Hart chose to use it in the creation of Sacred Gin after his extensive study of the 12 volumes of a Seventeenth-Century botanical work *Hortus Indicus Malabaricus*.

Geranium

The genus *Geranium* comprises around 422 species of flowering plants. Wild geraniums are commonly known as Cranesbills due to the beak-like shape of the fruit capsules. (The Greek name for crane was *geranos*.)

Many geraniums have highly scented leaves, and have been used in herbal medicine to relieve anxiety and boost the lymph system.

Geranium features as a botanical in Henrik Hammer's Dry London Gin of the same name: Geranium Gin.

Ginger

Zingiber officinale, or ginger, originates from China, and is still a staple of Chinese cookery. Both dried and fresh ginger is used in Chinese medicine, and it was mentioned in the writings of Confucius. Now, it is grown in many parts of the world, including India, South-east Asia, West Africa and the Caribbean. In the West, ginger is often thought of as more sweet than savoury, and is candied and also used in baking.

Did you know?

In the 1800s, saucers of powdered ginger were to be found in taverns and inns, so that drinkers could take a pinch and spice their ale with it. It's from this tradition that the modern ginger ales and beers have developed.

Ginger brings a spicy note to gin, both warm and dry in quality. It's to be found both in the very traditional Gordon's, and also in the more controversial Hoxton Gin. Tanqueray 10 and the spicy German Adler Gin also use ginger as a botanical.

Grains of Paradise

This West African spice (*Aframomum melegueta*) is a relative of ginger and grows in swampy areas. The seeds that form inside the trumpet-shaped flowers have a very pungent, peppery flavour which is used in African cuisines. Grains of Paradise are found as a botanical in several gins including Bombay Sapphire.

Honeysuckle

The sweet scent of honeysuckle, which is strongest at night, is one of the most familiar and best-loved smells of British hedgerows and woodlands. This twining climber grows wild in many places, but is also found in many gardens, where it has been a favourite since the Sixteenth Century.

Honeysuckle's delicate sweetness is used in the fragrant, floral Bloom Gin. It's also found in Damrak Amsterdam Original.

Did you know?

One of the great pleasures of childhood is to pick a honeysuckle flower and suck the sweet nectar from the base of it.

Kaffir Lime Leaves

Citrus x hystrix, or the kaffir lime, grows in the Far East and India. The fruit is a knobbly, dark green lime – but it's the leaves that are important as an ingredient of many South-east Asian dishes. When crushed, the volatile oils released give off a subtle blend of green herbal notes and light citrus.

As a gin botanical, kaffir lime leaves bring a clean, crisp note of subtle dry citrus. They were used to create Beefeater Market Edition, and are also one of the botanicals found in Berkeley Square.

Lavender

The chymical oil drawn from Lavender, usually called Oil of Spike, is of so fierce and piercing a quality, that it is cautiously to be used, some few drops being sufficient, to be given with other things, either for inward or outward griefs.

The Complete Herbal

The *Lavandula* genus comprises many varieties of this fragrant herb. It's common in gardens throughout Europe, and is commercially grown for the extraction of the essential oil, which is very popular as a relaxing and antiseptic aromatherapy remedy.

Lavender is used as a botanical in Berkeley Square and Bulldog gins, where it brings a clean, bright herbal note.

Lotus Leaves

The lotus (*Nelumba nucifera*) is not related to the European water lily, though it looks very similar. Its vibrant white or pink flowers, raised high above the flat, round leaves, are a common feature of water gardens in tropical countries.

In Chinese cuisine, lotus leaves are steamed and used to wrap dim sum.

Bulldog Gin uses lotus leaves as one of its more exotic botanicals, and they add a perfumy quality to the flavour.

Meadowsweet

Filipendula ulmaria, or meadowsweet, grows in damp meadows and shady hedgerows throughout Europe and the Near East – and has also been introduced to the US. The frothy white plumes of its flowers have a complex scent, which is somewhere between new-mown hay and sweet, musky honey. Used as a gin botanical, its light, wildflower-field notes evoke summer in the countryside. It can be found in Hendrick's, Oxley and Blackwood's.

Meadowsweet. (Image courtesy of Blackwood's)

Did you know?

Meadowsweet was once used to flavour mead – one of the earliest alcoholic drinks enjoyed in Britain. Its name may relate to this – 'mead-sweet' or 'mead-wort' – rather than to its location in fields and meadows.

Nutmeg

The nutmeg tree, *Myristica fragrans,* once grew only in the Banda Islands of Indonesia, and the fragrant seeds were a very highly-prized spice through the Middle Ages and also in Tudor times, when they were considered a powerful remedy against the plague. Like many of the spices from the Far East, the supply of nutmeg was hotly contested by the Dutch and British East India Companies.

Nutmeg features as a botanical in many classic London gins, including Broker's, Gordon's and Portobello No. 171, bringing a delicate, lingering note of spice and pepper to the taste profile.

Olive

The silvery leaves and oval fruits of the olive tree are a common sight in many Mediterranean countries. *Olea europea* is best known for providing oil and preserved olives which are eaten as snacks, but a touch of its quintessential Mediterranean flavour is found in Gin Mare, which uses Arbequine olives as a botanical.

Pepper

A peppery, lingering after-taste is much sought after in many of the lighter, modern spicy and floral gins. This can be obtained by using nutmeg as a botanical, but some gins, including the Swedish Right Gin, use black pepper (*Piper nigrum*) to gain the effect.

Pine Shoots

These are the little fluffy buds that are the beginning of a pine cone. Used by Desmond Payne in the creation of Beefeater Winter Edition, their light, piny essence has a natural affinity with the deeper notes of juniper.

Pomegranate

The pomegranate tree (*Punica granatum*) grows throughout the Eastern Mediterranean and the Near East, where it is used in numerous recipes. The juice is highly-prized and has become very popular in Western Europe and America due to its high level of antioxidants. It's believed to guard against heart disease and many other ailments.

A pomegranate is actually a berry, around the size of a large orange, with a thick, smooth, reddish skin. Inside the pomegranate are hundreds of small seeds surrounded by a juice-bearing pulp, and embedded in a spongy, bitter pith.

Pomegranate was used in the creation of Beefeater Market Gin – which was a tribute to James Burrough, who sourced many of his botanicals in the 1800s from London markets. Pomegranates are a relatively new arrival to the market stall and, no doubt, the curious and innovative Victorian distiller-chemist would have been keen to try them out in the distillery.

Did you know?

The name *pomegranate* derives from the Latin words for apple, *pomum,* and seeded, *granatum.*

Poppy Seeds

The tiny, kidney-shaped seeds of *Papaver somniferum* are widely used in baking, especially in Eastern Europe, and they can also be pressed to yield poppy-seed oil. In herbal medicine, they are believed to have relaxing, soporific qualities. Bulldog Gin includes poppy seeds in its list of botanicals to bring a sweet nuttiness to the flavour profile.

Rose

An infusion of rose petals is added to Hendrick's after distillation, bringing a distinctive silky, floral smoothness to the gin.

The distilled Water of Roses, Vinegar of Roses, Ointment, and Oil of Roses, and the Rose leaves dried, are of great use and effect. To write at large of every one of these, would make my book swell too big, it being sufficient for a volume of itself, to speak fully of them.

The Complete Herbal

Rosemary

> *The leaves are very much used in bathings; and made into ointments or oil, are singularly good to help cold benumbed joints, sinews, or members.*
>
> The Complete Herbal

Rosmarinus officinalis, or rosemary, is a woody perennial herb with fragrant, spiny leaves which are extensively used in cookery. Its Latin name means 'dew of the sea', which possibly refers to the plant's high tolerance of dry conditions, implying that all it needs to drink is sea-mist.

Rosemary is found in Gin Mare, where it adds to the gutsy, Mediterranean flavour profile, and also in the classic old favourite London Dry Gin, Boodles.

Saffron

> *It grows frequently at Waldon in Essex, and in Cambridgeshire. It is an herb of the Sun, and under the Lion, and therefore you need not demand a reason why it strengthens the heart so exceedingly.*
>
> The Complete Herbal

Saffron, the world's most expensive spice, is made from the crimson stigmas of the purple *Crocus sativus* flower. Around 14,000 of these stigmas, or 'threads' as they are known, are needed to make 1oz of saffron.

Saffron is prized not just for its delicate, spicy flavour (an essential ingredient of Spanish paella) but also for the intense colour it brings. Boudier Saffron Gin owes its fabulous tangerine hue purely to natural saffron, and the spice also brings a light yellow hue to Cadenhead's Old Raj.

Sage

Sage (*Salvia officinalis*) has been grown in gardens for centuries, both as a herb for cooking and for its healing properties. The Latin name *officinalis* refers to the *officina* or storeroom in a monastery which was used for keeping herbs and medicines. So familiar was the herb in Culpepper's time, that he states: 'Our ordinary garden

Sage needs no description' before listing the considerable healing attributes it was believed to have.

Its light, peppery flavour, more commonly used for stuffing poultry and in Sage Derby cheese, is used as a gin botanical in Berkeley Square and Boodles.

Savory

There are two types of this herb – Winter Savory (*Satureja montana*), a perennial; and Summer Savory (*Sautureja hortensis*), which is an annual. Summer Savory has the lighter flavour, and is a classic ingredient in *Herbes de Provence*. Both are common garden herbs, and widely used in cookery.

Savory is a folk remedy for wasp and bee stings, and is also considered to be a good digestive.

Outwardly applied with wheat flour, in manner of a poultice, it gives ease to the sciatica and palsied members, heating and warming them, and takes away their pains. It also takes away the pains that come by stinging of bees, wasps, &c.

The Complete Herbal

Savory is used as a botanical in Citadelle and also in Edgerton's Pink Gin.

Spruce

Spruce is a large coniferous tree of the pine family – genus *Picea* – found in the northerly temperate regions of the earth.

As its name would imply, Rogue Spruce Gin uses local Oregon spruce as a botanical. The thick, fruitiness of the piny spruce marries well with the lighter, more herbal pine fragrance of the juniper berries.

Star Anise

Star anise (*Illicum verum*) is so called because, when cut into slices, the eight-cornered, aniseed-flavoured fruits resemble stars. The small evergreen trees are native to China and Vietnam, and the fruits contain anethole – which also gives the distinctive flavour to aniseed. As star anise is not as expensive as aniseed, it has become a very popular culinary ingredient, and is also used in the Galliano liqueur and in the making of absinthe.

Citadelle Gin employs star anise as a botanical.

Did you know?

Star anise is one of the classic 'Five Spices' used in Chinese cookery, and is also a regular ingredient of Indian cuisine, especially in Biryanis.

Tea

Tea (*Camilla sinensis*) is a quintessentially English beverage – but it's had a recent introduction to the gin botanicals list, too – in Beefeater 24. Japanese Sencha tea is used here. The aromatic green tea leaves are steamed after picking to prevent oxidisation, and Sencha is the most popular type of tea in Japan.

Desmond Payne, Master Distiller at Beefeater, took a tea-tasting course and experimented with various green teas (our traditional English black tea is too tannin rich, and the 'bite' of this in the flavour profile would compete too strongly with the juniper) before settling on Sencha.

Did you know?

The Sencha tea works in two ways in the Beefeater 24 taste profile. First up, even before the citrus, the aromas of the green tea come through on the nose and the palate. Then, right at the end of the profile, there is a light, lingering bitterness from the tannins.

Thyme

Thymus mongolicus is a common garden herb with a long history as a healing and culinary herb. Its warm scent evokes summer on a Mediterranean hillside, and it's one of the botanicals used in Gin Mare from Spain. It's also found in the Hebridean Gin, The Botanist.

Did you know?

The Ancient Greeks burnt thyme as an incense in their temples, and believed it to inspire courage. This belief persisted into the Middle Ages, when ladies would offer their favoured knights a bunch of the herb. It was also laid on coffins, to ease the passage of the occupant into the next life.

Vanilla

The seeds of the Vanilla orchid (*Vanilla planifolia*) are the second most expensive spice after saffron, largely due to the labour-intensive harvesting of the pods. (The name is derived from the Spanish word *vaina* and means 'little pod'.)

Did you know?

Before Columbus arrived in the Americas, the indigenous people of Central and South American cultivated the vanilla orchid, and the conquistador Hernán Cortés is crediting with bringing the spice to Europe in the early 1500s.

Vanilla's complex, sweet, floral aroma is much in demand for perfumes and aromatherapy, and also in baking. It's only in recent years that it has become a gin botanical, featuring in Sacred, Oxley, Adnam's First Rate and Sloane's, and bringing a creamy smoothness to the profile.

Vine Blossoms

The sweetly perfumed flowers of the grape vine (*Vitis vinifera*) are used as botanicals in the French G'Vine gins Floraison and Nouvaison, which were created as a tribute to the two brief periods in the life cycle of the grape, when the flower is out and when the young berry first forms.

G'Vine also uses neutral spirit which is distilled from grapes.

Scottish Local and Wild Botanicals

A whole new family of Scottish gins has emerged in recent years. Some, like London Hill Gin, are classic London Gins. Some, including Caorunn Gin, are made in the London Gin-style, but use the delicate local northern flora in addition to the more conventional botanicals. Yet others, such as the The Botanist and Blackwood's, have a unique Scottish quality which is all their own.

Blackwood's harvest wild herbs and flowers from the Shetland Islands to make their Viking gin. Local crofters gather meadowsweet, sea pinks, wild water mint and violet flowers for the distillery. Since Shetland lies so far to the north, the climate can be very variable, and this has an effect on the wild plants, so the mix of botanicals can vary year on year – giving Blackwood's its Vintage title. The Botanist, made on Islay in the Hebrides, includes local juniper berries among an astonishing list of 22 local plants used as botanicals. Caorunn Gin has the wonderful Coul blush, Britain's most northerly apple, as well as rowan berries and heather.

Scottish Botanicals

Birch Leaves

> *This grows a goodly tall straight tree, fraught with many boughs, and slender branches bending downward...*
>
> The Complete Herbal

After the retreat of the Ice Ages, silver birch (*Betula pendula*) was one of the earliest trees to start growing in Britain. Now, the hardy birch does well in the Scottish Highlands, where not many trees are robust enough to survive. There, you can find woods composed purely of birches – forming an entrancing picture with their exquisite white trunks and delicate twigs and leaves.

For many centuries, Highlanders built their houses, made their furniture, smoked their haddocks and fired their whisky stills with birch wood. Now, the sap is very popular for making birch wine, and local birch leaves from Islay feature as a wild botanical in The Botanist.

Bog Myrtle

Bog myrtle (*Myrica gale*), also known as Sweet gale or Gold withy, likes to grow on wet moors and heathlands with acid soil. It's a drab-looking shrub, with bronze catkins which appear in spring and early summer but, when in flower, bog myrtle

Bog myrtle. (Image courtesy of Blackwood's)

Did you know?

Bog myrtle has had many uses over the centuries. It's been used to add a pleasant scent to mask the odour of tallow candles, and also as a fragrant insect repellent when stored with linen. In Scotland, anglers will sometimes add a sprig of the shrub to their buttonhole to keep the midges away, and in an experiment using the essential oil of Bog myrtle, it was found to have excellent results in repelling insects when applied to the skin.

makes its presence known with an intense, balsamic fragrance that can carry for hundreds of yards.

This sweet-scented plant has been frequently used in the brewing of homemade beer, and now it is found as a gin botanical in Caorunn and The Botanist.

Coul Blush Apple

The Coul blush – one of the botanicals in Caorunn Gin – is Britain's most northerly growing apple, first raised in Ross-shire, Scotland in 1827. Many of the old orchards are now lost, but young trees are still available, and are being grown on to plant out in Scotland's Highland gardens and orchards.

The Coul blush is a sweet dessert apple, with a reddish flush to the skin – hence the name.

Dandelion

The familiar bright yellow flowers and fluffy 'clocks' of the dandelion – a member of the *Taraxacum* species – are known to all. The leaves are currently enjoying a rise in popularity as a healthy 'wild food', featuring in salads, stir fries and the classic French dish *pissenlit au lard* – fried bacon and croutons served on dandelion-leaf salad. Dandelion coffee, made from the dried roots, was a staple of the Second World War rationing era, when real coffee was unavailable. And dandelion wine, made with the flowers, has long been a country favourite, as described in Laurie Lee's *Cider with Rosie*.

Caorunn Gin features local dandelion leaves, prized as a valuable herb in ancient Celtic culture, as a botanical.

Caorunn Gin's stylised representation of bog myrtle.

The Coul blush apple, as represented by Caorunn Gin.

Caorunn's dandelion.

Did you know?

Dandelion's long usage as a herbal diuretic has earned it many nicknames, including Jack-Piss-the-Bed, Pissy-Beds, Tiddle-beds and Wet-the-Bed.

Gorse

The bright yellow flowers of gorse (*Ulex europaeus*) are one of great beauties of the Scottish moorland landscapes, especially when combined with the deep purple of the heather blooms. 'When gorse is in blossom, kissing's in season' is a well-known saying throughout Britain, and the wonderful smell of vanilla and coconut given off by the flowers is certainly very lush and sensual. Gorse-blossom wine captures some of this fabulous, perfumy sweetness and local gorse from the island of Islay brings its special fragrance as a botanical for The Botanist.

Hawthorn

The hawthorn or May tree (*Crataegus monogyna*) is the only British plant which takes its name from the month in which it flowers. The saying 'Cast ne'r a clout till May be out' almost certainly refers to the eruption of white May blossom that marks the start of summer, rather than the end of the month. Hawthorn from Islay is just one of the 22 wild botanicals listed for The Botanist.

Did you know?

There are many superstitions attached to the hawthorn. Its leaves are one of the foliages that adorn the faces of the ancient carved Green Men that are found in old churches, and warnings about the ill consequences of bringing May blossom into the house have persisted into the Twenty-first Century.

Heather

The great expanses of purple, honey-scented heather blossoms (*Calluna vulgaris*) which can be seen on Scotland's moors are not a completely natural landscape – they have evolved on acid soils where trees were cleared and their re-growth prevented by the grazing of animals.

Did you know?

Heather was once used in all sorts of ways – as fuel, as a building material, for ropes and twines, and also for mattresses. In Scotland, a lucky heather sprig is still sometimes placed under the bed, perhaps as a memory of this. The sweet-scented flowers have also been made into an excellent beer.

A number of gins use heather as a botanical, including Caorunn, The Botanist, Edinburgh Gin and Knockeen Hills Heather Gin.

Lady's Bedstraw

Lady's bedstraw (*Galium verum*) has a soft, honey scent when fresh and, when dry, it smells of new-mown hay. It was once included in mattresses stuffed with straw, from which use it gets its name.

Lady's bedstraw is one of the 22 local botanicals which contribute to the complex, wild-flowery freshness of The Botanist.

Caorunn's Heather.

This rises up with divers small brown, and square upright stalks, a yard high or more; sometimes branches forth into divers parts, full of joints and with divers very fine small leaves at every one of them, little or nothing rough at all; at the tops of the branches grow many long tufts of yellow flowers ... which smell somewhat strong, but not unpleasant.

The Complete Herbal

Lemon Balm

Melissa officinalis or lemon balm originates from Southern Europe, and is now naturalised in Britain, where it grows on roadsides and waste grounds. It's also frequently found in herb gardens, where bees love to bustle among its white flowers. The leaves have a very soft, fresh, lemony tastes, and Lemon balm is often used in herbal teas – as well as providing one of The Botanist's wild botanicals.

Mint

Wild mints feature in the botanicals of two Scottish gins. Blackwood's Vintage has wild water mint (*Mentha aquatica*), the scent of which is somewhere between Eau-de-Cologne and a damp, smoky chimney. The Botanist also has water mint, as well

Wild mint leaves. (Image courtesy of Blackwood's)

as two other mints: apple mint (*Mentha x villosa*), which is found growing wild, though it originated as a herb-garden plant, and peppermint (*Mentha x piperita*) a species which has been used for many centuries to flavour sweets and cordials.

Mugwort

Mugwort (*Artemisia vulgaris*) is a common plant of roadside verges. It was once known as 'the Mother of Herbs' and was used widely as a medicinal plant and also as a charm. It was often placed inside shoes to prevent sore and tired feet when travelling. Sprigs of mugwort are worn as a charm at the 4th July annual Tynwald Parliament on the Isle of Man, a custom going back many centuries.

Did you know?

Country children still sometimes use mugwort leaves to make 'cigarettes', rolling them up inside newspaper and smoking them.

Mugwort leaves are found as one of The Botanist's many botanicals.

Rowan Berries

Rowan trees (*Sorbus aucuparia*), or mountain ashes as they are also known, were once planted outside houses as a protection against witches. Now, you are more likely to find them growing along city pavements as an urban planting, where they thrive well. In many parts of Scotland, there is still a strong superstition which forbids the cutting down of a rowan tree, especially one which is close to a house.

Caorunn's rowan design.

The rowan's bright-red berries and pale bark make it a striking sight against a dark moorland or wild hillside. The berries can be made into a jelly with crab apples, which is good for eating with game meats. Rowan berries, with their long history of significance in Celtic tradition, are a signature botanical in Caorunn Gin – which takes its name from the Gaelic word for rowan.

Sea Pinks

Sea pinks (*Armeria maritima*) – more commonly known as thrift – are one of the Shetland botanicals used in the distillation of Blackwood's Vintage Gin. The small cushions of hardy leaves with their clusters of pink flowers borne on slender stems grow freely on walls and cliffs near the sea and have a delicate fragrance.

1943 threepenny bit, showing the thrift on its reverse/tail side. (Image courtesy of Welkinridge)

Did you know?

The old 12-sided threepenny bit, which was often given to children to put into their money boxes, carried an image of thrift on one side – a clever pun, perhaps intended to encourage the habit of saving.

Tansy

The ferny leaves of tansy (*Tanacetum vulgare*) have a pungent smell and a very bitter taste. They were once cooked with eggs, milk and flour and eaten at Easter, as a purgative, and the oil of tansy can be used as to expel worms from the body. Its round button-like yellow flowers are a common feature of riverbanks, roadsides and rough ground. Tansy is one of the wild botanicals in The Botanist.

Thistle

Thistles are often considered to be tiresome weeds, but in the past they have sometimes been used as food plants, the shoots being peeled and served as salads and the kernels of the flowers eaten like small artichokes. Fittingly, since it has been used as an emblem of Scotland since the late-Middle Ages, two varieties of thistle are employed as botanicals in Scottish Gins. Edinburgh Gin has milk thistle (*Silybum marianum*) and The Botanist uses wild creeping thistle (*Cirsium arvense*).

Violet

> *The dried flower of Violets are accounted amongst the cordial drinks, powders, and other medicines, especially where cooling cordials are necessary.*
>
> The Complete Herbal

The Sweet violet (*Viola odorata*) grows in woods, hedgerows and scrublands. Its purple flower is very fragrant, and has been used as a perfume ingredient since Ancient Greek times. Sweet violets have been used as a strewing herb, to freshen the floors of medieval homes, and in herbal medicine they were a remedy for headaches, low spirits and insomnia.

Violet flowers. (Image courtesy of Blackwood's)

Wild violets are used as a botanical in Blackwood's and also in Citadelle, which is made in France.

White Clover

The three-leafed white clover (*Trifolium repens*) is a very common plant throughout Britain, wherever there is grassland. It's also know as 'bee-bread' due to the bead of honey-like nectar that can be sucked out of the white flowers. Four- or five-leafed clovers are considered to be very lucky.

White clover from the island of Islay is one of the wild botanicals used to make The Botanist.

Did you know?

You may wonder, when sniffing a violet flower, why the lovely fragrance seems to fade so quickly. This is because one of the chemicals which makes up the violet's scent is ionine, which can have a deadening effect on the smell receptors in the nose.

Wood Sage

Teucrium Scorodinium, or wood sage, has sage-green leaves and straw-yellow upright flowers, and likes to grow in woodlands and heaths. It's very similar to cultivated sage, though the smell of the leaves is much more delicate. It is gathered on Islay to add to The Botanist's many wild botanicals.

Chapter Ten

London Dry Gin Brands

HERE, you will find a comprehensive list of the most of the London Gins that are currently available. Many of their distinctive bottles can be seen behind the bars listed in *Chapter Eighteen – Where to Drink Gin in London* and most of them can be bought in the bigger supermarkets and specialist off-licences, (see *Chapter Nineteen – Where to Buy Gin in London*). Online retail will supply anything that can't be tracked down here.

I've focussed mainly on the brands that bear the title London Dry Gin on their labels. This means they are in accordance with the EU specification (see *Chapter Eight – How Gin is Made*) although the title doesn't guarantee that the gin is made in London. Where known, I've indicated the provenance of each brand.

There are some gins which I've described as 'London Dry Gin Style' – these may not meet the EU criteria exactly, but they clearly belong with the London Gins which do.

Home-produced gins which are not in the London Dry Gin style are to be found in *Chapter Eleven*.

As the popularity of premium gins grows, more and more are being developed by independent enthusiasts and also by the big brands. It's always worth checking with some of the specialist websites in *Chapter Twenty-two* for new arrivals.

6 O'clock Gin

www.bramleyandgage.com
London Dry Gin Style

ABV 43%

Botanicals: Seven, including elderflower and orange peel

Bramley and Gage, the producers of 6 O'clock Gin, operate from their fruit farm in South Devon, and their philosophy for growing good fruit – from letting it ripen fully and naturally on the tree, to choosing only the varieties that give great flavour – applies equally to their famous fruit liqueurs, and now also to their gin.

Method of Distillation
Made at Thames Distillers, in a traditional pot still.

Tasting Notes
A beautifully balanced gin with plenty of juniper. It's very dry, in true London Dry style, but, within the dryness, the citrus and elderflower come through with a

---

Did you know?

6 O'clock Gin was dreamt up by Michael Kain – whose great-grandfather, Edward Kain, was an engineer on board the British and East India Steamship Company's vessels. The crew were given tonic water to stave off malaria, and mixed it with gin to improve the flavour. Edward loved his gin, but observed great restraint in its consumption, and always waited for 6 O'clock – hence the name of his great-grandson's creation. The Victorian engineer applied 'balance, poise and precision' to his projects, and the blueprints for these are still in existence today. Michael applied the same qualities as his ancestor when developing 6 O'clock Gin. Juniper, elderflower and orange peel must balance in perfect harmony with the other botanicals, chiming together perfectly as the hour approaches…

See the Bramley and Gage website (www.bramleyandgage.com) for details of the publication of Edward Kain's diaries online and on Facebook.

luscious freshness. The light aftertaste lingers well in the mouth and, overall, you will find sipping this gin a beautifully balanced, yet also complex, experience.

Combined with Bramley and Gage's own 6 O'clock tonic, the gin makes a superb gin and tonic, which is very flavourful, but also soft and light. The juniper and quinine come through well but, at the same time, it's a very easy and relaxing drink – perfect for the wind-down at the end of the day.

In a Martini, 6 O'clock Gin comes through with an engaging blend of citrus and juniper. It makes a fine, balanced Tom Collins, too.

Bramley and Gage also make **Damson and Sloe Gins**, as well as a large selection of fruit liqueurs.

Their 6 O'clock Tonic Water is zesty and bright, containing essence of lemon and lime as well as quinine. (See *Chapter Fourteen, Tonic Water*).

Beefeater

www.beefeatergin.com
London Dry Gin

ABV 40% (UK, Europe), 47% (US, Japan, and in Travel Retail outlets)

Botanicals: Angelica root and seed, bitter almond, coriander seed, juniper, lemon peel, orris root, Seville orange peel

Beefeater is a classic London Dry Gin. It's the only major international London Gin that continues to be distilled in London – in quantities in excess of 2,400,000 cases per year.

Just about every bar you visit – be it in your local pub, or a luxurious nightclub in Mayfair – you'll find a bottle of Beefeater on display, for the simple reason that it is a reasonably-priced and truly excellent gin.

The brand has survived when many of its competitors from the last century have either disappeared without trace or are now located in obscure corners of the globe. This is no small part due to the fine recipe developed by Beefeater's founder, James Burrough, in the 1870s, and also to the extraordinary skill and dedication of

---

Did you know?

A gin recipe from 1879 and noted down in James Burrough's own handwriting, marks the first use of the bitter Seville orange as a botanical. These oranges were purchased from a Mrs Isaacs at Covent Garden market.

---

the distillers who have maintained the consistency and excellence of the spirit for almost 200 years.

Desmond Payne, the current Master Distiller, has held the position since 1995. His knowledge and experience are legendary.

Great care is taken at every stage of the process; from sourcing the finest quality juniper and other botanicals (and ensuring that the huge quantities required offer consistency of flavour from year to year) to choosing exactly the right moment to 'cut' the spirit.

Method of Distillation

Desmond Payne claims that the high quality of flavour found in Beefeater is due to the 24-hour steeping of the botanicals in the neutral grain spirit. The stills are 'charged' with neutral grain spirit, diluted with water to 60% ABV. The botanicals are then weighed out and added to this, and the still is then left for 24 hours. Distillation takes place over around seven hours. Only the 'heart' of the spirit is taken, and the 'heads' and 'tails' are discarded. Demineralised Scottish spring water is used to reduce the ABV before bottling takes place at a location in Scotland.

Did you know?

The Beefeater Distillery doesn't operate over the weekend – so botanicals which are put into the still on Friday night have a longer steeping period than those which go in during the week. To guard against any subtle differences of flavour resulting from this, all the batches produced in any one week are blended together, thus ensuring consistency.

Tasting Notes

There's nothing reticent about Beefeater Gin. The classic London Gin flavour is balanced, but it's full-on, too. An 'urban gin' as Desmond Payne describes it, which stands up well with tonic and other mixers.

Beefeater is citrus-led – the lemon and bitter orange peels come through strongly on the nose as well as the palate. Citrus is the first taste you experience, and then there's what could almost be described as a 'click' or 'slash' of bitterness across the middle of the tongue: the signature juniper. Behind the juniper, there's a gentle fade away through the rest of the botanicals – the coriander, angelica and orris. You might even pick up a hint of something like liquorice from the angelica at the end – giving a soft feel in the mouth. In fact, the sequence of flavours as you savour each sip follows exactly the evaporation of the different essential oils in the still.

There's no doubt that the steeping of the botanicals in the pure alcohol for 24 hours is a major contributor to this clarity and complexity of flavour. It gives the gin a great vitality and intensity: ideal in a spirit which is so often – if not almost always – drunk with something else. A gin needs to make its presence felt in a highly-flavoured cocktail such as a Negroni – where the sweet vermouth and the bitter Campari offer their own strong notes. A timid gin simply wouldn't work here. And, of course, the citrus in Beefeater chimes perfectly in a fruit-led cocktail such as a Singapore Sling.

An absolutely honest, totally genuine London Dry Gin; and always reliable and consistent in its outstanding quality, thanks to the skill and commitment of the Master Distiller and his team.

Did you know?

Beefeater Crown Jewel, a premium brand issued in 1993 and aimed mainly at the export market is no longer produced. With the addition of grapefruit to the botanicals, and at an ABV of 50%, do try this if you get the opportunity. Bottles are still available sometimes online, but the price tag reflects the scarcity of the remaining supplies.

The 47% ABV version available in the US, Japan and at airports and other travel retail outlets offers the same quality and consistency, and the complex flavour profile is enhanced by the higher alcohol content. Well worth trying if you get the opportunity.

Beefeater 24

www.beefeater24.com
London Dry Gin

ABV 45%

Did you know?

The design of the Beefeater 24 bottle harks back to the early 1900s and the time of the Arts and Crafts movement, when the Beefeater distillery was next door to Royal Doulton's Lambeth Pottery. Many of the Burrough liqueurs from that time were bottled in Royal Doulton vials.

Botanicals: Angelica root and seed, bitter almond, coriander seed, grapefruit peel, Japanese Sencha tea, juniper, lemon peel, liquorice, orris root, Sencha green tea, Seville orange peel.

It took 40 years of working as a distiller before Desmond Payne got the opportunity to create his own gin – and the result is outstanding. In 2008, Beefeater launched a 'super premium' gin – Beefeater 24. At that time, only Hendrick's and Tanqueray 10 occupied this area of the market, and Beefeater 24 (named after the 24-hour distillation process) very quickly established itself as a classic yet outstanding gin.

It was quite a challenge to create something new alongside the traditional, and highly successful Beefeater Gin. Desmond Payne felt compelled (metaphorically if not literally) to turn the James Burrough portrait in his office to the wall as he worked on the innovative recipe. But he needn't have feared. The redoubtable founder of the Beefeater distillery would have been delighted with the results. In the year it was launched, Beefeater 24 won two gold awards – the IWSC trophy for best gin and the San Francisco award for best gin – and has gone on to be consistently successful in tastings and competitions. As its creator Desmond says: 'It shows well!'

Method of Distillation

As with standard Beefeater, the botanicals are steeped in the spirit for 24 hours. However, the 'cut' is much shorter, and around 30% of the distillation is discarded. This is because of the tea. The tea aroma comes through very quickly in the still, even before the citrus but, towards the end of the distillation, the tannins kick in. The cut is finished here, to avoid the tannins becoming too dominant.

Did you know?

It took a year and a half to develop Beefeater 24 – a key concern for Desmond being that it should have the same quality of 'balance' as Beefeater. It's built around the recipe for a discontinued line called 'Beefeater Crown Jewel' – which also contained grapefruit.

One impetus for developing Beefeater 24 was to create a gin that would work well with Japanese tonic water, which contains no quinine. In order to achieve this, Desmond lighted upon tea as the right botanical to give the drink the necessary light bitterness. Green tea offered the right aromas and flavours but after distillation, the tea flavour was not coming through. Eventually, Desmond tried aromatic Japanese Sencha tea (which is steamed when picked to prevent oxidisation) and this gave the desired result in the still.

Tasting Notes

Softer on the nose than Beefeater Original, the first flavour to come through is the delicate hint of the Sencha tea. Then, there's a pulse of citrus – much less orange than in Original, as the fresh tang of the grapefruit is clearly in evidence. As the citrus dies away, a classic 'stripe' of juniper hits the middle of the tongue in the perfect 'gin experience'. But there's more to come. The long, exquisite taste profile comes to a close with a light touch of tea again – only, this time, more tannin-based.

Due to the delicate flavours and the length and subtlety of the taste profile in the mouth (which can last from 45 seconds to one minute), Beefeater 24 is a very good gin to enjoy neat. It also makes a great and very 'soft' Martini, with wonderful complexity of flavour.

At 45% ABV, 24 has a slightly higher alcohol content than Original – but this helps to bring through the volatile and delicate nature of the tea flavour.

Beefeater Limited Editions

Hot on the heels of Beefeater 24, came three limited edition gins – all developed by Desmond Payne. These can still be found offered for sale online, from some of the outlets listed in *Chapter Twenty-two.*

Beefeater Summer Edition Gin
ABV 40%

With botanicals that include hibiscus, blackcurrant leaf and elderflower, this floral, refreshing gin is perfect for a summer picnic, served up in a jug with cranberry juice, or mixed with soda and grapefruit juice.

Like Beefeater 24, the taste profile is long and complex, but offers lighter, more floral notes. The sweetness of summer fruits comes through first, from the elderflower and blackcurrant, followed by juniper. There's a contrasting, but refreshing astringency towards the end, but this is softened by the creaminess of the hibiscus. All the flavour notes chime well with mixers – this isn't a gin that cries out to be tasted neat – as does Summer Gin's predecessor, Beefeater 24.

Beefeater Winter Edition Gin
ABV 40%

This is, perhaps, a slightly more conventional gin than its sister, Summer Edition Gin, with cinnamon, nutmeg and pine shoots (the small fluffy buds that start off the pine cones) all bringing a seasonal twist to the more usual botanicals.

Winter Edition Gin works beautifully as a warming winter drink with apple or pineapple juice.

The taste profile sings with the fresh woodland notes of the pine shoots, which harmonise perfectly with the juniper. The cinnamon and nutmeg, which can bring very strong, aromatic notes, are used with a very light touch. They are very present in the profile, but not dominant.

Market Edition Gin
ABV 40%

Issued in the summer of 2011, and with botanicals including pomegranate, kaffir lime leaves and cardamom, this recipe was inspired by James Burrough. Desmond Payne scoured the contemporary markets in London to see what was on offer – and noted how much things have changed since Burrough's day – there are far more products from around the world available now.

Pomegranate – currently experiencing a huge rise in popularity due to the health-giving properties of its luscious, dark-red juice – was an obvious choice but, due to the exceptional bitterness of the pith, only the seeds are used. Desmond's first choice for the citrus element was pomelo – that large, green and rather ugly fruit from South-east Asia which is the ancestor of our modern grapefruits. However, since the Spanish word for grapefruit is *pomelo*, and the citrus peels for Beefeater are sourced from Spain, the nuances would have been lost in translation, so to speak. Instead, he decided to use kaffir lime leaves – frequently employed in Thai cuisine – for the exotic citrus tang. Cardamom, a key ingredient in curries, brings a spicy note.

Market Edition Gin has a full flavour of great richness and softness, right from the initial berry note of the pomegranate. The tradition Beefeater lemon and bitter orange notes are lifted by softer kaffir lime leaves, the juniper comes through clearly but not too strongly, and a touch of spice from the cardamom brings the profile to a soft, smooth conclusion on the palate.

A great contemporary gin, yet firmly rooted in the tradition of gin distilling in London.

Berkeley Square

www.gjgreenall.co.uk/berkeleysquare-gin/
London Dry Gin

ABV 40%

Botanicals include: Angelica, basil, coriander, cubeb, kaffir lime leaves, juniper, lavender, sage

The name of this sophisticated premium gin from G&J Greenall conjures up – with an unmissable echo of the eponymous nightingale singing away – the essence of London squares and crescents in a bygone and more elegant age. The old-school aquamarine bottle with its square shoulders and finely fluted sides is rather masculine in appearance, and – in contrast to Greenall's other premium garden-themed gin, Bloom – would seem to be aimed at the gentleman gin-drinker. Interestingly, Berkeley Square Gin was developed by Joanne Moore, Master Distiller at G&J Greenall. Joanne is one of the very few women in the world to hold this title – if not the only woman. Berkeley Square was inspired by the herbs that grow in a timeless English garden – but the more unusual botanicals, such as sage and basil, are complementary rather than antagonistic to the traditional juniper, coriander and citrus.

Method of Distillation
Berkeley Square Gin is made using a two-day *bouquet-garni* process. The core botanicals, including the kaffir lime leaves, are placed in a copper pot still with the triple-distilled neutral grain spirit, and left to macerate for 24 hours. Next day, the other botanicals are wrapped in muslin and also added to the still, where they steep for a further day, infusing their oils into the spirit. The still is then given a gentle, slow run to capture these subtle essential oils.

Tasting Notes
All the elements of a traditional London dry distilled gin are here. There's the pine of the juniper, and the sweetness of citrus, plus some earthy and pepper notes from the spices. The more unusual botanicals bring in additional notes: a green, herbal tang from the basil, a floral flourish from the lavender, and a subtle citrus finish from the kaffir lime leaves, which lingers in the mouth.

The green notes of the herbaceous botanicals work especially well in a Negroni cocktail, and also shine through when the neat spirit is poured over ice and sipped slowly.

Bloom

www.gjgreenall.co.uk/bloom-gin/
London Dry Gin

ABV 40%

Botanicals: Including angelica, coriander, cubeb, Roman chamomile, honeysuckle, juniper, pomelo peel

Bloom Gin comes in an elegant, vase-shaped bottle with sloping shoulders. The jewel-like green cut-glass, delicately embossed with a floral motif, signals that the target market is surely female. Even the vine design around the neck of the bottle could just as well represent the detailing on a couture dress as the historic design of the wrought iron garden gate which inspired it.

In 2007, the Head Distiller at G&J Greenall, Joanne Moore, drew on her wealth of experience and skill to create a gin which is absolutely recognisable as such, but which offers a sweeter, more floral taste profile. While sitting in an English country garden and sipping a cup of chamomile tea, Joanne was inspired to capture some of the quality of that moment within the 'nose' and flavour of Bloom Gin.

Method of Distillation
Bloom Gin is produced in small batches in a traditional copper pot still. Only the heart cut, which captures the subtle floral aromas, is used.

Tasting Notes
Honey and orange notes come through strongly, with the honeysuckle bringing a light layer of sweetness, but the angelica, coriander, cubeb and juniper help to keep Bloom Gin firmly in the London Dry Gin style. The pomelo peel adds a touch of sunshine with its warm citrus tang, and the soft, calming undertone of chamomile helps to bind the flavour profile together.

The sweeter, floral flavour of this very subtle, light gin works very well with soda as a mixer, rather than tonic. It is perfect to drink neat, and mixes beautifully in any fruit-based cocktail. An added bonus is that the honeysuckle and chamomile flowers used as botanicals can also be added fresh to the cocktail as a garnish.

Bombay Dry Gin

London Dry Gin

ABV 43%

Botanicals: Almond, angelica, cassia, coriander, juniper, lemon peel, liquorice, orris

The recipe for Bombay Dry is based on one dating back to 1761, and the exact details, including the 10 botanicals, are a well-kept secret. The Carterhead distillation gives a delicate, refined flavour which is balanced but complex. Bombay Dry has a stronger juniper note than its sister gin, Bombay Sapphire, and will be appreciated by those who enjoy a more traditional gin.

The image of Queen Victoria on the bottle links Bombay Dry to the days when gin and tonic was extensively drunk in the colonies of the British Empire; the quinine in the tonic helping to combat the symptoms of malaria.

Method of Distillation
Bombay Dry is produced using the Carterhead method, also known as vapour infusion. The botanicals are not immersed in the spirit during distillation, but are held separately in a perforated copper tray in the neck of the still, and the vaporised spirit picks up the flavours as it passes through the tray.

Tasting Notes
A crisp, clean gin which starts off slowly in the mouth, leading in with layers of citrus flavour, passing through the juniper and finishing with a hint of anise and a tingle of spice. No one botanical dominates, and this light, dry gin works very well in Martinis and gin and tonics.

Bombay Sapphire

www.bombaysapphire.com
Distilled Gin

ABV 47%

Botanicals: Almond, angelica, cassia, coriander, cubeb berries, grains of paradise, juniper, lemon peel, liquorice, orris

The distinctive blue bottle that contains Bombay Sapphire is easy to pick out behind most of the bars in the UK. Developed in the 1980s by Michel Roux (who was also instrumental in bringing Absolut Vodka into being) it has, over the last three decades, brought a whole new generation of drinkers back to gin. The august head of Queen Victoria on the label harks back to the formalities of colonial days – but Bombay Sapphire was a key cocktail ingredient in the bars and clubs of the partying 1980s.

Produced by the vapourising process of a Carterhead still, Bombay Sapphire brings a subtle, fragrant spiciness to the traditional juniper and citrus profile. Its innovative use of cubeb and West African grains of paradise has opened the door for other distillers to start experimenting with unusual botanicals.

Method of Distillation

As with Bombay Dry, the botanicals are not immersed in the spirit during distillation, but are held separately in a perforated copper tray in the neck of the still, and the vapourised spirit picks up the flavours as it passes through the tray.

Did you know?

Bombay Sapphire and Bombay Dry were distilled by G&J Greenall in Warrington for many years but this changed in 2013. A new, purpose-designed Bombay Sapphire distillery and visitors' centre opened at the old Laverstoke Mill in Hampshire. The Mill, which is named in the Domesday Book, was owned by Portals and run as a paper mill for many years. It's interesting to note that Portals printed rupee banknotes for India until 1950 – a nice link with the Bombay name.

As part of the project, the original water mill will be restored, and an area beside the River Test will be landscaped and opened to the public. There will be a heritage centre, and a glasshouse is also planned, in conjunction with Kew Gardens, in which the botanicals used in Bombay Sapphire will be grown for visitors to view.

Tasting Notes

A very light, subtle gin which gradually unleashes its delicate, spicy complexity in the mouth. The Carterhead process allows the gentle incorporation of all the aromas from the botanicals, resulting in a balanced, yet crisp flavour profile. Layers of light citrus zest yield to the nutty spiciness of almond, cubeb and grains of paradise and a sweet hint of lavender finishes with a long, peppery aftertaste. Juniper is there, but it is much less predominant than in gins which are traditionally distilled.

A very good mixer, in both traditional cocktails and longer drinks.

Boodles Gin

London Dry Gin

ABV 45.2%

Botanicals: Angelica seed and root, caraway, cassia, coriander, juniper, nutmeg, rosemary, sage

Boodles Gin is named for the famous Boodles Gentlemen's Club in St James's, which celebrated its 250th anniversary in 2012. Through the Nineteenth Century, it was very popular in the British Colonies – and is still a firm favourite with many of the current gin aficionados.

Did you know?

One of the most famous members of Boodles Club, Winston Churchill, is reputed to have enjoyed Boodles Gin – though Plymouth Gin is also said to have been a favourite of his.

Method of Distillation
Produced by Chivas, the malt whisky distillers now owned by Pernod Ricard, at their Strathisla Distillery.

Tasting Notes
Boodles is unusual in having no citrus botanicals – yet the flavour profile is that of a classic London Gin, being crisp and very fresh. It's light and sharp and very complex on the nose. Juniper's there, and a hint of citrus (despite the dried peels not being used) and the aroma is also very floral and lightly spicy.

When you taste, Boodles starts out very sweet and mellow, expanding into juniper, with some sharp, sweet spice notes. Following through, there's a touch of light mint and a sweet, fruity quality, followed by a long, herbal finish.

With the length and complexity of the flavour profile, this classic gin is an excellent choice to try neat – or in a Martini.

Booth's Finest Dry

London Dry Gin Style

ABV 40%

Botanicals: Not listed

Sadly, since it's one of the oldest gin brands still going, Booth's Gin is no longer made in the UK. The brand is now owned by drinks multinational Diageo and distilled in the US, and its distinctive blue bottles have a loyal following across the pond.

The Booth family are documented as operating as wine merchants in 1569 and, by 1740, they were also operating as distillers. Philip Booth and Company Distillers of Clerkenwell are listed in a 1778 Directory of Merchants.

With Sir Felix Booth, Philip's son, at the helm, the company continued to expand through the Nineteenth Century, building another distillery in Brentford and eventually becoming the largest distilling company in England. Felix Booth was keen to open up an international market for gin, and lobbied successfully for legislation to enable this.

Did you know?

In 1829–33 Felix Booth funded an expedition, led by John Ross, to chart the Northwest Passage in Canada. The expedition failed to achieve this aim, but Ross named some newly discovered areas after his patron, notably Boothia Peninsula in Canada.

Booth's remained a top brand into the first half of the Twentieth Century and, through the 1930s, was frequently mentioned in recipes for cocktails.

Bottles of Booth's Gin dating back to the 1950s and 1960s may still be obtained from some online retailers and specialist dealers.

Method of Distillation
Booth's Finest Dry is distilled using 100% grain neutral spirits. In the past, its distinctive pale gold colour was due to the gin's being aged in oak sherry casks.

Booth's High and Dry

London Dry Gin Style

Until the mid 1980s, the stylish frosted bottle (bearing a red plastic lion on a silver chain around its neck) containing Booth's High and Dry was a common sight in the drinks cabinets of Dry Martini lovers.

Vintage bottles of this gin are still available from some retailers.

Broker's Gin

www.brokersgin.com
London Dry Gin

ABV 40% and 47%

Botanicals: Angelica root, cassia, cinnamon, coriander, juniper, lemon peel, liquorice, nutmeg, orange peel, orris

Martin and Andy tipping their bowlers.

Broker's Gin was created by two brothers, Martin and Andy Dawson, in 1998. A robust gin with a strong, aromatic nose and an intense flavour, Broker's plays up its London heritage with a quirky and very 'British' humour. The traditional bowler-hatted City-of-London stockbroker on the bottle is as old-fashioned and proper as one could wish – but his formal elegance is deliciously undercut by the fact that the bottle itself is wearing a bowler!

Martin Dawson, with 20 years experience of working in the spirits industry, was keen to create a very high-quality gin that was also approachable and even 'fun-loving'. His creativity and innovation are supported and realised by brother Andy, whose strategic planning and financial skills have helped to make Broker's a very successful worldwide brand.

Winston Churchill Martini

The Broker's brand of very 'British' humour is delightfully reflected in their suggestion for a 'Winston Churchill Martini'.

Ingredients: 4fl oz (120ml) Broker's Gin
Ice
Twist of lime or olive, to taste

Shake the Broker's Gin over ice and pour into a chilled Martini glass while looking at the vermouth bottle on the other side of the room. Add a twist of lime or an olive.

Method of Distillation
Broker's Gin is made in a traditional copper pot still at the Langley Distillery near Birmingham. The botanicals are steeped for 24 hours in a quadruple-distilled grain spirit made from English wheat before being redistilled. As with all good quality gins, only the heart cut is taken.

Tasting Notes
A very clear, intense flavour with the up-front citrus peels coming through with a ripe, almost candied sweetness. The juniper is as spicy as one would expect, and is followed through with a long, smooth, peppery fade that leaves the mouth feeling warm. A very good gin for a stylish and flavourful Martini, but also one which really comes across well with tonic.

Bulldog Gin

www.bulldoggin.com
London Dry Gin

ABV 40%

Botanicals: Almond, angelica, cassia, coriander, dragon's eye, juniper, lavender, lemon, liquorice, lotus leaves, orris root, poppy seeds

Former American investment banker Anshuman Vohra gave up his job to create Bulldog Gin, which shouldered its way onto the market in 2007. The stocky, smoked-glass bottle with its spiky collar moulded into the glass is striking different from anything else on the shelves. It also bears a Union Jack label, carried on a chain, which adds to the bulldog image.

The name of this unusual gin was inspired by that independent spirit Winston Churchill – perhaps the most iconic embodiment of the 'British Bulldog' ideal.

As a young man, Vohra enjoyed drinking traditional gin and tonics with his father. He was keen to create a perfect gin – both defiant and delicious – that, while maintaining the very best of the tradition, also brought a new vitality and 'sexiness' to the spirit, attracting younger drinkers.

Method of Distillation
Small-batch distilled in England, using a traditional copper pot still. The grain spirit is made from Norfolk wheat, and pure spring water from Wales is used to bring the gin to bottling strength.

Did you know?

Bulldog Gin contains some very unusual and exotic botanicals.

Dragon's eye, a relative of the lychee, is so-called because the black seed is visible through the flesh of the fruit, and looks rather like the pupil of an eye. In Chinese medicine, it's reputed to generate 'internal heat' – creating vitality and sexual energy.

Lotus leaves bring a perfumy quality to the flavour, and are thought to invigorate the blood.

Poppy adds a sweet nuttiness to the gin – and is considered to have a sedative effect.

Tasting Notes

Very strong and perfumy on the nose, with the traditional London Dry juniper coming through well, and a slight spikiness following through from the other botanicals. The flavour is exciting. It's very balanced, but with strong, exotic herbal notes pushing through. On the palate, the first sensation is creamy but quite dry, almost chalky – this dryness possibly generated by the dragon's eye. The mid-palate juniper rush is followed by a gentler, herby and citrusy finish.

The mix of stronger, exotic notes backed up by the gentler, balanced creaminess make this an excellent gin for sipping neat, or for creating sophisticated cocktails such as the Plumdog Millionaire from the Bulldog Gin website, which utilises Japanese plum wine and lavender.

Burnett's White Satin Gin

London Dry Gin

ABV 40%

Botanicals: Not listed

Burnett's White Satin was once a very big seller in the UK, but as with many of the oldest brands, it has had a very chequered career in recent years. The brand was established by Sir Robert Burnett in the late-Eighteenth Century, and was made at his Vauxhall distillery – which was then the biggest in London.

The Sir Robert Burnett Co. at the Heaven Hill Distillery in the US now owns the Burnett's brand name, and make a Burnett's London Dry Gin. It's good to know that, in 2007, the Burnett's 'White Satin' brand was bought back by a UK company to be distilled according to the original recipe.

Did you know?

Sir Robert kept 2,000 pigs at the Vauxhall distillery, which were fed entirely on the waste grain from the distilling process.

Method of Distillation
As for a traditional London Dry Gin, using a pot still.

Tasting Notes
A crisp, clean-tasting gin, with the classic juniper and spice notes.

Darnley's View

www.darnleysview.com
London Dry Gin

ABV 40%

Botanicals: Angelica, coriander, elderflower, juniper, lemon peel, orris

Like some other gins – Hendrick's and The Botanist, to name two – Darnley's View includes elderflower in the list of botanicals. It's a light, contemporary take on the classic London Dry Gin, and the creators of the brand, the Wemyss family, aim to combine the best of both English and Scottish distilling in this gin.

Did you know?

The Wemyss family seat at Wemyss Castle, on the Firth of Forth, once housed Mary, Queen of Scots, who spied her husband, Lord Darnley, through one of the castle windows. This was the inspiration for Darnley's View Gin.

Method of Distillation
Made at the Thames Distillers by traditional methods – despite the Scottish connection, the Wemyss family wanted their gin to be made in London, the historic home of London Dry Gin.

Tasting Notes

Plenty of classic juniper on the nose. The taste profile is light, smooth and quite sweet for a dry gin, with juniper and peppery spice at the end. With the addition of ice, or a little water, the floral notes come through more strongly. Makes a lovely, delicate Martini with floral overtones.

Edgerton

Distilled Gin

ABV 47%

Botanicals: 14, including almond, angelica, cassia, cinnamon, coriander, damiana, grains of paradise, juniper, lemon peel, liquorice, nutmeg, orris and savory

The pink glow of this premium gin stands out immediately on the shelf and behind the bar. It's not the bottle, either, that is so brightly coloured – it's the spirit itself. Though not listed in the botanicals, the makers say that pomegranate has been used to add warm blush to the spirit.

Did you know?

Edgerton Gin is not to be confused with the Pink Gin cocktail which came to popularity in the mid-Nineteenth Century. This was a mix of Plymouth Gin with a dash of dark red Angostura bitters – giving a similar rosy colour.

Method of Distillation

Small-batch distilled at Thames Distillers.

Tasting Notes

Sweet floral notes strike the nose first, followed by dry, powdery cinnamon and spice. In the mouth, there is an interesting mix of sweet and bitter. Sweet orange and juniper are up front, leading through to a slightly bitter, grapefruity finish with an aftertaste which is almost like chocolate. The damiana adds a smoky mint quality.

The high ABV of 47% gives Edgerton Gin an overall strength of flavour, in spite of the delicacy and complexity of the profile, and this makes it ideal for cocktails.

Edgerton's character comes through as very fresh and fruit-laden in a gin and tonic, and it creates an intriguing balance of flavours with the lime in a Gimlet. The floral notes add a touch of lilac to the lemon juice, maraschino and crème de violette in an Aviation. In a Martini, Edgerton brings lasting and unusual berry flavours.

Finsbury

www.borco.com
London Dry Gin

ABV 37.5%

Botanicals: Including juniper and coriander

Finsbury Distillery was one of the big names in London though the Eighteenth and Nineteenth Centuries, but now this historical brand is owned by Borco International, a German company.

Did you know?

The Finsbury Distillery was founded by Joseph Bishop in 1740, and was situated near Clerkenwell Springs in the Borough of Finsbury, London. It remained in the ownership of the Booth family until its closure in the early-1900s. Finsbury Gin is still made to a secret recipe, handed down through the family for more than 200 years.

Finsbury Gin is now a top seller in Germany. It can be obtained in the UK, but mostly through online retailers.

Method of Distillation
Finsbury Gin uses neutral spirit made from molasses rather than grain. It's made at the Langley Distillery near Birmingham in a traditional copper pot still known as 'Jenny'.

Tasting Notes
On the nose, plenty of juniper and coriander. A sweetish, smooth taste profile with spicy undertones. Great in a gin and tonic, where the juniper provides a good backbone.

Finsbury Platinum

ABV 47%

This is the premium range from Finsbury, with the higher ABV of 47% bringing a much more intense complexity to the flavours.

Tasting Notes

On the nose, Finsbury Platinum offers a strong presence of black pepper, with coriander and juniper underlying. The flavour profile has lots of juniper, backed with gingery spice, zesty lemon, and herbal sage. Citrus and a slight, dry, musky note of angelica end the experience, together with a return of juniper.

Brings plenty of juniper and spice to a gin and tonic, and is also very mellow and soft in a Negroni. A Finsbury Platinum Martini is very light and delicate with a good balance of gin and vermouth on the palate.

Finsbury Export Strength is also sometimes available, with an ABV of 60%.

Foxdenton

www.foxdentonestate.co.uk/
London Dry Gin

ABV 48%

Botanicals: Organic angelica, coriander, juniper, lemon peel, lime flower, orris

Foxdenton Estate Company dates back to 1935, when it was set up by Major CRE Radclyffe to provide revenue for the Estate that had belonged to his family since 1367. Still a small family firm, Foxdenton Estate specialises in gin and gin liqueurs. Their high-strength gin is intended to capture the intense flavour of the old 'Export Strength' gins.

Method of Distillation

Traditionally distilled at Thames Distillers by Charles Maxwell, in full conformity with the EU specification for London Dry Gin.

Tasting Notes

A classic, juniper-led London Dry Gin. The punchy intensity of flavour that comes with the high ABV is well-balanced, and the lime flower adds a clean, refreshing note to the taste profile.

This is a gin which will stand up to lots of tonic – so you can stick to a single measure, but make your gin and tonic into a long drink.

Geranium Gin

www.geraniumgin.com
London Dry Gin

ABV 44%

Botanicals: 10, including angelica, cassia, coriander, geranium, juniper, lemon, liquorice and orris

Norwegian Henrik Hammer, creator of Geranium Gin, has long been a fan of London Gin. Aware of the therapeutic properties of scented geranium leaves, which are an old remedy for depression and low spirits, he wanted to utilise them as a botanical. It took many months of work with his father, a chemist with many years of experience in the perfume and food industries, to work out how to distil geranium in alcohol. Once father and son were satisfied with the result, they came to the Langley Distillery near Birmingham with the recipe, and Geranium Gin was born.

Henrik Hammer with a bottle of Geranium Gin.

It brings a pleasing floral note to the traditional London Gin flavour profile, without moving too far away from it.

Method of Distillation
Botanicals are steeped for 48 hours before distillation in a traditional copper pot still at the Langley Distillery.

Tasting Notes
A soft mix of juniper and floral notes strikes the nose. On the palate, there is a strong rush of juniper before the floral hints of rose and violet come through. Juniper surfaces again, together with citrus and a pleasantly bitter dryness as the profile fades.

Makes an impressive Martini, combined with Dolin vermouth. The hint of violet is picked up well in an Aviation, and with so much classic juniper present in the profile, Geranium works very well in a gin and tonic.

Gilbey's Special Dry Gin

London Dry Gin

ABV 37.5%

Botanicals: Including juniper

Sadly, this once popular gin – still remembered with affection by many older gin drinkers – is now produced outside of the UK. Now owned by drinks giant Diageo, Gilbey's is still a huge brand in the US, and in Commonwealth countries such as Australia, Canada and South Africa, but it's rarely seen for sale here – and mostly online.

Brothers Walter and Alfred Gilbey established a very successful wine and whisky business on their return from the Crimean War in 1857 – and, by 1872, they were making gin at their distillery in Camden Town. Soon, they were exporting to the British colonies.

Did you know?

Gilbey's was very popular in the US during the Prohibition years. It would be shipped to the 12-mile limit just off the US coastline and, from there, it would be smuggled ashore. It became so popular at this time that there were many attempts to counterfeit it and, as a result, Gilbey's manufactured an unusual frosted bottle that was almost impossible to copy.

Method of Distillation
As for EU London Dry Gin specification.

Tasting Notes
A light-bodied gin with a creamy texture and a rich but delicate flavour, spicy and aromatic with a hint of dried herbs. Once very popular in all kinds of cocktails.

Did you know?

Gilbey's distillery, bonded warehouses and bottlestore occupied a huge site at Chalk Farm, close to the canal and railway, for many years. They established the distillery in the 1870s, on land belonging to the London and North Western Railway Company (LNWR). For some years previous to this, they'd also leased a warehouse on Oval Road, known as 'A' shed – and, in 1895, three underground tunnels were dug to transport goods from the distillery to this warehouse.

The iconic Roundhouse building (once used for turning steam locomotives and now a performance space) was also taken over by Gilbey's, who used it as bonded warehouse between 1869-1963 – a span of almost 100 years.

Gordon's Original Special London Dry Gin

www.gordons-gin.co.uk
London Dry Gin

ABV 37.5% (UK), 40% (US)

Botanicals: Including angelica, cassia, coriander, ginger, juniper, nutmeg

For many people, not just in the UK (where around 15 million consumers purchase it regularly), but throughout the world, Gordon's is the definitive gin, and has been so for many years. It's strong on juniper and, with a hint of lemon, too, in the flavour profile, it makes an excellent gin and tonic, which means that it's always been popularly with traditional gin drinkers.

Did you know?

Gordon's 'G&T Society' can be accessed through their website, and offers regular competitions, news, and plenty of ideas for cocktails.

Like so many other classic London gins, Gordon's dates back to the Eighteenth Century. Alexander Gordon first set up a distillery in Southwark, in 1769, before moving to Clerkenwell in 1786. One of his 10 children, Charles, took the family business into the next century. In 1878, Gordon's was sold to John Currie and Co Distillers (who had supplied the raw spirit for the gin for many years) at the Four

Mills Distillery in Bromley-by-Bow, East London. Twenty years later, Tanqueray, who had also had a long relationship with Curries, amalgamated with Gordon's to become Tanqueray, Gordon and Co – a powerful partnership which has endured to this day.

Did you know?

In its recent advertising campaigns, Gordon's has taken a bold and creative approach. Some years ago, they took on feisty chef Gordon Ramsay to promote the brand, but his reputation for bad language and explosive behaviour didn't appeal to the traditional customer base, and sales went down. Currently, actors Philip Glenister and Emilia Fox are reinventing the Gordon's image, with tough guy Philip (who starred in *Life on Mars*) being gently and wittily reminded of his manners in various social situations by upper-class Emilia. Three of these amusing scenarios, plus a 'behind the scenes' documentary, can be seen on the Gordon's website.

Method of Distillation
This conforms to the EU criteria for London Gin – but the details are confidential, as is the full list of botanicals.

Did you know?

Some years ago, Gordon's Distiller's Cut was created, with ginger and lemongrass botanicals adding an exotic slant to the flavour profile. Though it's no longer made, it's worth trying if you can find a bottle online or at a specialist retailer.

Tasting Notes
The UK strength Gordon's is strong on juniper and citrus, with a pleasant lemony tang, which leaves the mouth feeling clean and fresh. The strong presence of juniper, alongside the lemon, makes Gordon's ideal for gin and tonic. The US version, with a higher ABV, is much more aromatic, and the flavours come through much more powerfully through the taste profile.

Gordon's Sloe Gin

Made with steeped wild sloe berries, Gordon's Sloe Gin has a deep purple colour, and marries the dryness of the spirit with a cassis-like sweetness. Makes a great alternative gin and tonic, and also works well in Brambles and other fruit-based cocktails. For more details, see *Chapter Thirteen*.

Other Products
Gordon's also specialise in ready-mixed gin and tonics in a can, which are perfect if you're on the move.

Greenall's Original London Dry Gin

www.gjgreenall.co.uk
London Dry Gin

ABV 40%

Botanicals: Including almond, cassia, coriander, juniper, lemon, liquorice

This classic London Dry Gin has been produced in much the same way at the Warrington distillery for almost 200 years.

Method of Distillation
Traditionally distilled in a copper pot still.

Did you know?

There has been a distillery at Warrington, in the heart of the rolling Cheshire countryside, since Thomas Dakin began producing gin there in 1761. The business was bought in 1870 by Edward Greenall, and continued to flourish. It was rebuilt and expanded in the 1960s, enabling G&J Greenall to take on contract distilling, including the hugely successful Bombay Sapphire brand in the 1980s.

Tasting Notes
A very soft feel in the mouth initially, which expands into a slash of juniper and a rush of fresh citrus. The long taste profile eases into a finish of earthy and spicy

notes. A traditional, no-nonsense London Gin which works beautifully in a gin and tonic.

Hayman's Gin

www.haymansgin.com
London Dry Gin

ABV 40%

Botanicals: Angelica, cassia, cinnamon, juniper, lemon peel, liquorice, nutmeg, orange peel, orris

The Haymans have been in the distilling business for longer than any other family in the UK. Christopher Hayman developed Hayman's Gin after a 40-year career, which included working for James Burrough Ltd to distil and produce Beefeater Gin from 1969 until the late-1980s when the company was sold. Christopher set up Hayman Distillers in 1989.

Did you know?

James Burrough, creator of Beefeater Gin in the Nineteenth Century, is Christopher Hayman's great-grandfather. His father, Neville, married Marjorie Burrough (James Burrough's granddaughter) and joined the James Burrough Board in 1950. James Hayman, Christopher's son, together with his wife, Miranda, are now carrying on the Hayman's tradition as they work to develop and promote the Hayman's brands.

Method of Distillation
Botanicals are steeped in the alcohol for 24 hours before distillation, to ensure that the flavours are fully developed. Only the best of the middle run from the distillation is used.

Tasting Notes
Clear strong notes of citrus and juniper come through on the nose, and the taste profile is beautifully balanced (in the James Burrough tradition) between juniper, citrus and coriander, finishing with a crisp, delicate taste which lingers in the mouth. Perfect for a Martini or a gin and tonic.

Other Products

Hayman's also make an **Old Tom Gin**, an **1820 Gin Liqueur** and an **1850 Reserve** which are listed in *Chapter Twelve* with the Old Tom Gins. They also make a **Sloe Gin**. For details, see *Chapter Thirteen*.

Hendrick's Gin

www.hendricksgin.com
Distilled Gin

ABV 41.4% (UK), 44% (US and Spain)

Botanicals: Angelica, caraway, chamomile, coriander, cubeb, cucumber, elderflower, juniper, lemon peel, meadowsweet, orange peel, orris, rose petal

Hendrick's is the innovative creation of whisky distillers William Grant & Sons, and was one of the first new gins that led to the current rebirth of interest in the spirit. The traditional flavours of a British summer were the inspiration, but it took two long years of hard work in the laboratory before the recipe was complete.

The dark-brown, squat and square-shouldered bottle is reminiscent of an old apothecary's bottle, evoking the days when gin and other liqueurs were considered as remedies.

Everything about Hendrick's Gin is unusual, from the distillation method, to the wacky humour of the very distinctive retro-styled marketing campaign. Hendrick's run frequent events through the summer at Fringe Festivals and literary gatherings, and if you're a fan, it's well worth checking the website regularly to see what's going on.

Method of Distillation

Hendrick's is small-batch distilled, but uses two different methods. A traditional Bennett copper pot still dating from the 1860s is used to steep some of the botanicals, before boiling them in the traditional way. A Carterhead still is also used to infuse other botanicals, ensuring a fresh, subtle flavour. The exact details of these processes are kept secret but, after the results of the two distillations have been combined, separate distillates of

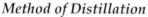

Hendrick's signature cucumber and rose botanicals are added. Local spring water from Ayrshire is used to dilute Hendrick's before bottling.

Tasting Notes

The marriage of strong, aromatic flavours from the traditional distillation with the more subtle flavours from the infusion is complex but gentle, and the addition of the unusual cucumber and rose notes give Hendrick's a very distinctive nose and flavour.

Fresh, delicate, floral aromas are a delicious introduction to the taste experience, which is silky smooth in texture, and very balanced. Juniper is there, but is less predominant than in the more traditional gins. Hendrick's is perfect in cocktails such as Elderflower Collins, and also makes a wonderful Elderflower Martini. Adding a slice of cucumber as a garnish makes a very special Hendrick's gin and tonic.

Hoxton Gin

www.hoxtongin.com
Distilled Gin

ABV 43%

Botanicals: Coconut, ginger, grapefruit, iris root, juniper, tarragon

This is one that you will either love or hate. Launched in 2011 by Gerry Calabrese, son of legendary London bartender Salvatore Calabrese and owner of the über-cool Hoxton Pony Bar in East London, this punchy, in-your-face, gin-with-attitude is not for the faint-hearted. The label bears the words: 'Warning! Grapefruit and Coconut'. That's just about right, as those are the flavours that come through right up front, and very strongly, too.

Some traditionalists have claimed that Hoxton Gin isn't, strictly speaking, a gin at all since the juniper is overshadowed by the more exotic botanicals. But juniper does comprise 55% of the botanical mix, and Gerry is adamant that he is operating well within the historical context. To get a fuller flavour of the debate, you might enjoy the 'traditional versus innovative' debate between Gerry and Beefeater Master Distiller Desmond Payne on the Imbibe.com website.

And – to be fair – it does say 'Warning!' on the label...

Method of Distillation

The botanicals are macerated and distilled in a 150-year-old copper pot still by Gabriel Boudier in Dijon, France. (See also **Boudier Saffron Gin**.)

Did you know?

EastEnder Gerry Calabrese took three years to create Hoxton Gin. Concerned that gin – a fantastic spirit, as far as he was concerned – was not relevant to younger people, he wanted to come up with something that would really grab their attention.

At first, he had no idea how to do this but, on the way to a preliminary discussion with the French expert distiller Gabriel Boudier, Gerry popped into his local corner shop and came out with three coconuts and three grapefruits. Then he jumped on the Eurostar and, later that day, over dinner with Boudier, the concept of Hoxton Gin came into being.

The botanicals worked well in Boudier's laboratory, but Gerry set the bar very high for his gin – he wanted it to be extremely versatile, not only as a neat gin, a striking Martini and in a gin and tonic, but also with coke, cranberry juice, ginger beer and even Red Bull. Adjusting the ABV was crucial for this. Changing just one or two per cent made all the difference, and samples crossed and re-crossed the Channel until Gerry chose an ABV of 43%.

Tasting Notes

A very strong hit of coconut on the nose as soon as you raise your glass. Some have described the initial experience on the palate as being like 'drinking a liquid Bounty Bar'. Tangy grapefruit follows through, also very strongly. If you are patient, and savour the neat spirit, which lingers for a long, strong, while in the mouth, you'll get a warmth that comes not just from the slightly high ABV, but also from the ginger. And there *is* juniper there, too – but it takes a while to tune in to it as it kicks in somewhere in the middle of the experience.

Drunk neat, Hoxton Gin makes a very unusual 'contemporary Martini'. It holds its own very well with tonic, blending nicely with the bitterness of the quinine and is very good in exotic cocktails such as Daiquiris, and the Hoxton Pony's Shoreditch Sour, made with lemon and orange juice, grapes and honey.

One big benefit of Hoxton Gin in cocktails is that you can have the flavour of coconut without having to add coconut cream or rely on sickly-sweet coconut liqueurs. This means that you can create a drink that tastes of coconut, yet retains the characteristic dryness of the gin.

-Ish Gin

www.ishgin.com
London Dry Gin

ABV 41%

Botanicals: Almond, angelica, cassia, cinnamon, coriander, juniper, lemon peel, liquorice, nutmeg, orange peel, orris

The startling red bottle gives a hint as to the racy approach the producers have taken to marketing this stylish London Dry Gin. Go to the website, and you'll find an intriguing and unusual list of 'fet-ish' cocktails that you can make using -Ish Gin. Handcuffs, high heels, feathers, whips – whatever takes your fancy, there's a cocktail to match.

The spirit itself has a 'twist', too – an additional shot of juniper to boost the distinctive London Dry Gin profile.

Method of Distillation
Small-batch distilled at The London Distillery using high-quality English grain spirit. The botanicals are macerated for 12 hours before distillation and, after distillation, the sprit is rested for two weeks to allow the flavours to integrate.

Tasting Notes
A full-bodied gin, with the slightly higher ABV of 41% bringing the mix of flavours through with complexity and balance. The extra hit of juniper makes -Ish Gin a good candidate for a Dry Martini. It comes through well in a gin and tonic, too.

Jensen's

www.bermondseygin.com
London Dry Gin

ABV 43%

Botanicals: Including angelica, coriander, juniper, liquorice, orris

Jensen's Bermondsey London Dry Gin comes in an elegant, simple, frosted glass bottle which looks very modern – but the contents hark back some 70 years, to the golden age of cocktails.

Christian Jensen was working in Japan when he encountered some old-style British gins in the bars there. After trying samples of gins which were popular in the cocktail heyday of the 1940s, he found that he liked their heavier, more flavoursome quality – in contrast to the lighter modern gins.

A Japanese bartender noted Christian's enthusiasm and sent him back to London with a challenge – 'Make your own old-style London Gin!'

On his return, bearing a sample of one of the old gins, Christian worked with the Thames Distillers to develop a recipe (reputed to be based around the once-famous Nicholson's Lamplighter Gin) and the result is Jensen's Bermondsey London Dry Gin.

Method of Distillation
Small-batch distilled and bottled in London.

Tasting Notes
Jensen's London Dry Gin is juniper-led, and the signature botanical comes through with a fresh, clean hit of aroma and flavour. The texture in the mouth is silky, lingering on the palate with a soft intensity and weight which is very distinctive. Makes a great gin and tonic, and is also ideal for bringing an authentic taste to a Negroni or a Ramos Gin Fizz.

Jensen's Old Tom Gin is listed in *Chapter Twelve*.

Juniper Green Organic Gin

www.junipergreen.com
London Dry Gin

ABV 43%

Botanicals: Angelica, coriander, juniper, savory

Launched in the UK in 1999 as 'the world's first organic gin', Juniper Green is still in the forefront of the organic spirits movement after more than a decade of success on supermarket shelves and in health food stores.

There are quite a few gins which use organically produced botanicals but, with Juniper Green, even the neutral spirit is made from biodynamically grown and certified organic grain.

The gin is distilled and bottled at Thames Distillers in London, under the skilled nose of Charles Maxwell, Master Distiller and Managing Director. An eighth-generation distiller, Charles has inherited one of the oldest unbroken family involvements in gin distilling.

At first, like many others, Charles Maxwell was unsure of the wisdom of using organic neutral alcohol. The distillation process is an industrial one, and the resulting spirit is extremely refined – so, surely, anything impure would be removed. What difference could it make? Also, organic grain spirit is extremely difficult to source. It can only be made in a still which has been thoroughly cleaned of all non-organic residues, and the small quantities required for Juniper Green make this process uneconomical for alcohol producers in this country.

Eventually, a distiller was found in Eastern Europe who could offer a reliable supply, and Charles was pleased to note that their organic spirit has a quality of exceptional softness, as can be experienced with some very old whiskies. Perhaps this is due to the fact that, as the creators of Juniper Green stress, organic grain has a better cell structure than grain grown with unnatural, chemical fertilisers – and the fact that no chemical fungicides are used means that the grain will undergo a very deep and complex fermentation, all of which results in an extremely fine alcohol.

Despite being organic, Juniper Green is very reasonably priced, and its simple green-and-white label (sporting the Royal Warrant 'By Appointment to HRH Prince Charles') can be found on the shelves of many supermarkets.

Method of Distillation
The organic grain spirit and botanicals are distilled together at Thames Distillers in the smallest pot stills in the UK – Tom Thumb and Thumbelina.

Tasting Notes
An outstandingly bright, clear flavour, with a very intense hit of juniper. The clean note of the juniper is strong on the nose, and also on the palate, and the other botanicals bring lighter, herbaceous spicy notes. Works well in a gin and tonic.

Knockeen Hills Heather Gin

www.heather-gin.com
London Gin

ABV 47.3%

Botanicals: Angelica, coriander, heather, juniper, savory

The name is a little misleading on this one. Knockeen Hills are well-known for producing a range of high-strength Irish Poteens, but their light, smooth Heather Gin is made in London and fulfils the criteria for London Dry Gin. It sells very well in Spain, where gin is currently very popular, but isn't often seen in the UK.

Method of Distillation
Distilled in London at Thames Distillers. Botanicals are steeped for 24 hours prior to distillation.

Tasting Notes

A hit of juniper up front on the nose, with lighter, floral elements coming through from the heather. On the palate, very smooth, with a dry finish of fruit and flowery notes.

Makes a very good gin and tonic, and is also lovely as a long drink with pink lemonade, where the tartness of the lemons blends refreshingly with the strong juniper and the floral heather notes.

London Hill Gin

www.ianmacleod.com
London Dry Gin

ABV 43%

Botanicals: Angelica, cassia, coriander, ginger, juniper, liquorice, nutmeg, orange

Made in Scotland by whisky distillers Ian Macleod, London Hill Gin is a premium quality traditional London Dry Gin which deserves to be much better known.

Method of Distillation

Small-batch distilled in a traditional copper pot still.

Tasting Notes

A very balanced London Gin, with juniper coming through just a little ahead of the other botanicals. Smooth on the palate, and very balanced. Coriander and angelica lead through into a fresh, bright finish.

An excellent gin for a Martini.

Martin Miller's

www.martinmillersgin.com
London Dry Gin Style

ABV 40% and 45.2% (Martin Miller's Westbourne Strength)

Botanicals: Angelica, cassia, cinnamon, coriander, Florentine iris root, juniper, orris, lemon peel, lime peel, liquorice, nutmeg, Seville orange peel

This premium gin was first envisioned in a bar in Notting Hill in the summer of 1998. Antiques guru and *bon viveur* Martin Miller of *Miller's Guide* fame was disappointed in the quality of the gins on offer – and decided the only solution was to create his own. Time and money would be no object. He simply wanted to create a 'gin from the heart' that would be a modern classic, but still retain a twist on tradition.

Martin Miller's Gin at Gerry's of Old Compton Street.

The gin is distilled in England, but is blended and bottled 1,500 miles away in Iceland, at Borgarnes on the remote west coast. The icy cold water which is drawn from the spring there has been underground for perhaps 800 years, and brings great clarity and softness to the gin.

Method of Distillation

Martin Miller's Gin is distilled at the Langley Distillery near Birmingham, in the 100-year old copper pot still known as Angela. Before distillation, the botanicals are left to steep in the still overnight. The citrus peels, however, are not included in this. They are distilled separately, and the resulting distillate is added to the earthy, spicy, juniper-based main distillate later. (Since the botanicals are not all distilled together, Martin Miller's cannot fulfil the EU criteria for London Dry Gin, but it is most definitely of that style.)

Tasting Notes

A fresh, smooth gin which has a very soft quality in the mouth. It's gently aromatic, with a touch of Parma violet from the orris and iris roots, and the spices come through in a subtle and balanced way. Ideal for the mixing lighter, fresher, contemporary cocktails.

Martin Miller's Westbourne Strength

The botanicals and the distillation process are exactly the same as for Martin Miller's Gin, the only difference being that it is bottled with a much higher alcohol content. This changes the taste profile, bringing juniper, spice and citrus through much more strongly, and giving much more of a classic London Gin flavour profile.

No. 3

www.no3gin.com
London Dry Gin

ABV 46%

Botanicals: Angelica, cardamom, coriander, grapefruit peel, juniper, sweet orange peel

This classic, assertive London Dry Gin is as neat and finely tailored as a well-cut suit. This is hardly surprising, since it is produced by the famous London Wine and Spirits Merchants Berry Bros. & Rudd. It's named for the address of their premises – dating back to 1698 – at No. 3 St James's Street. No. 3 Gin is the creation of Simon Berry, Chairman of Berry Bros. & Rudd. His love of a fine Martini – and the need to have the finest possible gin for the creation of this most elegant of cocktails – was the starting point.

Method of Distillation
No. 3 is made in Schiedam, Holland – where there is still a thriving distilling industry, making both gin and genever.

Tasting Notes
A characterful and balanced classic London dry, with plenty of juniper up front. The profile has clean, fresh citrus to start and a strong, piny stripe of juniper followed by cool, acerbic spice.
    Makes a very classy Martini, and a robust, refreshing gin and tonic.

Oxley

www.oxleygin.com
Distilled Gin

ABV 47%

Botanicals: 14, including fresh citrus peels, juniper, meadowsweet and vanilla

Oxley Gin is the result of a major technological development. It's made not in a conventional still, but in a cold distillation process, using vacuum technology. The lack of heat means that some of the botanicals, especially the citrus peels, can be used fresh rather than dry. This gives a purity and soft texture to the spirit that is unique. Developed at Thames Distillers, the process and the recipe took eight years to perfect.

Method of Distillation

The botanicals are macerated in the spirit for 15 hours before being added to the custom-built still. Instead of heat being used, a vacuum reduces pressure in the still, until the temperature is lowered to –5°C, and the spirit vapourises. The vapour rises to meet a cold-finger probe at around –100°C and converts back to liquid. No heads or tails are produced with this method, so all the spirit is used for bottling.

Only 120 bottles per distillation are produced, so Oxley is a genuinely small-batch gin.

Tasting Notes

On the nose, Oxley is very fresh, soft and complex, with an aroma of sweet lemons predominating. There is light juniper, too, and hints of aniseed, almond and lavender.

On the palate, a juicy hit of citrus is the first sensation, followed by an elegant, subtle dash of juniper. The strong pine notes of juniper, which are generated in a conventional heated still, are much less in evidence here, allowing the subtler qualities of the berry to come through. The overall effect is creamy and lush, with soft, scented floral notes, too, and the meadowsweet bringing a touch of almond flavour.

A great way to savour this unique gin is to serve over ice in a balloon glass. A twist of grapefruit will help to enhance the flavours.

Perivale Gin

www.fabulousvodkacompany.co.uk
Distilled Gin

ABV 40%

Botanicals: Angelica, coriander, juniper, lemon, orange

Did you know?

The narrowboat featured on the green-and-white label gives a clue to the name – Chris once lived on the canal in Perivale. And the lack of pubs he experienced while in the area gives an added piquancy to the title 'Dry'.

This clean, fresh-flavoured gin is the creation of Chris Spiller of the Fabulous Vodka Company. It's a great value gin, good in its own right, and extremely versatile for mixing.

Chris, an experienced distiller, makes the gin himself at Thames Distillers. His aim is to produce a subtle and delicate gin which is firmly in the London Dry style.

Method of Distillation

Small-batch. Botanicals are steeped in the spirit overnight before distillation. Chris pays great attention to the taking of the cuts, using only the heart from each distillation. Heads and tails are saved for redistillation in the next batch.

Tasting Notes

On the nose, Perivale Gin is very clear and clean, with juniper, angelica and coriander present. In the mouth, juniper is predominant, but the overall feel is very soft and silky. The profile follows through with freshness and clarity.

Very good sipped extra cold (from the freezer), with a wedge of lime. Makes a great gin and tonic, a crisp Martini, a fine Pink Gin and also comes through very well in fruit-based cocktails.

Did you know?

The Fabulous Vodka Company, as their name would imply, also make speciality vodkas, including caramel-flavoured Caralicious and a Polish-style potato vodka, Krol Kazimiersz.

Portobello Road No. 171

www.portobellostarbar.co.uk
London Dry Gin Style

ABV 42%

Botanicals: Angelica, bitter orange peel, cassia, coriander, juniper, lemon peel, liquorice, nutmeg, orris

The exquisite vintage styling of the label on the simple, corked bottle says it all. This classic and very versatile London Dry was launched in 2011 and is the creation of Ged Feltham, proprietor of the award-winning Portobello Star bar in Notting Hill, and his colleague, mixologist Jake Burger.

No. 171 Gin was inspired by some of the antique gins in the collection at The Ginstitute Museum above the Portobello Star. The nine traditional botanicals, sourced from Europe, The East Indies and The Commonwealth, make no concessions to the modern trend of esoteric and unusual fruits, herbs and spices.

Method of Distillation
This is a small-batch gin, distilled by eighth-generation London distiller, Charles Maxwell, at Thames Distillers.

Tasting Notes
As befits a classic London Dry, there's a big hit of juniper and a burst of citrus from the lemon and bitter orange. Liquorice and cassia follow through, and the taste profile slowly builds to a long peppery finish from the nutmeg.

No. 171 is exceptionally versatile. It makes a superb Martini, a delicious Negroni and, with the strong juniper presence, it has no problem holding its own in a gin and tonic. The depth of character and the long, spicy and peppery finish also make it ideal for drinking neat.

Sacred Gin

www.sacredspiritscompany.co.uk
Distilled Gin

ABV 40%

Botanicals: 12, including angelica, *Boswellia sacra* (frankincense), cardamom, juniper, fresh lemon, lime, nutmeg, fresh orange

This elegant bottle with the purple-and-gold label stands tall behind some of the most distinguished bars in London. Micro-distiller Ian Hart (see *Chapter Seven*) once worked in the financial sector but, having left all that behind him to indulge his passion for fine spirits, he has created a distinctive and high-quality gin, which is vacuum-distilled for a very fresh, soft flavour.

The 'Sacred' name is a reference to the unusual botanical frankincense – unique to this gin.

Method of Distillation

Sacred Gin is handmade in small batches. Each botanical is macerated and distilled separately under a vacuum, which enables distillation to take place at a low temperature. This is very energy efficient and also preserves the fresh flavour of each botanical so that there are no harsh or 'cooked' notes coming through. These distillates are then blended together to create Sacred Gin. Each bottle carries a 'batch number' as a record of when it was made.

Tasting Notes

This is a very smooth, delicate gin which is exceptionally clean and light. On the nose, there are soft citrus hints and a slight sense of spice, with hints of vanilla. To taste, distiller Ian Hart recommends trying Sacred Gin neat with no ice, so that you can discover the full potential of the taste profile. It starts very smoothly, with light citrus and spice coming through, and then the warm, clean flare of the juniper tails off into a creamy, complex finish.

Very good indeed neat. Makes a great Martini, a fine Gimlet and also works well in a Negroni. Despite its delicacy and softness, Sacred Gin makes a fabulous gin and tonic, especially when topped off with a swirl of Sacred Spirits' Cassia distillate. See also *Chapter Twenty-one – Blend your Own Gin*, for details of the Sacred Spirits Open Sauce Distillates.

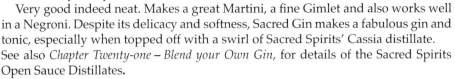

Did you know?

Sacred Christmas Pudding Gin is also available from the Sacred Spirits Company. It's made by infusing Christmas pudding in Sacred Gin for three months before redistilling and bottling.

As with Sacred, the flavour starts gently, building to a very warm sensation in the mouth. There are strong, slightly bitter overtones of dark fruitcake overlying the juniper. At the end, your mouth feels as if you have just eaten a spoonful of Christmas Pudding – even down to the texture of it.

Very good drunk chilled, and makes a smashing seasonal Hot Toddy, and a lovely and very unusual 'Christmas Martini'.

Sacred Vodka and also Spiced English Vermouth are also now made by the Sacred Spirits Company.

Sipsmith

www.sipsmith.com
London Dry Gin

ABV 41.6%

Botanicals: Almond, angelica, cassia, cinnamon, coriander, juniper, lemon peel, liquorice, orange peel, orris

This classic, high-quality London Dry Gin was inspired by the many small-batch artisan gins made in the US. After many years of working in the drinks industry, Sam Galsworthy and Fairfax Hall set up Sipsmith, installing (after a two-year battle with Customs and Excise) the first new copper pot still in London for 189 years. In collaboration with Master Distiller Jared Brown, they've created a gin which has been outstandingly successful.

The Sipsmith bottle is pleasingly solid, with an elegant, copper-tinted label featuring a graceful swan's head inspired by the elegant beauty of Prudence, the Sipsmith copper pot still. The gin-bottle top is sealed with a cork covered with dark green wax and a black ribbon – and when you pull out the cork, you'll hear an inviting pop and squeak, just as happens with a top quality whisky bottle.

At the top of the bottle, you'll find a small label bearing your batch number, which you can use to check on the Sipsmith website to find out what was happening there on the day your gin was distilled.

Did you know?

The Sipsmith Distillery is to be found in a modest garage on a quiet street in West London – which once housed the office of a famous whisky and beer expert and writer, Michael Jackson. Its residential location is a resonant link with the days of the Eighteenth-Century Gin Craze, when every fourth household in the parish of St Giles was producing gin.

Method of Distillation

This is definitely a small-batch gin. Only around 200 bottles are made from each charging of the still.

The Sipsmith distillery also produces the neutral alcohol, or vodka, which forms the base spirit for the gin. This is an exceptionally pure spirit, with a light, sweet quality, made from English barley in Prudence's fractional distillation column (which is disengaged for the final distillation of the gin).

The evening before the gin is distilled, Prudence is charged with Sipsmith vodka and the botanicals. The still is heated up to around 60%, and then switched off, leaving the botanicals to macerate for 12 hours in the gentle warmth. The next day, the distillation process takes around eight hours. Only the heart cut is used, and around 20% of the total volume of liquid will be discarded.

Sam, Fairfax and Jared wanted to keep the London connection very much to the fore when they created Sipsmith London Dry Gin. The water which is used to dilute the spirit to bottling strength comes from the source of the River Thames, at Lydwell Spring in Gloucester – necessitating many a rushed early-morning drive to pick up this vital ingredient.

Tasting Notes

Up front, a clean, clear aroma of juniper comes through on the nose, tempered with flowery, citrus notes. On the palate, this gin is exceptionally smooth, with strong juniper and sweet, almost marmalady citrus flavours which support, rather than distract from, the juniper. The taste profile tails off with some peppery, savoury end-notes. A classic London Dry Gin, with just a little of the softer, more floral style of that other classic – Plymouth Gin.

An ideal spirit for a gin and tonic, bringing a creamy, juniper laden intensity to the mix, which is enhanced by the addition of a slice of lime. Also works well in a Collins.

Other Products

Sipsmith also make a **Sloe Gin**, an excellent **Vodka**, a **Damson Vodka** and a **Summer Cup**. All of these are very subtle and distinctive, with a complexity and delicacy of flavour that evoke the tastes of the past. Further details can be found in *Chapter Thirteen*.

Sloane's

www.toorank.com
London Dry Gin Style

ABV 40%

Botanicals: Angelica, cardamom, coriander, juniper, lemon, liquorice, orris, orange, vanilla

Sloane's Gin is a relative newcomer to the scene, being developed and launched by Toorank Distillers in 2010. It can't be classified as 'London Dry Gin' due to the botanicals being distilled separately and not all in one still, but it is firmly in the tradition. The Master Distiller at Toorank took his inspiration from Sir Hans Sloane, the famous Eighteenth Century botanist, who, by bringing exotic fruits and herbs to England, inadvertently contributed to the rise of gin as we know it.

Sloane's is a balanced and very smooth gin, and made its mark almost immediately by winning gold medals in both the 'Best un-aged White Spirit' and

---

Did you know?

Sir Hans Sloane (Royal Physician and Botanist) after whom this gin is named, is remembered in London as a lifelong benefactor and landlord of the famous Chelsea Physic Garden, where plants for medicinal purposes have long been grown. His botanical collection formed the basis of the Natural History Museum collection, and it is likely that he was instrumental in introducing into this country some of the key exotic gin botanicals such as orris, cardamom, coriander, liquorice and vanilla.

Hans Crescent, Sloane Square and Sloane Street in the Borough of Kensington and Chelsea were named after him.

'Best Gin' categories at the San Francisco World Spirits Competition.

Method of Distillation

Distilled and bottled in the Netherlands by Toorank Distillers. The botanicals are distilled separately, and then blended by the master distiller. Whole fresh botanicals are used, and the fresh citrus fruits are left macerate for 24 hours to add freshness to the flavour.

Tasting Notes

Juniper and spice dominate on the nose, with a hint of vanilla. The taste profile is extremely smooth; soft and creamy at the start, then you will experience a strong hit of juniper, followed by the spiciness of the coriander. The citrus is fresh, but not too strong, and the angelica is very present, balancing and smoothing the other flavours. All the separately distilled botanicals make their mark, but there's an overall impression of smoothness and creaminess, and a light freshness.

Lovely in a gin and tonic, and makes a crisp, clean Martini. Works well in a Gimlet, with light notes of juniper and cardamom. Overall, a great and very versatile gin in the classic style.

Sloane's Bottle and botanicals.

Tanqueray London Dry Gin

www.tanqueray.com
London Dry Gin

ABV 47.3%

Botanicals: Angelica, coriander, juniper, liquorice

The solid, iconic bottle of Tanqueray London Dry bears the red seal of all the Tanqueray Gins. There is a long history behind this gin; The Tanqueray Distillery was founded in Bloomsbury in 1832 – a Tanqueray Dry Gin bottle from 1912 is held in the Diageo archive. (Both Tanqueray and Gordon's Gin are now under the umbrella of drinks multinational Diageo.)

It's a very distinctive London Dry Gin with a neat, crisp spiciness and a very powerful lead from the juniper. Despite having only four botanicals, Tanqueray London Dry is a masterpiece of the distiller's art, being balanced and yet also boisterous and fresh.

Method of Distillation

This is confidential – no details of the process are revealed by the Tanqueray distillery in Scotland.

Tasting Notes

Up front, juniper is very strong on the nose. On tasting, the juniper is still very predominant, but liquorice comes through strongly, too, with a subtle dash of spice from the coriander. The high alcohol content adds an extra warmth and dryness, and helps to keep the botanicals coming through clear and balanced after mixing and dilution.

Tanqueray No 10

www.tanqueray.com
Distilled Gin

ABV 47.3%

Botanicals: Including chamomile, coriander, juniper, lime, orange, white grapefruit

Launched in 2000, Tanqueray 10 was one of the earliest super-premium gins to come on the market. It was created as a perfect gin for making Martinis. The key difference from Tanqueray London Dry is the citrus element. Fresh oranges, lemons and white grapefruits are added to the botanicals, instead of the usual dried peels.

The owner of Tanquerary, drinks multinational Diageo, set up the Tanqueray 10 Guild in 2008, with 10 famous bartenders from 10 cities around the world – Athens, Barcelona, London, Mexico City, Miami, Milan, Paris, New York, Shanghai and Tokyo. Each bartender has developed a signature Martini using Tanqueray 10.

Method of Distillation

Tanqueray 10 is made in very small batches in a copper pot still. The citrus fruits are distilled separately in a small still known as 'Tiny Ten', and this spirit is then redistilled with the more traditional botanicals. Extra, fresh citrus is then blended with the final spirit.

Tasting Notes

A much gentler, softer experience than Tanqueray Dry, with a clean, fresh tang. As you would expect, it's very citrusy, with light notes of the chamomile chiming in. juniper is very much present, but is not as central to the flavour as it is in a traditional London Dry Gin.

Works very well as it was originally intended, in Martinis. Also great in all fruit-based cocktails, as well as drunk neat over ice.

Tanqueray Rangpur

www.tanqueray.com
Distilled Gin

ABV 41.3%

Botanicals: Including angelica, bay leaves, coriander seed, ginger, juniper, Rangpur lime

This is the latest Tanqueray gin, introduced in the US in 2006, and now readily available in the UK. The light, almost lime-green of the glass gives a clue to the spirit's key flavour. There is juniper here, but not as much as in the classic London Dry. It's the citrus freshness of lime that strikes both nose and palate.

British colonials living out in India used to add a twist of Rangpur lime to their gin to add smoothness. Tanqueray pay tribute to that heritage by adding a distillate of the fresh fruit to their Rangpur Gin.

Did you know?

A Rangpur lime (*Citrus x limonia*) is actually a hybrid between a lemon and a mandarin orange. It has a bright orange skin, looks very similar to a mandarin, and has a very strong, acidic taste.

The name of the fruit comes from the town of Rangpur in Bangladesh; it's also known as the mandarin lime or the Canton lime.

Method of Distillation
Presumably similar to Tanqueray 10, though the makers are reluctant to give away too many details. The Rangpur limes are distilled as fresh fruit, and added separately to the other botanicals.

Tasting Notes
A lot of citrus strikes the nose, and (although Rangpur limes are not actually limes) there's almost a hint of Rose's Lime Cordial coming through. There's a good aroma of juniper, too, despite the other unusual botanicals. On the palate, you'll experience a strong lemon-and-lime rush, backed up by juniper and coriander. The flavour profile comes to a close with an almost fizzy sensation of lemon and lime.

Very good indeed mixed with cranberry juice or ginger ale and a drop of bitters.

The London Gin No 1

www.thelondon1.com/
Distilled Gin

ABV 47%

Botanicals: Almond, angelica, bergamot, cassia, cinnamon, coriander, juniper, lemon peel, liquorice, orange peel, orris, savory

The first thing you'll notice about The London Gin No 1 is its colour – turquoise blue. Not the bottle glass, as in Bombay Sapphire, but the spirit itself. The vivid colouration of The London Gin No 1 derives from gardenia petals, which are macerated in the spirit. However, once you have got over the initial shock, and braved a sniff and sip, you will find a delicate and sophisticated gin in the classic English style.

Despite the name, The London Gin No 1 is produced by Spanish sherry giants Gonzalez Byass (makers of Tio Pepe and Croft) – another sign of the outstanding popularity of quality London gin in Spain.

Method of Distillation
Made from spirit using grain from Suffolk and Norfolk, and distilled in a traditional still at Thames Distillers. After distillation, the gin is rested for three weeks, which helps to create its very rounded and balanced quality.

Tasting Notes
Despite the high ABV of 47%, The London Gin No 1 is light and aromatic on the nose, with notes of spice and balsam. The bergamot gives a hint of Earl Grey tea which mingles well with the freshness of the orange and lemon peel. The mouthfeel is soft, mellow, and very balanced.

This is a versatile gin which delivers a great taste experience when sipped neat over ice, but also mixes well in most cocktails.

Whitley Neill

www.whitleyneill.com
London Dry Gin

ABV 42%

Botanicals: Angelica, baobab fruit pulp, Cape gooseberries (*Physalis*), cassia, coriander, juniper, lemon peel, orris, sweet orange peel

Created in 2004 by Johnny Neill (a fourth-generation member of the Greenall Whitley family, whose distilling heritage dates back to 1761) this gin is unusual in that owes its inspiration to Africa. Johnny's wife is from South Africa, and the unique African botanicals of Cape gooseberries and baobab are a tribute to the couple's love for her homeland.

As well as honouring the African connection, independent distiller Johnny wanted to bring a fresh vitality to the London Gin tradition, and he found the ideal botanical for this in the fruit of the wild baobab tree – also known in Africa as 'The Tree of Life'.

Did you know?

Five per cent of the net profit from Whitley Neill Gin goes towards the charity Tree Aid, which assists some of Africa's most disadvantaged communities to make a sustainable living from trees.

Method of Distillation
Botanicals are steeped in grain spirit overnight, before distillation in an antique copper pot.

Tasting Notes
A fresh aroma of spices is first on the nose. In the mouth, juniper is quite understated, with a robust, fresh, fruity quality from the baobab and Cape gooseberries mingling with citrus tones. The finish lingers pleasantly on the palate, holding all the flavours in balance.

A warm and vibrant gin to enjoy neat, Whitley Neill also works very well indeed in fruit-based cocktails.

Chapter Eleven

The Competition: Other Great Gins

L ONDON Gin is at the forefront of the current Craze – but there are many other varieties of gin to be found on bar shelves in the hotels, clubs and bars where Londoners love to drink gin and gin cocktails.

You'll find American gins from some of the artisan distillers who inspired British producers like Sipsmith to set up in business. You might be intrigued to see Scottish gins, made north of the Border by some of the famous malt whisky distillers. There's even a Welsh gin – the only one currently flying the flag for the country. And, last but not least, there are many excellent European gins, too, which bring something very different to the mix.

It's hard to precisely pin down a specific set of flavour characteristics common to, say, Scottish gins, or American gins. There are definite trends, though, within the different countries. The US artisan distillers have a rugged independence. They'll sometimes pay homage to the British heritage, but they like to be very clear that they are striking out on their own. In Scotland, there's a vogue for using wild, locally sourced plants and herbs as botanicals – though the results across the distilleries are very different. And the Europeans, for the most part, delight in stepping away as far as they can from the London Dry style.

Even the quiet countryside of England can bring some surprises to the glass, with innovative ideas both for the base spirit and the botanicals.

Adler

www.adlergin.de
Distilled Gin

ABV 42%

Botanicals: Including coriander, ginger, juniper, lavender, lemon peel

This German gin, re-released onto the market in 2004, is based on a recipe from 1874 and made in a 150-year-old distillery in Berlin – though the method of distillation is definitely from the Twenty-first Century.

The label on the bottle has a very striking 'Eagle' design (Adler is the German word for eagle), with a distinctive 1930s look.

Method of Distillation

Neutral wheat-based spirit is redistilled with the botanicals under a vacuum, at temperatures below 80°C. The distillate from this process is then left to rest in earthenware crocks for at least three months.

Tasting Notes

A light, mild gin with a complex flavour, which isn't dominated by juniper. On the nose, Adler Gin is fresh and bright, with a hit of cardamom up front, followed by juniper, ginger and coriander – there are hints of gingerbread in the aroma.

The taste profile is intense. Juniper and cardamom are followed by sweet ginger and lemon, with some herbal and floral lavender notes. Pine and eucalyptus linger in the mouth at the close, with some pepper, too.

In a gin and tonic, Adler Gin is refreshingly spicy, though the lack of strong juniper may not be to everyone's taste. Makes an excellent Aviation, and a very good Pink Gin, where the bitters combine well with the ginger and spice. Works well, too, in a Gimlet.

Adnam's Copperhouse

www.adnams.co.uk
Distilled Gin

ABV 40%

Botanicals: Coriander, cardamom, hibiscus flower, juniper, orris, sweet orange peel

Adnam's, the Suffolk brewers, have always been well known for their outstanding real ales, but in 2010 they launched a small-scale distillery at their Sole Bay Brewery in the small coastal town of Southwold.

You will often find a small distillery attached to a brewery on the continent, but Adnam's new venture is very innovative for the UK.

Method of Distillation

Copperhouse Distilled Gin is made from Adnam's Barley Vodka, a very pure spirit made in the copper rectifying still from East Anglian malted barley. This is redistilled with the six botanicals in a copper pot still made by Carl of Germany. Master Distiller John McCarthy fine-tuned the recipe over several months to get just the right balance of flavours.

Did you know?

The brand new Copperhouse Distillery has a glass frontage so, if you are passing, you can peer in at the gleaming copper fittings. In line with the latest energy-efficiency initiatives, the hot water which is a by-product of the distilling process is used to wash out casks in the main brewery, and any waste products are put through Adnam's anaerobic digester and converted into renewable gas.

Tasting Notes

A light and very smooth gin, with fragrant herbal notes on the nose. Very soft and creamy on the palate, with plenty of juniper and coriander. There's a long, warm, and quite spicy end to the taste profile.

You'll find Copperhouse Distilled makes a wonderfully refreshing gin and tonic, with citrus and spice coming through strongly. It's also great in a Gimlet, the sweet and spicy elements holding their own beautifully against the lime.

Did you know?

If you are in need of a bracing, no-nonsense pick-me-up, then combination of a pint of one of Adnam's excellent ales, plus a generous shot of Copperhouse Distilled Gin makes an excellent Dog's Nose.

Adnam's First Rate

Distilled Gin

ABV 48%

Botanicals: As for Copperhouse, with the addition of angelica, caraway, cassia, fennel, liquorice and vanilla

Method of Distillation

As for Adnam's Copperhouse Distilled, except for the use of a different base spirit – Adnam's Longshore Premium Vodka, which is made with wheat, barley and oats.

Tasting Notes

On the nose, juniper is up front, backed by vanilla, and there's an overall sweet creaminess to the aroma. In the mouth, First Rate is very silky, with a complex, spicy rush of cardamom overriding the juniper. Due to the higher ABV, all the flavours come through warm and strong, and the profile tails off with cinnamon and liquorice.

In a First Rate Martini, the pleasant vanilla and herbal aroma pervades, with hints of juniper and anise. Makes a very intense gin and tonic, with lots of cardamom and citrus. As with Copperhouse Distilled, the Gimlet is outstanding. And last, but not least, the Dog's Nose is strong on cardamom, and very warm and spicy.

Did you know?

If you would like to see the Adnam's Distillery from the inside, there are regular tours. As well as viewing the state-of-the-art stills, you can also enjoy some wonderful panoramas of Southwold and the North Sea coastline. After the tour, there is a tutored tasting session and an opportunity to buy some of the products at a discounted rate.

Booking is essential, and all tour participants must be over 18.

Contact www.adnams.co.uk or call 01502 725256

Blackwood's Vintage

www.blackwoodsgin.net
Distilled Gin

ABV 40%

Botanicals: Angelica, coriander, cinnamon, citrus peels, elderflower, juniper, liquorice, meadowsweet, nutmeg, orris, sea pinks, turmeric, violet flowers, wild watermint. (There may be a slight variation in the Shetland botanicals used from year to year, as the climatic conditions where they grow are very variable. See the next page.)

Blackwood's Gin bears a Viking Ship on the label and, despite its unusual provenance in the far north of Britain, it's certainly carried off plenty of trophies in the various competitions for white spirits – and also managed to invade some supermarket shelves, too.

Now owned by Blavod Extreme Spirits and distilled on the Scottish mainland, Blackwood's started out with the aim of founding Scotland's most northerly distillery, on the Shetland Islands. Sadly, this didn't work out – but the connection with the Islands is still integral to this unique gin.

Method of Distillation
Small-batch distilled. Neutral grain spirit is distilled in a small copper still, and the vapour passes through perforated trays on which the botanicals have been layered. The slow infusion process allows maximum contact between the alcohol and the delicate essences of the botanicals.

Did you know?

Each summer – and that season can be a moveable and somewhat brief feast in this northerly outpost of Britain, taking place any time between June and September – local Shetland crofters harvest the wild botanicals for Blackwood's. They do this in a sustainable way, ensuring no damage is done to the fragile ecosystem. The weather conditions on Shetland are very variable, due to the maritime climate – and each year, this affects the wild botanicals in different ways. The resulting subtle variations in Blackwood's ensure that its 'Vintage' title is genuine. Each bottle is dated and signed, and carries brief tasting notes and a list of the wild botanicals used for that particular batch.

Tasting Notes
Very strong and sweet on the nose, with zesty lemon and fresh mint combining with a delicate, earthy note from the juniper. The taste profile is soft and floral, with piquant herbal tones. Finishes with a lingering frisson of lemon and lime.

Lovely to sip neat, and with its strong citrus emphasis, makes an excellent gin and tonic.

Blackwood's Superior Strength

ABV 60%

This gin is made in the same way and with the same botanicals as the standard Blackwood's Vintage, but has a higher alcohol content. The very high ABV is based on the location of the Shetland Islands where the wild botanicals are picked – they lie at a latitude of 60° north and it enhances the delicate flavours and aromas of the wild Shetland botanicals. When you uncork the bottle, you can almost smell the sea mist drawing up the sweet, fresh scents of vegetation at sunrise on a summer day. This is a Limited Edition, so well worth snapping up if you find a bottle.

Method of Distillation
As for Blackwood's Vintage, but with a higher alcohol content.

Tasting Notes
On the nose, a complex and very soft experience, fresh and lightly herbal, with a fine balance of all the botanicals.

The addition of water or tonic brings out the more traditional juniper, but the complexity is still there, and the taste experience is so satisfying that, luckily, you'll find yourself taking it slowly to savour each nuance. It's all too easy to forget how strong this one is!

Did you know?

If you hold a bottle of Blackwood's up to the light, you'll notice that the gin has a very slight sea-blue tint. This comes from the infusion of the sea pink and meadowsweet botanicals.

Bluecoat

www.bluecoatgin.com
American Dry Gin

ABV 47%

Botanicals: Organic juniper berries, American orange and lemon peel and other botanicals which the distillers prefer not to reveal

Bluecoat gin was created in 2006 at Philadelphia Distilling, the first distillery to open in Pennsylvania since Prohibition was repealed in the state of Pennsylvania on 5th December, 1933. It celebrates the spirit of independence and rebellion born over 200 years ago in the American Revolution. 'Be revolutionary. Proudly assert your independence with Bluecoat' – its creators exhort. It has won gold medals at both the International Wine & Spirit Competition, and the San Francisco World Spirits Competition.

The striking, intense cobalt blue of the bottle with its fine gold lettering reflects the blue cloth and gold trimmings of the Revolutionary militia's coats in 1776.

Method of Distillation
This is a small-batch highly crafted gin, made in a single old-style copper pot still. The distillation takes 10 hours and a relatively short cut is taken to ensure purity of flavour.

Tasting Notes
The organic citrus peels bring a very bright citrus note, complemented by the organic juniper berries which are very distinctive here, bringing a rather spicy, earthy note to the flavour. The high ABV brings out fresh but delicate notes of black pepper and lemon.

Available from online retailers in the UK.

The Botanist

www.bruichladdich.com
Distilled Gin

ABV 46%

Botanicals: Angelica, cassia, cinnamon, coriander, juniper, lemon peel, liquorice, orris, orange peel

Hand-picked Islay wild botanicals: Apple mint, birch leaves, bog myrtle, chamomile, creeping thistle, elderflower, gorse flower, hawthorn flower, heather flower, lady's bedstraw, lemon balm, meadowsweet, mugwort leaves, peppermint, red clover flowers, sweet cicely leaves, tansy, thyme leaves, watermint, white clover, wild Islay juniper, wood sage

The progressive Hebridean Bruichladdich Distillery, which specialises in the production of characterful whiskies, prides itself on a non-conformist approach. This is certainly reflected in the creation of their unique Islay Dry Gin – which boasts an unprecedented 31 botanicals, including 22 which are collected from the wild plants which grow on the windswept hills, peat bogs and Atlantic shores of the island of Islay where the distillery is based.

The Botanist comes in an elegant bottle made from clear, flint glass with a simple but attractive label. The contents reflect the stylish design. Master Distiller Jim McEwan has exercised all his skill and experience to marry together the vast range of flavours and aromas into a soft, creamy spirit which retains the fresh, bright nature of its Hebridean home.

Method of Distillation

The Botanist is made in a low-pressure 'Lomond' still, affectionately known at the Bruichladdich Distillery as Ugly Betty. Due to the low pressure, distillation takes place over 17 hours – a very long time compared to most traditional copper pot processes. The vapour passes through a custom-made basket which holds the botanicals, and is infused with their flavours. The spirit is reduced to bottling strength with Islay spring water.

Ugly Betty – clearly someone at the distillery loves her!

Did you know?

Ugly Betty is the last Lomond still which is still in existence. She was made in 1955 and was intended to be used for distilling different types of whisky. Key to her versatility was her thick column of a neck, which was designed to have three removable sections, so that the length could be altered, and rectifying plates inserted if necessary. She was named 'Ugly Betty' because of her thick neck, not after the popular TV series.

Tasting Notes

You'd be forgiven for expecting – given the vast array of botanicals – that the taste experience of Botanist Islay Gin might be a bit of a muddle. But that's not the case. It is complex, but very balanced. The aroma is light and floral, with a sweet undertone of juniper. The taste profile starts rich and creamy. Floral notes of chamomile, meadowsweet and soft mint vie for precedence with the juniper, before a zesty and lightly spicy finish.

Perfect to drink neat over ice by the fire on a northern winter night – and also works beautifully in a gin and tonic, the high ABV helping the delicate flavours to hold their own against the quinine in the tonic water.

Did you know?

With the new Gin Craze growing year on year, it's no wonder that so many die-hard malt whisky producers are turning to gin, including the Bruichladdich Distillery.

Boudier Saffron Gin

www.boudier.com
Distilled Gin

ABV 40%

Botanicals: Angelica seeds, coriander, fennel, iris, juniper, lemon, orange peel, saffron

Boudier Saffron Gin (seen here glowing to great effect in a miniature bottle on the shelf at Gerry's Off-Licence) owes its startling but all-natural tangerine hue to the most expensive spice in the world – saffron.

The Boudier micro-distillery in Dijon, Northern France has been making fine spirits – especially crème de cassis and other liqueurs – since 1874.

The Saffron Gin is based on a recipe discovered in France's Nineteenth-Century colonial archives, when India and the Far East brought exotic botanicals onto the agenda. But it's also a nod to the Eighteenth Century, when Northern France was considered part of the Low Countries – the birthplace of genever – and distiller Gabriel Boudier also cites the fine qualities of classic London Dry Gin as an inspiration.

Method of Distillation
A small-batch, pot-distilled gin.

Tasting Notes
This is a delicate, complex gin. Saffron pervades, and there are subtle undertones of spice from the fennel and the angelica seed.

A great way to appreciate the delicacy of the flavour profile is to drink Saffron Gin neat with ice. It also works beautifully with tonic, as the marriage with the quinine seems to enhance, rather than swamp, the subtle, Campari-like bitterness of the gin.

Did you know?

Despite Gabriel Boudier's position in a traditional and historic French distillery, it was he that London bar-owner Gerry Calabrese turned to when he wanted to create his innovate and shocking gin-with-attitude, Hoxton Gin.

Brecon Special Reserve

http://www.welsh-whisky.co.uk/
London Dry Gin Style

ABV 40%

Botanicals: Angelica, cassia, cinnamon, coriander, juniper, lemon peel, liquorice, nutmeg, orange peel, orris

---

Did you know?

The Visitors' Centre at the Pendryn Distillery.

The Visitors' Centre at the Penderyn Distillery offers an ideal day out if you are holidaying in the Brecon Beacons National Park. It's a very modern and stylish complex, clad in dark timber, and fits beautifully into the wild mountain landscape. The distillery's main focus is Welsh whisky, but you will be able to see the still where the neutral alcohol for the gin is made, as well as the traditional copper-pot still. Tours run from 9.30am-5pm every day with the last admission at 4.00pm, and pre-booking is advised. Evening tours and corporate events are available by arrangement. A chance to sample some of the products is included in the fee for the tour (currently £6, with a £4 concession for pensioners, under-18s and students). Under-18s must be accompanied by an adult.

For details, call 01685 810651 or email visitorcentre@welsh-whisky.co.uk.
See the website for details of visiting hours.

Brecon Gin, made in the heart of the hill country of South Wales, is currently the only Welsh gin in production. It was first launched in 2000, before being re-launched in its current, elegant and tall bottle in 2006.

You will find Brecon Gin behind bars and on the shelves of retail outlets throughout Wales (especially when the famous Brecon Jazz Festival is up and running) but it's also to be found in specialist suppliers in other parts of the UK, as well as in Europe.

Method of Distillation
Made to a 100-year-old recipe, and small-batch distilled from Welsh spirit (also made at the Penderyn Distillery) in a traditional copper pot still.

Tasting Notes
The citrus freshness of Brecon Gin works well in a gin and tonic, and also in long, refreshing cocktails such as a Tom Collins. With plenty of juniper and warming spice, it's also a lovely drink to sip neat over ice, when snuggled up in a *cwtch* (as they say in Wales) by a winter log fire.

Cadenhead's Old Raj

www.wmcadenhead.com
Distilled Gin

ABV 55% and 46%

Botanicals: Including angelica, cassia, coriander, juniper, lemon peel, orange peel, orris

Cadenhead's Old Raj is an unusual premium gin in that it is made by the two-shot method (see Method of Distillation). Due to the skill and experience of the

---

Did you know?

Saffron is a yellow powder derived from the stigmas of the crocus flower. Each thread-like stamen must be picked by hand, before gently drying to protect the delicate but intense flavour and aroma. Around 14,000 threads are needed to make 1oz of saffron.

distillers, and possibly also aided by the high alcohol content – this gin is very good indeed. It's aromatic and balanced, and has a distinctive flavour and colour.

Method of Distillation
Made in Scotland at the William Cadenhead Distillery. The botanicals are steeped separately in an alcohol-and-water mix for 36 hours, and then distilled together – this is known as the two-shot method. Saffron is added to the spirit in the final stage of the process, giving Cadenhead's Old Raj an extra boost of flavour – and its typical light-straw colour.

Tasting Notes
Juniper leads in strongly on the nose, with citrus following, and nutty spice chiming in at the end. The flavour on the palate is very dry, with green, herbaceous notes and a strong hit of juniper. This softens to a subtle blend of spices and the long aftertaste is crisp and clean.

The weaker strength, at 46%, is lighter and slightly peppery compared to the full, rounded, aromatic quality of the 55% bottling – but both are excellent drunk neat over ice, and also make a superb Martini, with just a dash of vermouth.

Caorunn

www.caorunngin.com
Distilled Gin

ABV 41.8%

Botanicals: Including angelica, cassia, coriander, juniper, lemon peel, orange peel

Five local botanicals from the environs of the distillery: Bog myrtle, Coul blush apple, dandelion, heather, rowan berries

Caorunn Gin is made in a malt whisky distillery, and stands proudly with one foot in the Celtic past, and one in the exiting future that's opening up for gin in the UK.

Inspired by the Celtic tradition, Caorunn ran a Storytellers Global Cocktail challenge, inviting fans worldwide to focus on re-imagining the past and on shaping the future by inventing new classic cocktails using Caorunn Gin, and also creating a story to go alongside this. See the website for full details.

The stocky Caorunn gin bottle has five sides, one for each of its Celtic botanicals, and is decorated with designs that reflect the influence of the Scottish Art Nouveau movement. Caorunn takes its name from one of these botanicals – since *caorunn* is the Gaelic word for rowan.

Method of Distillation
Caorunn Gin is made on Speyside at the Balmenach Distillery using a copper berry still from the 1920s. The botanicals are laid out on four large trays inside the still, which is then charged with high-quality neutral grain spirit. When the still is heated, vapour from the spirit passes over the trays and is infused with the flavours of the botanicals. Before bottling, pure and very soft Highland water is added to dilute the gin to the required ABV.

Did you know?

Caorunn is prononced *'ka-roon'*.

The Coul blush is Britain's most northerly apple, and will grow throughout the Highlands and as far north as Inverness.

Tasting Notes
Despite the Celtic botanicals, juniper is very up-front on the nose, with plenty of fruit from the apple and rowan. Caorunn is a mellow, complex gin and you will find that the taste profile pretty much mirrors what you get on the nose, although the unusual, fruity tang lingers into a crisp, dry fade-out that's softened by a touch of heather honey.

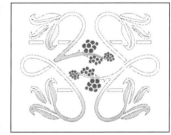

Caorunn's rowan design.

Ideal to drink neat, as you accustom yourself to the unusual botanicals. In a gin and tonic, a slice of apple can replace the more usual lemon. Caorunn Gin is especially good in gin punches, and is great to experiment with in any of the fruit-based cocktails.

Cascade Mountain

www.bendistillery.com
American Gin

ABV 47.5%

Botanicals: Including Oregon wild juniper

As you check out the very sparse list of botanicals, you'd be forgiven for thinking that there is some kind of 'secret recipe' involved with Cascade Mountain Gin. Nothing could be further from the truth. This small-batch, artisan-made American gin relies almost solely on gin's signature ingredient – juniper – with just a few other locally-sourced wild botanicals.

The makers believe that the unique, earthy complexity of their gin comes from their high-quality spirit, the local Cascade Mountain water (both of which are filtered through charcoal and crushed lava), and, last but not least, the hand-picked wild juniper berries from the high desert country.

Each bottle is given a batch number, which bears the initials of the person who bottled it. This enables drinkers to follow any slight variations in the batches, which may occur due to the nature of the wild botanicals.

Method of Distillation
The gin is distilled in an alembic pot still. The infusion of wild juniper berries adds a straw-yellow colour to the spirit.

Tasting Notes
As you would expect, juniper is very dominant, both on the nose and in the mouth. Due to the use of wild local berries, though, the juniper has a complex and earthy quality, and is not quite so 'piny' as in more conventional gins. This rich taste experience gains even more intensity from the high ABV at 47%. Great drunk neat, if you enjoy juniper and are not averse to a walk on the wild side.

Citadelle Gin

www.citadelle.com
Distilled Gin

ABV 44%

Botanicals: Almond, angelica, cardamom, cassia, cinnamon, coriander, cubeb, cumin, fennel, grains of paradise, juniper, lemon rind, liquorice, nutmeg, orange peel, orris, savory, star anise, violet

This distinctive and very aromatic gin is made in France by Gabriel and Andreu (well known as makers of Cognac Ferrand). It is based on a 1771 recipe from the Citadelle Distillery which was sited in Dunkirk – then very much in the old, Lowlands genever territory. There is much less juniper in evidence than in a classic London Dry Gin, but Citadelle is a high-quality gin in the wider tradition.

Method of Distillation
Neutral spirit made using wheat from the Beauce region is distilled with the 19 botanicals. These are not steeped or macerated beforehand, but added to the spirit immediately, to capture all the freshness of the flavour.

Tasting Notes
A very perfumy, bright, floral quality on the nose, with hints of jasmine and cardamom. Spicy, herbal notes of anise and cinnamon follow. To taste, there's a dry hit of juniper to start, before the floral tones kick in, and the creamier texture of the herbs and spices comes through. The profile ends on a dry note once more.

An excellent, complex choice to drink neat over ice. In a gin and tonic, the mix of herbs and spices matches well with the quinine.

Cork Dry Gin

Distilled Gin

ABV 38% and 43% (export)

Botanicals: Including coriander, juniper, lemon, lime

Made by Irish Distillers at the Middleton Distilleries. Despite its name, Cork Dry is a somewhat sweet gin, with much more citrus flavour than most London Dry fans will be used to. Though not often seen in the UK, it's a hugely popular gin throughout Ireland.

Method of Distillation
Not listed.

Tasting Notes
Cork Dry is a very light, perfumey gin, with hints of coffee and soft vanilla on then nose. Despite the low ABV, the spice and juniper flavours come through well on the palate, and there is a lingering, warm finish.

Makes a good, creamy gin and tonic, with juniper and a touch of coffee coming through. A little overwhelmed in a Martini, but, with its hint of coffee, it makes an exceptional Alexander.

Damrak Amsterdam Original

www.damrakgin.nl
Distilled Gin

ABV 41.8%

Botanicals: 17, including aniseed, cinnamon, coriander, honeysuckle, juniper, lemon peel, orange peel

Made by Lucas Bols, makers of the famous Bols Genever, this fruity, intense gin has been created from a gin recipe dating back to the early-Eighteenth Century. The opaque white bottle is very reminiscent of the old Bols stoneware crocks, and has the type of swing top more usually found on beer bottles.

Did you know?

As a young man, Lucas Bols set up a distillery in the countryside near Amsterdam in 1575. He took advantage of all the exotic spices and herbs brought into the Damrak (Amsterdam's harbour) to create his products.

Method of Distillation
Five different distillations from different pot stills are brought together and left to rest for two weeks before bottling.

Did you know?

If you are visiting Amsterdam, The House of Bols Cocktail and Genever Experience at the Museumplein (Museum Square) is a great interactive experience involving all the senses. On your self-guiding tour you can find out all about the history of Lucas Bols, and also immerse yourself in the world of cocktails and bartending in a stunning, contemporary setting.

Visit www.lucasbols.com for details.

Tasting Notes

This is a citrus-led gin, with aromas of candied peel. On the palate, the hit of juniper is light and delicate, and there's a touch of liquorice, too. Perhaps too fruity for a London Dry Gin fan, Damrak makes a very good Negroni – its fruitiness marrying well with the bitter Campari.

Death's Door

www.deathsdoorspirits.com
Distilled Gin

ABV 46%

Botanicals: Organic coriander and fennel, organic juniper, wild Washington Island juniper

---

Did you know?

Picking juniper berries is an extremely slow and labour-intensive task. Every autumn (or 'fall', to be precise!) – usually the first week in November – when the wild berries are ready on Washington Island, Death's Door Spirits hold an open weekend and invite fans of their gin to come and help collect this vital ingredient. If you'd like to go along, check the website for details.

This artisan-crafted, small-batch gin has very strong links with the local community on Washington Island in Wisconsin, US. In 2007, the founders of Death's Door Spirits had been working for two years to help the local farming families regenerate their businesses. The wheat that was being grown as a result of this initiative was of exceptional quality – and distilled spirits were an ideal way to use and showcase the product. A local distillery worked with one of the nearby chefs to create a gin recipe that uses local ingredients and also reflects the tastes and character of the area. At a time when increasing importance is placed upon provenance, and upon the ethical production of foodstuffs and beverages, this gin ticks all the boxes.

There's nothing sinister implied in the name – Death's Door is the legendary wild waterway between Washington Island and the Door County Peninsula. A map of this can be seen on the Death's Door Gin label.

Method of Distillation

The Washington Island wheat is made into a beer mash and then given three runs through a column still. The botanicals pass through a botanicals extractor and are added before the third and final distillation.

Tasting Notes

The use of the local wheat spirit brings a malty quality – not unlike that of a genever – to the overall flavour, and there is a smoothness and sweetness, too, which is reminiscent of Old Tom Gins.

As you might expect from the important role of juniper in the botanical mix, it comes though strongly on the nose. On the palate, the coriander takes over once the juniper has faded, and the finish has a lingering note of aniseed from the fennel.

Great for sipping neat to warm your heart on a cold winter's night – and excellent also for using in some of the 1920s-30s cocktails which call for a more old-fashioned style of gin.

DH Krahn

www.dhkrahn.com
Dry Gin

ABV 40%

Botanicals: Californian citrus (grapefruit, lemon and orange) peels, coriander, ginger, juniper, Thai ginger

This unusual gin, made in a small distillery in upstate New York, lies somewhere between the classic London Dry Gins and the new American Dry Gins. It was created by Scott Krahn, a Canadian, in collaboration with his former teammate on the Cornell University Hockey Team, David Hughes from Long Island, and took two years of passion and commitment to develop.

Method of Distillation

The botanicals are macerated in a multi-step process before being distilled in an alembic pot still. The small batches then rest for three months in steel barrels, which helps to give DH Krahn Gin its characteristic mellowness.

Tasting Notes

DH Krahn's Gin has a very delicate, smooth quality, but there is plenty of flavour, especially citrus, due to the mix of peels used. The taste profile starts softly, building to a smooth, dry mix of light juniper, peppery spice and lemon peel. There's an almost powdery sweetness here, too, alongside the dryness. The profile tails off into pepper, more juniper, and a hint of lemon blossom. Makes a fantastic Tom Collins, a great gin and tonic and an unusual, slightly sweet Martini.

Edinburgh Gin

www.spencerfieldspirit.com
Distilled Gin

ABV 43%

Botanicals: Angelica, citrus peel, coriander, juniper, orris

Selected Scottish Botanicals: Including heather, Scottish juniper, milk thistle, pine

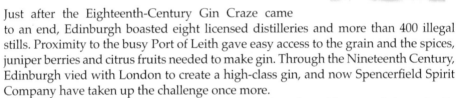

Just after the Eighteenth-Century Gin Craze came to an end, Edinburgh boasted eight licensed distilleries and more than 400 illegal stills. Proximity to the busy Port of Leith gave easy access to the grain and the spices, juniper berries and citrus fruits needed to make gin. Through the Nineteenth Century, Edinburgh vied with London to create a high-class gin, and now Spencerfield Spirit Company have taken up the challenge once more.

The bottle's Art Deco-themed design looks back to the golden era of gin cocktails in the 1920s, and reflects the crisp, clear quality of the gin it contains.

Method of Distillation
Small-batch distilled. Scottish grain spirit is mixed with the classic gin botanicals and distilled in Jenny, a 200-year-old Scottish copper pot still. The Scottish botanicals are added at the final production stage.

Tasting Notes
A very balanced, crisp gin. The pine of the juniper comes through well on the nose, with hints of fresh mountain air and delicate spice. Juniper leads in the taste profile, too, followed by a soft, heathery note. Spice and ginger, with a touch of citrus linger on the palate.

Ginebra San Miguel Red

www.ginebrasanmiguel.com

ABV 40%

Botanicals: Including juniper

The brand name Ginebra San Miguel first saw the light in Spain in 1834. It's now distilled in the Philippines where around 50 million cases of gin are drunk every year, and is the flagship brand of the huge San Miguel Corporation. The company claim their gin is the 'World's No. 1 Selling Gin'. It's certainly very popular in the gin-loving Philippines, where it holds more than half of the market share.

Method of Distillation
Not listed, although sugar-cane alcohol is used.

Tasting Notes
Not much aroma in evidence on the nose. Ginebra San Miguel comes over with a confectionary-style sweetness, and there's no juniper in evidence. On the palate, there's an intense hit of alcohol, and some fruity, sweet tones reminiscent of pear drops.

In a Martini, Ginebra San Miguel packs a good alcohol punch, but the gin flavour doesn't come through, so it acts more like a vodka. Plenty of earthy and fruity notes in a gin and tonic.

Did you know?

Ginebra San Miguel Blue, at 32.5% ABV and Ginebra San Miguel Premium at 35% ABV are also available. There is a 'Lite' version too, at 22% ABV, which is aimed at the younger end of the market. Ginebra San Miguel is also available in sachets – very handy for carrying in the pocket.

Gin Mare

www.ginmare.com
Distilled Gin

ABV 42.7%

Botanicals: Basil, cardamom, coriander, juniper, lemon, mandarin, Arbequina olive, orange, rosemary, thyme

Made on the Costa Dorada, near Barcelona, this is a very distinctive and striking gin, a long way from the Classic London Dry style. It's salty and savoury and a perfect complement to Mediterranean food, especially if a pre-dinner snack of olives is involved.

Method of Distillation

Prior to distillation, botanicals are steeped for three days – except for the citrus fruits, which are macerated in earthenware crocks for a whole year. Each botanical is distilled separately and then blended together to create Gin Mare.

Tasting Notes

As the list of botanicals would indicate, this is a very savoury gin, with a real taste of the Mediterranean. On the nose, it's quite salt-and-peppery, with strong herbal notes from the rosemary and thyme. The taste experience is intense, with the herbs outweighing the juniper.

Gin Mare makes an unusual Martini, with hints of thyme and soft anise coming through – and an olive garnish completes the experience. In a gin and tonic, Gin Mare keeps its herbal intensity, but there's some crisp dryness from the juniper, too.

Did you know?

Gin Mare make their own brand of Mediterranean tonic water, 1724 – so called because the quinine is collected at 1,724 metres above sea level. This is the perfect partner for Gin Mare.

G'vine Floraison

www.g-vine.com
Distilled Gin

ABV 40%

Botanicals: Green cardamom, cassia, coriander, cubeb, ginger, juniper, lime, liquorice, nutmeg, vine flowers

G'vine Gins are made in France, and use neutral spirit made from grapes, rather than the more usual grain-based alcohols. This brings a very floaty, smooth quality to the feel of the gin in the mouth. The grapes used by G'vine are of the Ugni Blanc variety.

Jean Sébastien Robicquet, a leading wine expert and master distiller from the Cognac region, wanted to break away from the juniper-based tradition of London Dry Gins. By looking back to the grape-based spirits of the Thirteenth Century, he's created a very modern, sophisticated gin that can be appreciated not only by gin connoisseurs, but also by those who don't consider themselves gin-drinkers.

Did you know?

Ripe grapes aren't the only vine products used to make G'vine Floraison. The key botanical is the deliciously fragrant green grape flower, which is in blossom for just a few days in June. It's quickly plucked from the vine, just before it develops into a young grape berry, and immediately macerated in the neutral grape spirit to capture the delicate floral essence.

Method of Distillation
The vine blossoms are macerated for several days before distillation in a small pot still. The other botanicals are macerated in separate groups (juniper, spices, aromatics) for two to five days in the neutral grape spirit, and then distilled in small copper liqueur stills. Finally, all the distillates are blended together and given a final distillation in a copper pot still affectionately known as Lily Fleur. (In true French style, Lily Fleur has been engraved with a slightly saucy 1940s-style girl sipping a cocktail!)

Tasting Notes
Delicate, sweet and floral on the nose, with a warm, spicy quality. In the mouth, G'vine Floraison is exceptionally smooth and heady, with subtle, grassy floral notes. The sweet vine blossoms come through first, followed by spicy juniper, cardamom and ginger. The clean, dry finish returns to the floral flavours.

If you love your juniper, then this may not be at the top of your list of favourites. But it is intriguing and almost seductive with its flowery spiciness, and it works very well indeed with citrus garnishes, and in any citrus-based cocktail.

G'vine Nouaison

www.g-vine.com
Distilled Gin

ABV 43.9%

Botanicals: As for G'vine Floraison, but with increased proportion of juniper and nutmeg, and less of the vine flower

G'vine's two gins, Floraison and Nouaison, are representative of the life cycle of the grape, from its brief, fragrant appearance as the vine blossom – a time known as 'Floraison' – to the days of the first forming of the tiny grape berry, which is traditionally called 'Nouaison'.

G'vine Nouaison Gin reflects the intense concentration of vibrant growth and energy that takes place in the vineyard as the blossoms fall and the power-packed grape berries begin to swell.

Method of Distillation
As for G'vine Floraison.

Tasting Notes
A more intense, warm experience on the nose than Floraison – due to the increased nutmeg and juniper. Very silky, sensual and robust in the mouth, with a strong hit of fruity, rich spice. The floral, viney element is still very present, but it's not as light and heady as in Floraison. It's more subtle against the stronger aromas from the spice, but definitely present at the start, and also as the taste profile fades to a close.

If you enjoy Floraison, but would like a slightly stronger and more intense flavour for drinking neat or for mixing, then Nouaison is definitely for you.

Junipero

www.anchordistilling.com/spirits
Distilled Gin

ABV 49.3%

Botanicals: 12 – but the details are kept secret

Junipero Gin, first launched in 1998 in San Francisco, was the first of the new American artisan gins to hit the market. Anchor Distilling, the makers, were also in the forefront of the new, craft-led, beer production movement in the US.

Method of Distillation
Small-batch distilled in a copper pot still, with the botanicals being soaked beforehand.

Tasting Notes
Very much in the classic London Dry style, with a good presence of juniper and citrus. The high ABV gives complexity to the profile, bringing through plenty of citrus and there are hints of softness, too, probably from liquorice.

Given the balance and strength of the flavours, this is a good gin for a Martini.

Larios

Distilled Gin

ABV 40%

Botanicals: Including angelica, coriander, juniper

There is a huge market for gin in Spain, and home-produced Larios Gin is the biggest seller over there. It's a high quality, Dry London Gin-style product and is also available worldwide.

Method of Distillation
Not listed.

Tasting Notes
Aromatic on the nose, with a strong juniper presence which comes through also in the mouth. Makes a good gin and tonic, and also works well with Coca Cola, a mix which is very popular in Spain.

Did you know?

Larios also make a premium gin, Larios 12, with a very high concentration of citrus. Lemon, lime, mandarin, orange, orange blossom, tangerine and watermelon are added to the juniper and spices.

Magellan

www.magellangin.com
Distilled Gin

ABV 44%

Botanicals: Cardamom, cassia, cinnamon, cloves, coriander, grains of paradise, juniper, liquorice, nutmeg, orange peel, orris

The striking colour of Magellan gin – bright blue – is achieved by adding an infusion of iris after distillation. It's the only gin to use cloves as a botanical.

Did you know?

This stylish French gin is named after the Portuguese explorer, Ferdinand Magellan, who sailed around the world in the Sixteenth Century. He never completed the fateful voyage, as he died in the Philippines, but his ship did make it home – loaded with the rare spice cloves from the Far East.

Method of Distillation

Neutral spirit made from wheat from the Beauce region of France and pure spring water from the Cognac area are used to make Magellan Gin. The 11 botanicals are sun-dried and then wrapped in cloth and put into a traditional still for the final distillation.

Tasting Notes

Magellan is a light, floral gin – very modern in taste and texture. Very good in fruit and berry-based cocktails, and as a light Martini.

No. 209

www.distillery209.com
Distilled Gin

ABV 46%

Botanicals: Including angelica, bergamot, cassia, coriander, juniper, orange peel

No. 209 is very much a modern gin, and the makers were keen to step away from the traditional London Dry Gin style when they created it. However, the method of production is very traditional.

Did you know?

The Distillery No. 209, sited at the Edge Hill winery in St Helena, California, was founded in 1882 – and was the 209th distillery to be registered in the US – hence the name.

Method of Distillation

Botanicals are soaked overnight in neutral spirit, which is then blended with water from the Sierra Nevada Mountains. Distillation takes place in a copper pot still custom made in Scotland. The still is heated by a steam-jacket, which allows a gentle, uniform heat. Only the heart cut is taken, and this is allowed to rest for few days, before purified Sierra Nevada water is added to bring the gin down to bottling strength.

Distillery No. 209.

Tasting Notes

On the nose, citrus and flowery notes are more prominent, though juniper and spice come through, too. On the palate, the first experience is citrus and bergamot, with cardamom and juniper following. There are hints of rose and mint, and the taste profile lingers through the slightly dryer, spicy cinnamon.

No. 209 gin works well in sweeter cocktails and, if you are not a great fan of gins with a high juniper content, it's pleasant sipped neat.

Plymouth

www.plymouthgin.com
Distilled Gin

ABV 41.2%

Botanicals: Angelica, cardamom, coriander, juniper, lemon peel, sweet orange peel, orris

This exceptionally fine gin, made to a recipe dating from 1793, takes its place alongside its cousin Beefeater as one of the leading gins in the world marketplace. It's not as robust and upfront as Beefeater, being perhaps more of a 'country cousin', but its smooth, sweet quality – given extra softness due to the addition of local Dartmoor spring water – has earned it many loyal fans over the years.

Did you know?

Plymouth Gin is unusual in being one of only 50 British foods and drinks to hold a 'Protected Geographical Indication' – similar to the French *appellation controlée*. It may only bear the name 'Plymouth Gin' if it continues to be made with Plymouth's city walls. This is due to a legal dispute in the 1880s, when a London distiller began producing something which he called 'Plymouth' Gin. Coates & Co, who owned Plymouth Gin in those days, took this gentleman to court and won.

Plymouth Gin has a long and illustrious heritage. In the Eighteenth Century, local and distinctive gins were produced in Bristol, Norwich, Plymouth and Warrington as well as in London. Through the later years of the Nineteenth Century, London Dry Gin gradually came to the fore and now, of all the regional gins, only Plymouth has survived. It's recommended in many of the early cocktail recipes, as can be found in *The Savoy Cocktail Book*.

Did you know?

Through the late-Nineteenth and early-Twentieth Century, Plymouth was the best-selling gin in the world. It's interesting to note that Plymouth Gin was listed as being carried on many of the White Star Lines Ships in the early 1900s – and, therefore, a bottle or two may well have gone down with the Titanic in 1912.

The Black Friars building, where the distillery is housed, was built in the 1400s, and distilling is thought to have taken place there as early as the Seventeenth Century. It's also possible that the Pilgrim Fathers may have gathered here, in what is now the Refectory bar, before they set off for America on board the Mayflower.

In 2012, the familiar Art Deco-style Plymouth Gin bottle (reflecting the spirit's predominance through the cocktail era in the 1920s and 1930s), was replaced with a design that harks back to earlier centuries in the spirit's long heritage. The new design features glass which is slightly uneven – looking almost as it if might have been made in the Nineteenth Century, and the copper cap is a reference to the still at Black Friars Distillery. The Mayflower features prominently on the label. Below the label, the figure of a monk can be seen on the glass. This is the famous 'Plymouth Monk', who first made his appearance on the Plymouth Gin bottle in the 1870s. As the folklore says – 'When his feet are dry, it's time to buy another bottle.'

Distiller Sean Harrison, who took over the role when Desmond Payne left to become Master Distiller at Beefeater in 1995, runs tours of the distillery. These offer a fantastic opportunity, not only to see a historic distillery in operation, but also to take advantage of Sean's expertise and knowledge, and partake in a tasting session or even have a go at distilling your own gin. (Details below.)

Did you know?

As with many historic buildings, there are rumours of ghostly presences at the Black Friars Distillery, which have been reported since Victorian times. These may be related to a period when the building was used as a debtors' prison, and some unfortunates inmates were actually hanged here.

Method of Distillation
Plymouth gin is made in a traditional 150-year-old copper pot still, and only the heart cut is taken by the Master Distiller.

Did you know?

Plymouth Gin was specified in the earliest-documented recipe for a Dry Martini, dating back to 1896.

Tasting Notes
On the nose, Plymouth Gin is a harmonious and complex experience. You'll find plenty of sweet citrus, and also spice from the juniper, coriander and cardamom. The earthy notes of the angelica and orris bring a delicate balance to the overall picture. To taste, it's light, smooth and creamy. Juniper and coriander are the first botanicals to come through, then the citrus flavours come into play. There is a soft, dry finish as the root botanicals, orris and angelica, complete the exceptionally long taste profile.

Perfect to drink neat, or to make Martinis.

The Black Friars Distillery, where Plymouth Gin is made.

Plymouth Navy Strength

www.plymouthgin.com

ABV 57%

Botanicals: As for Plymouth Gin

Through almost two centuries, Plymouth Navy Strength Gin was carried on board the ships of Her Majesty's Naval Fleet. An attempt was made to discontinue the line a few years ago, but a staunch defence from Plymouth Navy Strength's traditional fans saved this remarkable brand for posterity, and it now seems to be enjoying something of a revival.

Did you know?

It is claimed that the high ABV of Plymouth Navy Strength resulted from the fact that spirit at this strength could be spilt on stored gunpowder – and the gunpowder would still ignite. This was obviously important on board the Navy warships of the Eighteenth and early Nineteenth Centuries – the sailors needed to know that they would be able to use the gunpowder to fire their cannons.

This may be an urban legend – it's hard to imagine that Naval Officers would have allowed their precious gin ration to get spilt and wasted – or, indeed, that they would have been drinking it near the gunpowder stores – but the fact that both gin and gunpowder – valuable substances – were kept together, under lock and key onboard ship, adds credence to the story.

Tasting Notes
Plymouth Navy Strength has the characteristic Plymouth Gin smoothness, but the fragrance and complexity of the botanicals come through much more powerfully, with a very intense, rich flavour.

Great sipped neat over ice (go steady, if you're a Plymouth Navy Strength first-timer!) and also makes a fantastic gin and tonic. Well worth trying as a Gimlet – the lime-juice cocktail was invented as a pleasant way for sailors to get the vital vitamin C that would help prevent outbreaks of scurvy on board ship.

Did you know?

Gin was the officer's drink on board ship, while the ordinary sailors were restricted to rum – and the ubiquitous British Navy helped to carry the Plymouth brand around the world.

Navy Strength was very popular with submariners, where space was at a premium and the extra strength saved them having to carry more bottles. With the advent of nuclear technology, however, alcohol was banned on board, and sales began to slump. It was around this time that the brand was discontinued.

In 1993, Desmond Payne – now Master Distiller at Beefeater – was at Plymouth. When offered the opportunity to do something special for the 200th anniversary, he asked if he might reintroduce the old 57% ABV brand. Despite being told that it had only sold 25 cases over two years, he insisted that it should be reinstated. Plymouth Navy Strength was reintroduced, and sold by mail order from the distillery. Gradually, sales picked up, as the new wave of bartenders got to hear of it, and now is firmly back on the gin map.

Plymouth Sloe Gin

ABV 26%

Plymouth first produced Sloe Gin in 1883. Local Dartmoor sloes are steeped in Plymouth Gin for four months, and then a little sugar and some soft Dartmoor spring water are added to mitigate the bitterness of the sloes. (For more details, see *Chapter Thirteen*.)

Plymouth Distillery Tours

There are currently three types of tour at the Black Friars Distillery. To check times and details, and to book, contact:

Plymouth Gin Distillery
60 Southside Street
Plymouth PL1 2LQ
01752 665292
http://booking.plymouthgin.com/distillery-tours/cat_5.html

The Plymouth Gin Distillery Tour

This takes around 40 minutes, and offers an introduction to the history of the building, and to the botanicals and the method of distillation of Plymouth Gin. The cost is currently £7. At the end of the tour, visitors over 18 can choose between a free miniature of Plymouth Gin, or a gin and tonic in the Distillery Bar. Seventeen-year-olds and under may join the tours for free, if accompanied by an adult, but alcohol legislation applies.

At time of going to press, tours take place every half hour through the week and on Saturdays. Booking is advisable.

The Gin Connoisseurs' Tour

This is usually hosted by Sean Harrison himself and, in addition to the history and an introduction to the stills, offers an opportunity to taste and compare some of the different styles of gin. The experience takes around one and a half hours.

Booking in advance is essential – and the tours usually take place on Tuesday, Wednesday and Thursday afternoons.

The Master Distiller's Private Tour

Here, you can take a distilling masterclass under the expert eye of Sean Harrison. He will guide you through a comparative tasting, and assist you in blending your own gin in a micro-still using your own choice of botanicals. You will be able to take away a bottle of your 'single-batch' gin with you, and will also be offered a drink in the historic Refectory Bar.

You will need to set aside around two and a half hours for the Private Tour, and booking in advance is essential.

Right Gin

www.rightgin.com
Distilled Gin

ABV 40%

Botanicals: Bergamot, cardamom, coriander leaf, juniper, lemon, lime, bitter orange, black pepper

The Master Distiller who created Right Gin in 2005, W.L. Lyons Brown III, has a background in bourbon distilling. His aim was to make a crisp, clean gin that would be light, fresh and very mixable, and would appeal to the younger generation.

Right Gin is produced in Sweden, but its neutral spirit is made from American corn (as befits the bourbon connection) and has a lingering natural sweetness even before the botanicals are added.

Method of Distillation

Each botanical is distilled and then blended with neutral spirit made from corn. Before bottling, Right Gin is diluted with water from a lake near Malmö in Southern Sweden.

Tasting Notes

Right Gin is very upfront – all the botanicals come through boldly and warmly, and the lingering peppery finish to the taste profile is very more-ish.

Lovely to drink neat, and, as the distiller intended, works well in any cocktail.

Rogue Spruce

www.roguespirits.com
Distilled Gin

ABV 45%

Botanicals: Angelica, coriander, cucumber, ginger, grains of paradise, juniper, lemon peel, orange peel, orris, spruce, tangerine

Rogue Spruce is one of the many independent, small-batch, artisan gins to be developed in the US in recent years. The artwork on the distinctive label pays tribute to the Oregon Spruce Loggers who worked in the local forests in the 1880s.

As the name implies, spruce is an important ingredient of Rogue Spruce Gin. Despite spruce being a conifer closely related to the juniper bush, the combination of the two doesn't overload the gin with pine flavour. While juniper is fragrant, dry and herbal, spruce has a thicker, fruitier tang.

Method of Distillation

As the neutral spirit is heated in a Vendome copper pot still, the resulting vapour passes through the 11 botanicals and is infused with their flavour.

Tasting Notes

A very complex gin, very soft and slightly oily in texture. Clean, balanced, tangy notes of pine predominate.

Works very well in fruit-based cocktails such as the Bramble.

Seagram's Extra Dry

www.seagramsgin.com
Vacuum distilled gin

ABV 40%

Botanicals: Angelica, cardamom, cassia, coriander, juniper, bitter orange, orris

First made in 1939, Seagram's Extra Dry is a very popular gin in the US – by quite a long way. It's a smooth, very flavourful drink with a slight yellowish hue from being stored in oak barrels after distillation. It can often be found in travel retail outlets abroad, and thus has found a loyal following the UK, too. Available online in the UK.

Seagram's also make a wide range of bottled gin-and-juice mixes, with new introductions almost every year.

Method of Distillation
The vacuum process allows distillation at a much lower temperature than a conventional still, enhancing the freshness and purity of the flavours. Seagram's Gin is rested in oak casks, which gives a smooth and mellow quality to the spirit.

Tasting Notes
A slightly sweet and very flavourful gin, with plenty of juniper and spice and some floral notes and hints of candied peel.

Seagram's is excellent in a gin and tonic, and blends well in all fruit-based cocktails.

Seagram's Distiller's Reserve

ABV 51%

The Master Distiller at Seagram's selects the best of the barrels, and blends them to make Distiller's Reserve. The high ABV makes this a stunning gin to sip neat over ice, and it also makes a bold, spicy Martini and a very flavourful and bitter-sweet Negroni.

Other Products
Seagram's also produce a large range of fruit-flavoured gins, in their 'Twisted' range, including Twisted Apple, Twisted Grape, Twisted Lime, Twisted Orange, Twisted Pineapple and Twisted Raspberry.

Uganda Waragi

www.eabl.com
Gin

ABV 40%

Botanicals: Including juniper

The name *'waragi'* is a generic term for distilled beverages in Uganda, and the name dates back to the British colonial days, when the expats called the local *enguli* spirit 'war gin'. This was because the Nubian soldiers who helped with the colonisation of East Africa would quaff *enguli* to keep themselves in 'good heart' – an African version of the old 'Dutch Courage'.

From 1965 and the introduction of the 'Enguli Act', distillation was only allowed under licence, and Uganda Waragi Gin came into being then, made by East African Breweries Limited. Its quality has been variable over the years, due to use of neutral spirit from different local sources, but it's a very popular drink in Uganda and, as well as being bottled, is also sold in small pouches.

Uganda Waragi is hard to track down in the UK, though you may find a bottle (or pouch) for sale in areas where there is a large African community.

Method of Distillation
Not listed, although as the label states 'Gin' and not 'Distilled Gin' it is likely to be a compound gin, created by adding essences to the neutral alcohol, which is made from triple-distilled millet grain.

Tasting Notes
A soft, juniper-led gin, with a spicy, sweet quality. There's an earthy, spiciness on the nose, and on the palate, juniper and sweetness vie for attention, with a drier, slightly bitter aftertaste.

Makes a good, juniper-dominated gin and tonic, and a balanced, crisp Gimlet. Also mixes well with Coca Cola.

Williams Chase Gin

www.chasedistillery.co.uk
Distilled Gin

ABV 48%

Botanicals: Angelica, Bramley apple, coriander, elderflower, hops, juniper, lemon, liquorice, orange, orris

This unusual gin is made by the Chase family at their Herefordshire distillery, and many of the ingredients are grown organically on their nearby farm. When the Chase Gin was being developed, Chase Vodka, which is made with the farm's potatoes, was the first choice for the base spirit – but the creamy character of this was too predominant. A new, apple-based spirit was developed for Williams Chase Gin, and this proved so drinkable in its own right that it's now marketed as Naked Vodka.

Method of Distillation
Williams Chase Gin is made by vapour infusion in a small Carterhead still, known as Ginny.

Tasting Notes
Juniper and citrus are present on the nose, but there's a hint of woodiness and of the apple spirit, too. On the palate, juniper and citrus sweetness lead into a spicy, bitter, almost burnt finish.

Williams Chase Gin has a very distinctive, rural quality when drunk neat over ice, and it makes a lovely gin and tonic, especially with a slice of apple to garnish. Well worth trying in all fruit-based cocktails.

Xoriguer

www.xoriguer.co.uk
Distilled Gin

ABV 38%

Botanicals: A secret recipe, but definitely including juniper and other herbs

---

Did you know?

Xoriguer is pronounced *sho-ri-gair.*

You can buy Xoriguer Gin de Mahon in Menorca where it's made.

The Pons family have been making Xoriguer Gin – named after the old windmill built in 1784 which was the emblem of their milling business – for more than 100 years. The distinctive green glass bottle has a circular handle on the neck which mimics the handle on antique stone gin crocks.

Like Plymouth Gin, Xoriguer is subject to a geographical specification, and may only be made in Mahon on the island of Menorca. Sixty per cent of Xoriguer Gin is drunk on Menorca, but the Pons family are keen to keep up the British connection and share their spirit with the gin lovers over here, where it's available on line and from specialist retailers.

Method of Distillation

Xoriguer Gin is made by the infusion method, in very old copper pot stills heated by wood fires. The neutral spirit is wine-based, like G'Vine, and the botanicals are placed in copper baskets for a vapour infusion process. This process happens several times, to ensure that no botanical essence is missed. Unusually, Xoriguer is not diluted after leaving the still, but emerges at bottling strength – 38% ABV. After distillation, the gin is rested in oak barrels before bottling.

Did you know?

In the Eighteenth Century, Menorca (which belonged to the British Crown from 1713) was an important base for British soldiers and sailors. They missed their gin – which was at the height of its popularity back at home – and some local distilleries began to make it using juniper berries and a spirit made from the local wine. Now, Xoriguer is the last remaining distillery on the island.

Tasting Notes

Xoriguer is a floral, herby gin, with a soft and silky feel in the mouth. The flavour comes through strongly at first, with a burst of herbs and soft, piny juniper. The profile leads through into floral notes, and tails off with a subtle undertone of clove-like spice. Very pleasant to drink neat, and works well as a long cocktail, such as the traditional Pomada.

Xoriguer Gin is named after the Pons family's Eighteenth-Century windmill.

Zuidam

www.zuidam.com
Distilled Gin

ABV 44.5%

Botanicals: Angelica, cardamom, coriander, juniper, fresh lemon, liquorice, fresh orange, orris, vanilla

The Zuidam Distillery, in the heart of the Netherlands' genever country, brings together traditional methods and recipes with a very modern approach to making fine gins and genevers.

Zuidam Dry Gin is very traditional, utilising all the signature flavours of Dry Gin – but it packs a little extra punch, with the high ABV and the special method of distillation adding an extra, fiery spiciness. A great one to try if you want a little more 'oomph' from your gin

Method of Distillation
Each botanical is distilled separately. All the distillates are then blended and allowed to rest in stainless steel for six weeks.

Did you know?

Since each botanical releases its peak flavour in the still at a different temperature, distiller Patrick van Zuidam distils all the botanicals individually so that they will come through in as pure a form as possible before being blended together.

Tasting Notes
Zuidam Gin is very strong on juniper, and the use of fresh fruits rather than dried peels gives an extra citrus zing. The high ABV gives a powerful, explosive punch to the sweet, spicy flavours, but the use of vanilla balances this with softness and smoothness.

Zuidam Genever Gin

This is made with a malt spirit (comprising one third barley, one third corn and one third rye). After three distillations, this spirit is redistilled with the addition of aniseed, juniper, liquorice, marjoram and vanilla.

It's much sweeter than the Zuidam Dry Gin, and there is a distinct malty undertone, although the spirit is clear. It has an ABV of 40%.

Chapter Twelve

Old Style Gins

IF YOU were in need of refreshment in London before 1861 and you popped into a Gin Palace for a quick dram of gin, the bartender wouldn't serve it from a bottle. He or she would turn to the row of barrels that were lined up behind the bar and draw your drink from one of them. It wasn't until Gladstone's Single Bottle Act was introduced 1861 that spirits were permitted to be sold in bottles.

Old Tom Gins

As you sipped your gin, you'd notice the amber hue of the liquid and you'd taste much more sweetness than we now expect from the gins that are served up in most pubs and bars. London Dry Gin has yet to come on the scene, and what you'd be drinking is its predecessor, generally referred to as Old Tom Gin.

Old Tom would be sweetened, probably with sugar but possibly also with sweet botanicals such as liquorice. Your fellow drinkers in the Gin Palace, like all their contemporaries, had a very sweet tooth when it came to alcoholic drinks.

Did you know?

London was the centre of the worldwide trade in sugar in the Nineteenth Century. The West India Docks was built at this time to handle the vast amounts of the commodity being shipped into England from the Caribbean colonies. Distillers were quick to take advantage of the ready availability of sugar, and used it to disguise any unwelcome taints from the base spirit used to make their gin.

There wasn't much consistency between the gins that you would have been able to buy in London at this time. Some would have been exceptionally sweet – more like cordials or liqueurs than the gins we know today. Some would have fruit added. You would have been very hard put to find any gin that was dry.

Did you know?

The origins of the name 'Old Tom' are shrouded in mystery, and largely anecdotal. It's widely assumed that the name refers to the notorious Captain Dudley Bradstreet, and the sign of the cat on the door of his speakeasy. But there are other possibilities, too. Joseph Boord was the first distiller to register the image of a cat in his 1849 Cat and Barrel trademark for Old Tom Gin, which was also the earliest registered trademark for gin. He was prepared to go to court to defend his right to use it, as is detailed in the *Encyclopaedia Britannica* of 1910:

> *The precise origin of the term 'Old Tom' as applied to unsweetened gin, appears to be somewhat obscure. In the English case of Boord & Son v Huddart (1903), in which the plaintiffs established their right to the 'Cat Brand' trade-mark, it was proved before Mr Justice Swinfen Eady that this firm had first adopted about 1849 the punning association of the picture of a Tom cat on a barrel with the name of 'Old Tom' and it was at one time supposed that this was due to a tradition that a cat had fallen into one of the vats, the gin from which was highly esteemed. But the term 'Old Tom' had been known before that, and Messrs. Boord & Son inform us that previously 'Old Tom' had been a man, namely 'old Thomas Chamberlain of Hodge's Distillery'; an old label book in their possession (1909) shows a label and bill-head with a picture of 'Old Tom' the man on it, and another label shows a picture of a sailor lad on shipboard described as 'Young Tom.'*

One interesting point that emerges from the above extract is that Old Tom is described as 'unsweetened' – which seems to go against the general use of the term. But the situation was a complicated one. Perhaps, in the days when gins were all sweetened, 'Old Tom' had come to stand for a high-quality gin. After the advent of

Did you know?

The Beefeater Archive contains a recipe dating back to 1864, which is intended for both Dry and Old Tom Gins. For both varieties, it lists angelica, coriander, juniper, liquorice root and winter savory. The botanicals are exactly the same, but sugar is added to the Old Tom Gin in the proportion of 40lb of loaf sugar to every 100 gallons of spirit.

the column still, and the cleaner, purer spirits that resulted after the 1820s, gin no longer needed to be so sweet – but the name was continued with some of the dryer brands to ensure that they were still popular.

Even after the advent of Dry Gin to the scene, sweetened Old Tom remained popular. It was a key ingredient in many of the early cocktails books, dating from the 1880s through to the first half of the Twentieth Century. Even in the 1950s some cocktail experts wouldn't consider making a Tom Collins or a Martinez with anything other than Old Tom.

Titanic

When the 100th anniversary of the sinking of the Titanic was marked, there was speculation as to what drinks her unwitting passengers would have enjoyed as they sailed on, oblivious to the disaster to come. Not many wine lists and bar menus have survived, but a look at the details from other ships of around that time is very revealing:

In November 1907, the White Star Line Canopic carried three gins: Geneva, Warrington and Old Tom and, in 1910, the list for the White Star Arabic was exactly the same.

Nicholson's Old Tom was also listed as being carried by White Star ships around the date of the Titanic's sailing, so it's likely that this brand would have featured on board the doomed liner.

A wine list from Titanic's sister ship, RMS Olympic, dated 23rd July, 1924 lists three gins: Geneva, Gordon's London Dry and Nicholson's Old Tom.

It seems clear from this that the old-style Geneva and Old Tom Gins were very important to sophisticated drinkers of that time – and that London Dry was known to them, but hadn't yet taken the predominant position it would hold in a few years' time.

Old Tom and London Dry Gin marched side by side until the 1960s – being made in Plymouth and also at by G&J Greenall at Warrington, as well as by the big London names. It's good to see that, after a 50-year hiatus, Old Tom, riding on the crest of the new Gin Craze, is making a comeback.

Did you know?

Winston Churchill is reputed to have been a fan of Old Tom Gin – since he found London Dry too dry, and Geneva-style gin too sweet.

Old Tom Brands

Boord's

Old Tom Gin

Now made in the US, Boord's Old Tom Gin is a very old brand and, for many years until the current gin revival, was the only 'Old Tom' on the market. It's not now readily available in the UK.

Method of Distillation
Not listed.

Tasting Notes
On the nose, juniper and spice come through clearly. The taste profile has an initial rush of sweetness, but, despite the 'Old Tom' name, is much more like London Dry Gin or, possibly, the lighter, sweeter Plymouth. Juniper is very strong, with a touch of citrus and spice.

Makes a surprisingly dry and quite powerful juniper-led gin and tonic.

Both's

www.haromex.com
Old Tom Gin

ABV 47%

This is made at Both's Distillery in Germany and was created to be used in some of the cocktails, like the Martinez, which would originally have been made using Old Tom Gin. It's a true old-style gin, with plenty of lingering sweetness.

The long-necked bottle has a distinctly vintage look, as does the thick retro label with the cat and barrel, which is very similar to that of the discontinued, and once very popular, Booth's Old Tom Gin.

Method of Distillation
Not listed.

Tasting Notes
The aroma is light, sweet and very citrusy, with some floral and herbal hints. On the palate, Both's Old Tom has a very silky feel. The citrus is sweet, very fruity

and vibrant. The high ABV makes the floral notes intense, with juniper just about holding its own against a strong background of lavender, violet and fennel which lingers to a smooth finish.

Good to try neat, to get a good idea of the 'Old Tom' profile, though it is very strong, and is easier on the palate when a little water is added. Perfect for all old-style cocktails, or for any cocktail recipe where a shot of sugar syrup is called for. Since the Old Tom style of gin is so much sweeter than Dry Gin, you may need to omit the syrup or use much less, if any, than listed in recipes.

The Dorchester Old Tom Gin

www.dorchester.com
Old Tom Gin

ABV 40%

You won't find this gin for sale in a supermarket, or an off-licence, or even on one of the specialist online drinks retailer's sites. This Old Tom Gin was created exclusively and especially for The Dorchester Hotel, so that the barmen there could recreate some of the historic cocktails from the early years of the Twentieth Century. You will find it's well worth visiting the bar just to try some of these!

Method of Distillation
Made by William Grant & Sons, the whisky distillers, who also make Hendrick's Gin.

Tasting Notes
On the nose this is very light and perfumy, imbued with rose and sandalwood. It's sweet on the palate, and very floral. Lavender and violet predominate, and the juniper is very fresh and light.

Dorchester Old Tom Gin works perfectly in all the classic cocktails from the Cocktail Era which call for Old Tom Gin. You might also like to try it in a variation on a gin and tonic. Just add a dash of bitters to balance the sweetness, and you'll be pleasantly surprised at the complex, refreshing experience.

Hayman's Old Tom Gin

www.haymansgin.com
Old Tom Gin

ABV 40%

Botanicals: Including angelica, cassia, cinnamon, coriander, juniper, lemon peel, liquorice, orange peel, orris

This Old Tom Gin has an excellent pedigree, since it's made from an original recipe from the Hayman family archives, which dates back to the 1870s. It has a traditional gin profile of juniper and citrus, with plenty of light, but intense, spice. Sugar is added to give extra sweetness.

Did you know?

Hayman Distillers was founded in 1820, and in 1863 was acquired by James Burrough, founder of Beefeater and great-grandfather of the current Chairman of Hayman's – Christopher Hayman.

Method of Distillation
Traditional distillation. Sugar is added

Tasting Notes
The juniper comes through well on the nose, and there's very sweet citrus, too. The spices come through with a rounded, intense quality and there is a long, sweet finish in the mouth.

Hayman's Old Tom brings a great intensity of flavour to cocktails, the sweetness and the additional hit from the botanicals working really will with most mixes.

Hayman's 1820 Gin Liqueur

ABV 40%

This is similar to the cordial gins which were very popular in the early years of the Nineteenth Century. It is made in a traditional pot still, and then blended into a liqueur. It has strong juniper and fruit notes and is very good served neat with ice. It also adds a little extra 'oomph' to gin cocktails.

Hayman's 1850 Reserve Gin

ABV 40%

Newly launched in 2012, this is a scrupulous attempt to recreate as closely as possible the cask gin served in London's Gin Palaces. In the knowledge that this method of storage would undoubtedly have imparted some flavour and colour to the gin, Hayman's have taken their classic London Gin recipe and rested it in Scotch whisky barrels for four weeks. The barrels add soft and mellow notes to the juniper and coriander of the classic gin profile. The resulting liquid is pale yellow, with an intense juniper and floral flavour.

Overall, the texture is much softer than that of the gin which hasn't been 'rested', and Hayman's 1850 Reserve works wonderfully well as a base for a complex and very satisfying Martini.

Jensen's Old Tom Gin

www.bermondseygin.com
Old Tom Gin

ABV 43 %

Botanicals: Including juniper

This Old Tom Gin is unusual in that the sweet quality is obtained entirely from the botanicals (judging from the taste, there is probably some liquorice included in the list) and not from the addition of sugar. It's based on a recipe dating back to the 1840s, and while it's definitely not dry, like its sister, Jensen's London Dry Gin, it has a very light sweetness compared to some of the other Old Toms. It also lacks the floral, perfumey qualities of some of its competitors.

Did you know?

The high price of sugar at the time when Old Tom Gin was at the height of its popularity in the Nineteenth Century led to a search for other ingredients that would provide sweetness. Christian Jensen had this in mind when he created his Old Tom Gin as a complement to his London Dry Gin.

Method of Distillation
Small-batch distilled and bottled in London at the London Distillery.

Tasting Notes
Deep and complex aromas on the nose, with lots of juniper and spice. In the mouth, Jensen's Old Tom has strong, piny juniper and herbal tones well to the fore. It's

not particularly sweet upfront, but this kicks in through the long finish to the taste profile, which has a lot of liquorice.

Despite its bias towards sweetness, Jensen's Old Tom is not as smooth as Jensen's London Dry. It's a little rougher and warmer and, drunk neat, makes for a pleasant, invigorating experience.

Makes a very dry and aromatic Martinez. If you like the Old Tom style, comparing this one with one of the sweeter brands in some classic cocktails will make for an interesting experience.

Ransom Old Tom Gin

www.ransomspirits.com
Old Tom Gin

ABV 44%

Botanicals: Angelica, cardamom, coriander, juniper, lemon, orange

This American Old Tom Gin is intended to reproduce the gin that was popular in the US in the early 1800s. It was developed in collaboration with legendary drinks pundit and historian of the American cocktail, David Wondrich. It's barrel-aged, which gives it a deep amber colour, and this also adds a hint of toasty sweetness to the flavour.

Method of Distillation
Botanicals are infused in pure corn spirit, which is then blended with Ransom Spirits' in-house barley whisky. All of this is then put through a copper pot still. The heart cut is then barrel-aged before bottling.

Tasting Notes
Very strong on the nose, with a powerful hit of juniper and herbs. To taste, Ransom Old Tom isn't especially sweet. The juniper is intense, and there's a malty quality on top of some complex herb notes. You might also pick up some dried-fruit, too, somewhere around the middle, before cardamom and malt bring the profile to a finish.

Image courtesy of Ransom Spirits; picture by Eye of the Lady Photography Studio.

If you can get hold of a bottle of this unusual gin it's ideal for all pre-Prohibition cocktails. It makes a very striking Martinez, and also, with its warm, subtle toasty quality, it's an enjoyable gin to sip neat.

Dutch Genevers

Genever Timeline

- **Mid-1500s** – Grain starts being used for distillation in the Netherlands
- **1575** – The Bols family start distilling liqueurs in Amsterdam
- **1602** – The Dutch East India Company starts trading, bringing botanicals from around the globe back to the Netherlands
- **1664** – Lucas Bols starts production of genever
- **1820** – The Bols company start using a column still to make genever, creating a more sophisticated balance of flavour. Around this time, they also start exporting to America
- **1950** – '*Jonge genever*' invented, with a mix using less malt wine and more neutral alcohol than the old-style '*Oude genever*'
- **2008** – Genever gains a protected status from the European Union

The forerunner of today's distilled dry gins is alive and well, and still being produced in large quantities in Holland. Often in demand in the late-Nineteenth and early-Twentieth Centuries as a cocktail ingredient (sometimes described as 'Hollands Gin') genever is experiencing something of a revival in Twenty-first Century bars as bartenders and mixologists look for new and intriguing flavours to play with.

Genever is made with a whisky-like spirit known as malt wine, made by distilling a mash of grains. This is mixed with a neutral alcohol which has been distilled with botanicals (in other words – a gin). There are a number of varieties of genever, which have varying amounts of malt wine in them – and some of which have been aged. Over 200 brands are currently on the market, and many of them are made by small, local producers.

The large-scale genever producers – some of whom have names and traditions which go right back to the Sixteenth Century – include:

- Bokma (www.bokma.com)
- Lucas Bols (www.lucasbols.com)
- Boomsma (www.boomsma.net)
- De Kuyper (www.dekuyper.com)
- De Ooievaar (A. van Wees) (www.de-ooievaar.nl/english/)
- Zuidam (www.zuidam.eu)

If you are thinking of trying some of this historical spirit, you can find plenty of examples to buy online. Gerry's of Old Compton Street, London and Berry Bros. & Rudd of St James's Street, London always carry some brands.

The labels often have no English translation available, so you may find the explanations of some of the terms given below useful if you aren't familiar with all the different varieties of genever.

Genever Glossary

Graanjenever (**Grain Genever**) – A description of genevers which have been made with neutral spirit distilled from grain, as opposed to molasses

Moutwijnjenever (**Malt Wine Genever**) – This generally refers to a genever which consists of more than half malt wine

Korenwijn or *Corenwyn* (**Corn Wine Genever**) – This contains at least 51% malt wine and has an ABV of at least 38%. It must have no more than 20g of sugar per litre for sweetening. Corn wine does not have to be aged, although it often is. Bols Corenwyn has very little sugar added and is a blend of genevers that have been aged for three years in oak Cognac barrels

Oude or *Zeer Oude Genever* (**Old Genever**) – *Oude genever* has at least 15% malt wine, an ABV of at least 35% and no more than 20g of sugar per litre. It can be aged, but doesn't have to be. ('Old' refers to the style, not the age of the genever.)

Jonge Genever (**Young Genever**) – *Jonge genever* must not contain more than 15% malt wine, it must be at least 35% ABV and contain no more than 10g of sugar for sweetening. (As above, 'young' means new in style, rather than young in age.)

Aged Genever – If a genever label mentions aging, this must have taken place in a barrel of not more than 700l (154 gallons) for a minimum of one year.

Did you know?

Young Genever makes a great long drink, mixed with bitter lemon, ginger ale or lemonade – and it's very good, too, in cocktails as a variation from dry gin. You will get an authentic flavour of the early-Twentieth Century as you savour the smoothness and slight grainy aroma from the malt wine. Old Genevers and *Korenwijns*, which have a much higher proportion of malt wine, are great to sip neat with ice – much as you might enjoy a fine malt whisky.

To give an idea of what you might expect from these different types of genever, Bols Very Old has malt wine mixed with *gebeide* malt wine (which has been redistilled with juniper berries) and neutral alcohol distilled with botanicals. The malt wine content is 19% and there are only 6g of sugar per litre. Bols Jonge Genever has 3% malt wine, and no sugar. It contains extract of apricot, clove, ginger and liquorice, and a concentrate of distilled aniseed, angelica, caraway and liquorice.

Genever Museums

The Dutch and the Belgians – current inhabitants of what was once known as The Low Countries – are very proud of their distilling heritage, and there are a couple of wonderful museums to visit if you are in the area. The House of Bols Cocktail and Genever Experience is also not to be missed – more details are given with the brand in Chapter Eleven, or contact www.lucasbols.com.

Schiedam Jenever Musuem

The town of Schiedam, just outside Rotterdam, is a great place to visit if you are interested in the history of gin and her mother-spirit, genever. The Jenever Museum, sited on the canal at Lange Haven 74–76 is a charming old brick building which houses a huge number of exhibits and is also a working distillery. There are many festivals and events taking place there throughout the year, so it's always worth checking what's going on if you are in the area. Contact www.jenevermuseum.nl

National Jenever Museum, Hasselt

There is also the National Jenever Museum at Hasselt in Belgium, at Witte Nonnestraat 19, which hosts a genever festival every year during the third week in October. Contact www.jenevermuseum.be/

Did you know?

In the 1880s, there were almost 400 distilleries in Schiedam, and it took 20 windmills to grind enough grain to feed their stills. The economy of the whole town was focussed on the industry, with coopers, metalworkers, malthouses, yeast makers and glass blowers all gravitating to the area.

Chapter Thirteen

Sloe Gin and Other Delights

MAKING Sloe Gin was an annual ritual for my family. Picking sloes with my mother and father and carrying them home to make sloe gin is one of my happiest childhood memories. (Of course, in those days I was never allowed more than a tiny sip of the luscious purple liquid, but it was great fun watching all the grown-ups get extremely merry as they passed round the Sloe Gin after Christmas dinner!)

I don't remember a written recipe – the tradition had been handed down over the generations. My parents would add sloes to a gin bottle, pour some sugar over, and then top up with gin. By Christmas, the sugar would be gone and the delicious liqueur was ready to drink.

Sloe Gin has been a British countryside tradition for hundreds of years – its warming, bittersweet delights enjoyed by the upper-class hunting, fishing and shooting set as well as the working-class cottagers. In the Twenty-first Century, it's been reinvented as a cocktail ingredient – mostly due to the fantastic flavour, but also due to the fact that, in this ecologically conscious age, sloes tick all the boxes as a seasonal, locally-sourced ingredient.

Did you know?

The fruits of the blackthorn, or sloe, bush (*Prunus spinosa*) were known to the Romans, who used them as a foodstuff. Sloes also formed an important source of flavour in mead, one of the earliest alcoholic beverages to be drunk in Britain and made from honey, yeast and water. In Victorian times, sloes were used to bring tartness to jellies and jams.

The creation of sloe gin is a slow process (no pun intended). But it's well worth waiting a few months for the pleasure of pouring out a glass of your very own vintage to share with friends and family.

How to Make Sloe Gin

- Pick enough sloes to fill half a gin bottle (around 400–500g)
- If the sloes have not been 'frosted' (see below) you'll need to prick each one several times. Be careful not to prick the stone of the fruit, though, as this may release toxic cyanide compounds into your sloe gin! Alternatively, you can freeze the sloes for 24 hours before use
- Put the sloes in an empty bottle, together with around 150g sugar. (Caster sugar is good for this, though ordinary granulated will also work.) 150g is about one wine glassful
- Fill up the bottle almost to the top with gin (around 500ml)
- Leave a little room at the top of the neck, so it's easy to shake and mix the contents
- Now, place the bottle in a cool, dark place for at least two months
- Shake the bottle once a week, to mix the ingredients and help the sugar to dissolve
- Strain the sloe gin through muslin and pour into a sterilised bottle

If you can resist drinking all of your home-made sloe gin, it will keep well if stored in a dark cupboard. If kept for more than a couple of years, the flavour intensifies, with notes of almond becoming more predominant. You can also make Sloe Vodka, using the same method.

Did you know?

Like the plum, damsons are a cultivated relative of the sloe and make a very fine gin, too. They have a larger stone inside, and this adds a deliciously almondy note to the gin. However, the flesh of the damson is much sweeter, so you won't need to add so much sugar to the mix.

An ideal sloe gin should be quite tart, with just a little of the berry flavour coming through. The trick to making a successful batch every year is understanding that the flesh of each year's sloe berries will have different levels of sourness and acidity, and so the amount of sugar needed will vary. It should be just enough to enhance the soft berry flavour, but not so much as to cause a sickly sweetness. If it's been a hot summer, there'll be more sugar in the berries, and you'll need less sugar. Once you have had a few goes at making sloe gin, you will start to get a feel for this.

A bottle of Sloe Gin from Demijohn.

Did you know?

Traditionally, sloe pickers wait until the first frosts in October or November, before picking the purple-black berries. The frost ripens and softens the berries, helping to release the flavour. The berries are then described as 'frosted'. Sloes are found on blackthorn bushes, which grow in country hedgerows. You'll often find them along disused railway lines, too. Once you've spotted the telltale, plum-dark tint of the sloes in the hedge, approach with caution. Blackthorn is well-named; the twigs are covered in very sharp spikes. One tradition has it that only these thorns should be used if the sloes need pricking. If no thorns are available, a solid silver implement may be substituted.

The small, hard fruits are extremely sharp and bitter; but don't be discouraged by the mouth-drying, face-pulling experience if you're tempted to try one. Married with gin and sugar, the flavour is quite different – tart and poignant and absolutely mouth-watering.

If you don't have access to hedgerows, it's worth checking your local farmers' market in late-autumn. You will sometimes find sloes for sale there.

Some sloe-gin enthusiasts are happy to use cheap gin in their recipe. The sugar will mask a lot of evils (as the makers of Old Tom in the Nineteenth Century knew only too well) but a good quality gin will pay dividends. It will hold its own against the sweetness of the sugar and the tartness of the berries and bring something very special to the mix.

Ways to Enjoy Sloe Gin

- Sloe gin makes a superb after-dinner drink, sipped neat as an alternative to brandy or port
- A very little sloe gin in a glass of dry Champagne is an excellent aperitif. Don't overdo the sloe gin or the strong flavour will swamp the Champagne
- Sticking to an autumn theme, add freshly-pressed English apple juice to a measure of sloe gin, for a long, refreshing drink
- Why not substitute sloe gin for your usual gin in a gin and tonic? It's delicious with lemonade, too
- Don't just think about drinking sloe gin – you can use it in cooking, too. It will add a wonderful depth of flavour to a fruit crumble, and you can also add a few drops to the gravy if you are roasting game birds or other fowl

Sloe Gin Brands

Until the development of a sophisticated gin-distilling industry in the Nineteenth Century, the making of sloe gin was carried out in domestic kitchens – in farmhouses, country mansions and cottages throughout Britain.

Now, with the increasing popularity of sloe gin as a cocktail ingredient, many of the big-name brands are making their own variety.

Boudier Sloe Gin

www.boudier.com

ABV 25%

Gabriel Boudier, one of the most experienced liqueur-makers in France, pays tribute to the time-honoured British tradition with his high-quality sloe gin, which has a very intense flavour. The sloes are picked from the wild bushes which grow on the French limestone plateaux and are macerated in Boudier's own dry gin. After maceration, a little sugar is added to create the right blend of sharp and sweet.

Bramley and Gage Sloe Gin

www.bramleyandgage.com

ABV 26%

This sloe gin is made in the traditional way, using Bramley and Gage's own gin. It's drier than some of the other brands, as it's made with a high ratio of sloes to gin, and a moderate amount of sugar. However, a prolonged maturing process ensures that the flavour of the fruit is very much to the fore. Very warming sipped neat.

Did you know?

Sloe gin, carried in a hip flask, was an essential accompaniment to the British country sports which traditionally take place in winter – hunting and shooting. It's also a great reviver to carry with you on a long winter walk.

Bramley and Gage also make an **Organic Sloe Gin**, which has an intense, rounded flavour with gentle, plummy notes from the berries, and a rich **Damson Gin**.

Foxdenton Sloe Gin

www.foxdentonestate.co.uk

ABV 29%

With a slightly higher ABV than many of the other sloe gins, Foxdenton's is also less intense in colour, and quite dry in flavour. This doesn't prevent it from being an extremely warming tipple drunk neat on a cold winter day. In summer, it makes a great long drink with bitter lemon or tonic. The makers also recommend adding it to Champagne – to create what they like to call a 'Sloegasm'! It's a pleasure to linger over.

Other fruit gins made by Foxdenton include **Raspberry, Damson and Plum Gins.**

Did you know?

If you are intending to provide gin at a special occasion – a wedding, birthday or sporting event – Foxdenton Estate can provide personalised labels from your own photographs or artwork, and add these to their fruit gin bottles for you.

Gordon's Sloe Gin

www.gordons-gin.co.uk

ABV 26%

Did you know?

The Sloe Gin Fizz cocktail was invented in the early 1900s, and Harry Johnson, in his *Bartenders' Manual* of 1882, listed sloe gin as a must-have behind the bar.

Gordon's have been making sloe gin for around 100 years. Wild-picked berries are left to steep in Gordon's Gin – resulting in a deep garnet-coloured liqueur with a soft, balanced flavour.

Gordon's website offers an extensive list of cocktails for making with sloe gin.

Hayman's Sloe Gin

www.haymansgin.com

ABV 26%

This is made from an old family recipe. English sloe berries are steeped in Hayman's Dry Gin for some months, before the addition of sugar. The ruby-red liqueur is very smooth, with an intense, bittersweet flavour.

Hayman's also make a **Damson Gin**.

Plymouth Sloe Gin

www.plymouthgin.com

ABV 26%

Made to a recipe dating back to 1883, Plymouth Sloe Gin is made by steeping local sloes in soft Dartmoor water and Plymouth Gin. Very little sugar is added, allowing the sharp berry flavours to dominate.

Plymouth recommend trying their Sloe Gin in a West Country Long Pedlar. Take a tall glass, wipe the rim with lemon and dip with caster sugar. Then, add sloe gin and top up with plenty of bitter lemon.

Sipsmith

www.sipsmith.com

ABV 29%

Sipsmith have recently added a sloe gin to their range of small-batch, handcrafted spirits. Wild sloe berries are left to rest in Sipsmith Gin. For the first month, the gin is at the strength it comes out of the still, around 70% proof. This really extracts the flavour, even a hint of almond from the tiny stones of the sloes. After this, the gin is diluted and left to rest with the berries for a further two months. Sugar is only added right at the end of the process, with great care not to over-sweeten. The result is a velvety, rich taste profile with hints of cherry and cassis, finishing with a delicate, balanced sweetness.

Owing to the varying acidity of the sloes, year on year, Sipsmith have given their sloe gin a 'vintage' title.

Sipsmith also make a **Damson Vodka**.

Sloe Gin Cocktails

To be enjoyed sloe-ly, of course…

Shots

It's a good idea to use a measure, or 'jigger' when making cocktails. This will enable you to measure out your 'shots' accurately. Single and double measures are available. One single measure is equivalent to one shot – that's around 25ml or 1fl oz.

Sloe Bramble

A classic autumn cocktail, perfect for when the clocks go back.

Ice cubes
1 shot sloe gin
1 shot dry gin
5 tsp freshly squeezed lemon juice
1 tbsp sugar syrup
Crushed ice
Fresh or frozen blackberries and/or raspberries, to garnish

Fill a cocktail shaker with ice cubes and add the two gins, the lemon juice and the sugar syrup. Shake well and strain into a rocks glass containing crushed ice. Garnish with fresh or frozen berries, depending what's available.

Sloe Gin Royale

A stylish way to kick off a garden party, or any summer celebration.

1 shot sloe gin
Champagne, to top
Raspberries or redcurrants, to garnish

Pour the sloe gin into a Champagne flute, and top up with the Champagne. Gently stir. Add the berries to decorate.

Slo-Mo-Jito

Hedgerow and herb garden go Latin American in this tribute to the Cuban Mojito.

Basil leaves
1 tsp brown sugar
Lime wedges
Crushed ice
2 shots sloe gin
Soda water, to top

Toss the basil leaves, sugar and lime wedges into a rocks glass and muddle until the lime juice permeates the other ingredients. Add the crushed ice and then pour the sloe gin over it. Add soda water to taste. Stir.

Sloe-and-Spicy Eggnog

A wonderful treat for the festive season.

2 shots sloe gin
20ml spiced berry cordial
1 egg, raw
A little milk
Grated nutmeg, to garnish
Ice

Shake all the ingredients in a cocktail shaker with some ice. Strain into a wine glass and grate some nutmeg over the top.

Other Fruit Gins

Fruit gins had their heyday in the Victorian era, and only sloe gin has currently regained a foothold in the market. But there are a few notable exceptions:

Perthshire Raspberry Infused Edinburgh Gin

ABV 20%

Scotland is famous for the outstanding quality of its raspberries, so it's only natural that Spencerfield Spirit Company should choose these luscious little fruits to infuse in their Edinburgh Dry Gin (with the addition of just a little pure cane sugar). A glorious deep pink colour shines out from the bottle.

Tasting Notes

It's like raspberry jam on the nose, with touches of vanilla. To taste, it has the sweet spiciness of the Edinburgh Gin, with plenty of sweet, tart fruitiness from the raspberries.

Foxdenton Raspberry Gin

Foxdenton Estate also make a very good raspberry gin, which has a fabulous colour and is deliciously sweet – although very little sugar is added to the fruit.

Ways to Enjoy Raspberry Gin

- Chilled, raspberry gin is very crisp and fresh, so works very well over ice
- At room temperature (or body temperature if you're carrying it in your hipflask) it's more warming, with a pleasant softness
- Very good with Champagne, Cava or any sparkling wine
- In a gin and tonic, raspberry gin is unusually sharp and refreshing
- A Long Pedlar – often made with sloe gin – is delicious with raspberry gin. Just add bitter lemon to the pink fruit gin for a perfect summer pick-me-up

Raspberry Martini

A delectable bittersweet variation on the classic cocktail.

2 shots raspberry gin
1 shot dry vermouth
2 tsp maraschino liqueur
Dash of orange bitters

Stir the ingredients together in a chilled Martini glass, and enjoy the ensuing balance of sweet and dry, tart and creamy.

Damson and Plum Gins

The sloe's a wild ancestor of the cultivated plums and damsons, and you will find some similarities between sloe, damson and plum gins. They all come in shades of purple, and all have a bittersweet fruitiness. But the different characteristics of the fruits are very present. The larger, domesticated plums and damsons have a lot more sweetness than the dry, bitter, wild sloes, so less sugar will need to be added to the gin. The bigger stones, too, can add a hint of almond flavour.

Foxdenton Estate makes a **Winslow Plum Gin** using local plums of all varieties – Aylesbury, Czar and Victoria among them – going into the mix. The plum flavour comes through very well, and the dark skins of the fruit give the gin a very intense purple colour.

Foxdenton Damson Gin is made from Herefordshire damsons. It's slightly redder in hue than the plum gin and has a very tart flavour, somewhat like old-fashioned cherry drops.

More Fruit Gins

If you are keen to take your adventures with fruit gin even further, Demijohn – 'The Liquid Deli' – has shops in Edinburgh, Glasgow and York and also sells online (see www.demijohn.co.uk for further details). They stock a range of fruit gins that the Victorians would have been delighted to see. As well as sloe and damson, you will find a Seville orange gin (which featured in the recipes of Beefeater's James Burrough), a cranberry gin and a gooseberry gin. Sold as miniatures in a 'Gin Rack' collection, these make excellent gifts.

Many of Demijohn's fruit gins and liqueurs are made by Colin Hingston, of Tipsage Farm near Tenbury Wells in Worcestershire. Every year tons of fruits from his farm and from the local Teme Valley area are made into around 18,000 litres of his specialist Tipsy Fruit Gins, using old family recipes.

A Fruit Gin Rack from Demijohn.

Did you know?

Colin's family have been connected with Tipsage Farm for around 200 years. In the Nineteenth Century, damsons from the farm were sent to Manchester cotton mills to dye the cloth which was made there. Currently, new damson orchards are being planted at the farm, to ensure self-sufficiency in future years.

After the fruit and the gin have been put to steep, they are left for a minimum of three months, ensuring maximum flavour for the products.

You'll find Tipsage Tipsy Fruit Gins on sale in local National Trust properties, and also in many delicatessens, especially through Herefordshire, Worcestershire and Shropshire. Online marketing is done through www.hoppocketwine.co.uk.

The Hingstons visit many of the major agricultural shows, and you may be able to catch up with them there and sample the products. See www.tipsage.co.uk for further details.

Tipsage's Tipsy Seville Orange Gin – available from Demijohn.

Chapter Fourteen

Gin and Tonic

JUST as with gin, the tonic half of the gin and tonic started out as a medicinal remedy. Quinine, which gives tonic its characteristic bitterness, is an antidote to malaria – and in colonial days was prescribed throughout the tropical regions to both treat and prevent this potentially deadly illness.

At first, the British in India mixed quinine with sugar and diluted it with water to make it more palatable to the soldiers and other servants of Empire, who received daily prophylactic doses. It wasn't long before someone – Erasmus Bond, in 1858 – added a shot of gin to the mix, and the classic gin and tonic was born.

The first bottles of tonic water came on the market in 1858, when Erasmus Bond introduced his 'improved aerated tonic liquid'. This was so successful that other brands soon followed, including the iconic Schweppes.

Did you know?

Quinine (*Cinchona officinalis*) is extracted from the bark of the quina tree, which is native to the tropical western slopes of the Andes in South America. It was first discovered by the local Quechua people, and later brought to Europe by the Spanish colonists. It appears as a medical remedy for malaria in the Seventeenth Century. There's a story that, in 1638, the wife of the Spanish Viceroy in Peru was cured of her malarial fever by a local shaman, and took the miraculous bark he had used back to Spain when she returned. Countess Chinchon, for that was her name, is honoured in the tree's official name.

Due to its remarkable healing qualities, quinine became more valuable than gold dust. In the mid-Nineteenth Century, chinchona seeds were taken to the Far East and, soon, the trees were growing in Ceylon, India and Java. By the mid-Twentieth Century, quinine had been synthesised in the laboratory. Some of the tonic waters available today contain little natural quinine – though that has changed in recent years, with the advent of some new premium brands, including Fever-Tree.

More effective anti-malarial drugs are available today, though quinine is still used in some cases, especially in countries where the cost of these new drugs is prohibitive.

Did you know?

There would be no gin and tonic for us to enjoy if it hadn't been for a certain Joseph Priestly, who in 1767 invented a method of carbonating water. It was known at the time that the blanket of 'air' which hung above fermenting beer was poisonous to mice, and would kill them. In fact, this 'air' was actually carbon dioxide. Priestly found that, if he suspended water over the fermenting beer, the gas would infuse into it and create a bubbly liquid similar to the naturally carbonated waters so popular in the spa towns of the day.

Schweppes is what most people imagine when they think of tonic water. It's ideal to use in a gin tasting, if you want to measure up how different gins work in a gin and tonic. However, there are now – following in the footsteps of Fever-Tree – many premium tonics, such as 6 O'clock Tonic Water and Q Tonic, on the market. With some of these, the packaging is an important factor, especially in the bar and restaurant trade, where customers appreciate having something of high quality, which looks special and different. Some, too, focus on sourcing all natural ingredients and forgoing any artificial flavours and sweeteners.

It's important to remember what's really important in a tonic water:

- Tonic water needs to hold a good fizz. Especially important if you're buying the larger sizes of bottle
- A balance of sweetness and bitterness is vital to work successfully with the gin botanicals in a gin and tonic
- Any overpowering flavours, such as lemon, can distort the picture in a gin and tonic – though they might work well in some of the speciality gins
- Natural sweeteners sometimes unbalance the flavour of a tonic. Sometimes, though, and this is rather contra-intuitive – the tonics which use high-fructose corn syrup and other sweeteners are lighter, softer and work better in a gin and tonic
- You don't always have to pay a high price for quality – some budget lines are excellent, including Waitrose Essential

How to Make the Perfect Gin and Tonic

At the most basic level, all you need is some ice, some gin and some tonic.

Gin and Tonic

One part gin
Two parts tonic water
Ice cubes

Pour the liquids into a tumbler, add ice. Stir.

But there's so much more to think about, if you really want to make this quintessential English drink into something special:

- It's best to use a high quality gin, so the botanicals will marry well with the bitterness of the tonic. If you keep your gin in the freezer, all the better
- Always open a fresh bottle of tonic for the best bubbles and the freshest flavour. Don't use tonic that's been sitting in the fridge and has gone flat and tired
- Use a glass with a thick bottom – a tumbler or rocks glass. This helps the bubbles in the tonic to last longer

Chill your glass in the freezer if you have time, remove, and fill half of it with ice. Add the gin. Next, pour twice as much tonic as gin – so that it fills the glass. Add a freshly cut wedge of lemon or lime, if desired, then stir gently. Enjoy!

Another way to approach it – Gin Mare and Tonic with herbal garnish.

Did you know?

A great way to make a gin and tonic very special is to use a swirl of one of the Sacred Open Sauce Distillates to add extra flavour and pizzazz. Simply make your tonic as you like it, then drizzle a little of your chosen distillate over the top. Cassia works particularly well, adding a bright, fragrant depth to the drink as you sip.

Tonic Water Brands

1870

www.silverspring.co.uk

Silver Spring were founded in 1888 and are based in Kent – the Garden of England. Their mixers are based on English recipes first created at the very beginning of the Cocktail Era in the late-Nineteenth Century. Their 1870 tonic water is made with Brazilian essential oils and pure North Downs water, naturally high in calcium.

Fizz
A medium strength to the bubbles.

Taste
The Regular version has a thin flavour, quite bitter, with a long sweet aftertaste. The Light version is similar, but the artificial, dry quality of the sweetness is very apparent. Both Light and Regular versions of 1870 Tonic Water use the artificial sweetener, aspartame.

Gin and Tonic Recommendation
Since the flavour is not particularly pronounced, 1870 Tonic Water works best with a light gin. Plymouth Gin and a slice of lemon or lime would be excellent.

6 O'clock Tonic Water

www.bramleyandgage.co.uk

This tonic is designed to complement Bramley and Gage's 6 O'clock Gin. It's preservative, sweetener and artificial flavour-free.

Fizz
Light bubbles quickly disperse.

Taste
There's quite a strong lemon scent and flavour, and the quinine takes a little while to come through. Overall, quite a light, smooth tonic water.

Gin and Tonic Recommendation
6 O'clock Gin, of course – with a good squeeze of lemon.

Britvic Indian Tonic Water

www.britvic.com

A staple brand behind the bar in pubs and on supermarket shelves, Britvic is a traditional tonic water which contains sweeteners, preservatives and natural flavourings. It's lower in sugar than many other tonics, but tastes surprisingly sweet.

Fizz
Not great – doesn't sustain very well after opening.

Taste
Very light, in both Regular and Slimline versions. Not a great deal of bitterness, just a sweet, light flavour.

Gin and Tonic Recommendation
Good with Gordon's and Hayman's Dry Gins, garnished with lemon.

Fentimans Tonic Water

www.fentimans.com

This tonic, in its retro-styled bottle, is made by a family firm based in Hexham, Northumberland, and has an unusually sharp, bitter-lemon tang that works well with a strong, gutsy gin. Due to the 'botanical brewing' method of production, involving steeping, simmering and fermenting, Fentimans Tonic is probably very similar to the tonic water that the Victorians would have enjoyed.

Did you know?

Thomas Fentiman set up in business in 1905, when he lent some money to a friend, and was given a recipe for ginger beer as security. The loan was never repaid, and Thomas started making and selling ginger beer, which soon developed into a thriving business. In 1988, Thomas's great-grandson re-established the old production methods and created a new range of Victorian soft drinks and mixers, using 100% natural ingredients.

Fizz
Plenty of strong bubbles, which last well.

Taste
The woody note of the natural quinine has an intense depth, which marries well with the herbal and citrus of the lemongrass. A natural, light sweetness pervades, which is neither cloying nor has the flat, artificial quality of sweeteners.

Gin and Tonic Recommendation
Mix with Gin Mare, and add a wedge of grapefruit. Or, try Broker's Gin, and garnish with lemongrass.

Fever-Tree Premium Indian Tonic Water

www.fever-tree.com

The founders of Fever-Tree, Charles Rolls (ex-MD of Plymouth Gin) and Tim Warrilow, quite literally went to the ends of the earth to source ingredients for their groundbreaking tonic water which was launched in 2005. Tim spent many days in the British Library researching the archives of the British East India Company for references to quinine's medical properties. He found a farm in the Congo where *Cinchona ledgeriana* trees grew (There are many species of *Chinchona* tree, and this variety produces an exceptionally pure form of quinine.) Bitter oranges from Tanzania and marigold oil are two other ingredients, along with soft Buxton water and pure cane sugar. The full details of the company's recipes, though, are kept secret.

Did you know?

Fever-Tree Tonic Water takes its name from a book about the history of quinine, entitled *The Miraculous Fever-Tree: Malaria, Medicine and the Cure that Changed the World.*

The first consignments of Fever-Tree Tonic Water were delivered by the founders themselves, using a bicycle and a motorbike. Now, you can find Fever-Tree tonic in many supermarkets and in pubs and bars, too.

Fizz

Not Fever-Tree's strongest point. Despite (or perhaps because of) a Champagne-style method of carbonisation, the bubbles are intense to start with, but fade quite quickly. This is definitely not a tonic that will keep once opened – it needs to go in the glass and be drunk right away.

Taste

A smooth, balanced blend of luscious natural flavours, great as a soft drink, as well as a mixer. Fever-Tree Premium Indian Tonic Water is very vigorous and citrusy, with an overtone of lime. The quinine is soft and subtle. The Light version is made with fruit sugar, rather than artificial sweeteners, and is pretty close to the Premium in flavour – perhaps a touch more floral.

Gin and Tonic Recommendation

A very refreshing experience with Bombay Sapphire and a slice of lemon. For something a little more unusual, mix with Boudier Saffron Gin, and garnish with lime.

Fever-Tree also make a **Mediterranean Tonic Water** which is made with a little less quinine than the Indian Tonic Water. It's much more floral, and includes thyme, geranium and rosemary from Provence. Its flavour is very delicate, with dry notes of lemon sorbet and hints of rose. Intended primarily for use in vodka tonics, Fever-Tree Mediterranean Tonic Water can work well with the lighter, more floral gins, such as G'Vine.

Fever-Tree Lemon Tonic made with quinine and *sfumatrice* Sicilian lemon essence is their great version of a bitter lemon mixer but, apparently, sells more bottles under the tonic name.

Keyword

'*Sfumatrice*' – This lemon essence is of exceptionally high quality. It is extracted by hand, in a process that is normally reserved for the perfume industry.

Q Tonic

www.qtonic.com

This premium brand is made in the US, using quinine from the Peruvian Andes (the original source of the quina tree) and a natural sweetener extracted from the Mexican agave plant. It has around 60% fewer calories than other tonic waters. The clear, elegant bottle with the simple 'Q' logo on the label is strikingly different from other tonic packaging – reflecting the maker's collaboration with a top New York designer to create the look.

Fizz
Not bad. Just has the edge on Fever-Tree, which is interesting, given that both brands use the Champagne-style method of carbonation.

Taste
Very crisp, clean and complex, Q Tonic is soft and lightly fruity with some herbal bitter notes and some pepper, too. The natural quinine adds an almost medicinal tinge. A fair way from the usual tonic water experience.

Gin and Tonic Recommendation
Works well with a modern, characterful gin like Tanquerary 10 – with a generous squeeze of lemon.

Schweppes Indian Tonic Water

www.schweppes.com

Did you know?

The Schweppes Company was founded in 1783 by a Swiss watchmaker, Johann Jacob Schweppe. He utilised a new process, developed in the UK, to make carbonated mineral water and, a few years later, moved his business to London.

This is the classic tonic for many people. Balanced in flavour and very pleasant on the nose – it's what most people imagine when they think of tonic water. It's very versatile, blending well with most gins, and it's available in just about all supermarkets and corner shops.

Some years ago, Schweppes ran a highly successful advertising campaign, liking the brand name to the onomatopoeic hiss of the escaping fizz when the bottle or can was opened. *Schhhhh-weppes!*

Did you know?

One quirky gimmick – verging on bad taste – that I came across while researching this chapter is an ice cube tray which makes iceberg and Titanic liner ice cubes for your 'Gin and Ti-tonic'.

Fizz
Pretty good – lots of bubbles up front, and they last quite well, even when the bottle's kept in the fridge for a while. (Not recommended practice for the discerning gin and tonic maker!)

Taste
Clean, refreshing and neither too sharp, nor too sweet. There is some natural quinine in Schweppes tonic, but 'quinine hydrochloride' is also listed as a flavouring. There is high fructose in Schweppes Indian Tonic Water, but also saccharin. Some people don't like the taste of artificial sweeteners, even in small quantities, so they may be put off by this.

The Slimline version omits the sugar and adds aspartame as a sweetener – but is still a pleasant, balanced flavour.

Gin and Tonic Recommendation
This is perfect with a traditional, balanced gin such as Beefeater, garnished with a slice of lime.

Gordon's use Schweppes as the mixer in their ready-made gin-and-tonic-in-a-can product.

Waitrose Essential Indian Tonic Water

www.waitrose.com

This product from Waitrose's 'Essential' line gets consistently good reviews in gin and tonic tastings, and is very good value, too.

The ingredients are similar to Schweppes Indian Tonic Water, including high fructose corn syrup. Both Regular and Sugar Free versions have a similar taste profile.

Fizz
Pretty good level of bubbles which stays well.

Taste
Soft and floral, with some fruity, apple and pear notes. Both Regular and Sugar Free versions have a similar taste profile.

Gin and Tonic Recommendation
Like Schweppes, this one works well with a balanced gin – try Hayman's London Dry Gin and a slice of lemon.

A final thought

Quinine is exceptionally sensitive to UV light. But you don't need to be in a dark nightclub with UV lighting to observe this. Remarkably, quinine has the property of fluorescing under sunlight. If it's a bright summer day and you're having a gin and tonic mixed with one of the brands which uses a high proportion of natural quinine – pop outside and see your favourite drink in a whole new light – literally glowing.

Chapter Fifteen

The Golden Age of Cocktails

MIXED drinks have been popular since gin first arrived in London. In the Eighteenth Century, fruit punches with rum or gin were enjoyed by the upper classes. But the cocktail, as we know it today, didn't really start to make an appearance until the Nineteenth Century, when the invention of the column still led to a great improvement in the quality of distilled spirits. There are recipes dating back to the early 1800s, and by the late-1800s, bartenders were writing substantial books listing their own recipes. These early cocktails had names which are now largely forgotten, such as Daisy, Crusta, Shrub, and Smash and at that time were mostly made with Hollands (another name for a genever-style gin), and also with sweetened Old Tom.

A Brief History of Cocktails

The golden age of the cocktail began in the 1920s, in the US. Through the years of Prohibition, a lot of 'bathtub gin' was made, using low-quality spirit from illicit stills, and mixing it at home (often in the bathtub) with various flavourings. A glass of this harsh spirit really needed some mixers to make it more palatable.

Happily, in Britain there was no Prohibition. A fan of the new mixed drinks could go to any bar or hotel and enjoy their favourite mixed drink and, soon, early evening cocktail parties began to threaten the supremacy of that very English

---

Did you know?

The Great War of 1914–18 left considerable social upheaval in its wake. The old rules of polite society began to erode. Hemlines rose, and clothes in general became less elaborate. The days of the old ritual of dressing for dinner between 6–8pm were gone. But what else might one do to pass those two hours? Soon, enterprising hosts and hostesses were inviting friends to drink cocktails at 6pm, a revolutionary idea which soon became extremely popular, as the Bright Young Things – familiar from the writings of Evelyn Waugh – became the epitome of the Cocktail Age.

---

institution – afternoon tea. The novelist, Alex Waugh (elder brother of Evelyn), was one of the first to serve cocktails before dinner – but he took care to offer his guests tea at 4.30pm, before bringing out the stronger drinks at 5.30pm.

With the advent of transatlantic air travel, rich Americans were soon flying to London to partake of the glamorous new cocktail-fuelled lifestyle. They flocked to clubs and bars, particularly the American Bar at the Savoy Hotel, to taste the latest mixes.

At the height of the Cocktail Age, around 7,000 different varieties of cocktails were being made, and many non-drinks-based industries profited hugely from the craze, too. Couturiers, including Coco Chanel, produced cocktail dresses intended specifically for those early-evening parties, and novelty manufacturers flooded the shops with shakers, glasses, swizzle sticks, cocktail mats and invitation cards. Furniture manufacturers invented the cocktail cabinet, designing gleaming Art Deco edifices with chrome and glass shelves designed to hold all the necessary paraphernalia.

By the 1950s, after the Second World War and rationing had brought all this delightful indulgence to an end, cocktail drinking was largely confined to the affluent upper classes, and short drinks which provided a strong hit of alcohol, like the Martini and the Manhattan, were very popular both at home and in hotel bars.

For most people, the gin and tonic was the only gin-based mixed drink to be enjoyed, until the club and discotheque culture of the 1980s and 1990s revived the cocktail. At first, it was mostly vodka – made into long drinks with fruit juices – that was at the forefront of the revival. Then Bombay Sapphire came on the scene, and younger drinkers began to appreciate what their grandparents had loved – the complex and delicious marriage of the gin botanicals with mixers.

Now, in the Twenty-first Century, gin cocktails are back in vogue. New and different combinations of gin with fruit juices, bitters, liqueurs, teas and many other ingredients appear each season. There is so much to try, to enjoy, to experiment with. The world of gin has never been so expansive and diverse.

Famous Mixologists – Past and Present

There have been so many personalities in the world of cocktails – men and women who have brought new recipes to the bar counter and, with their welcoming and sometimes flamboyant characters, added fun, glamour and expertise to the experience.

Jerry Thomas, 1830–85

Jerry Thomas, nicknamed The Professor, was a pioneer of cocktails and is considered by many to the first mixologist. He learned his trade in New Haven, Connecticut before heading west to seek his fortune in the California Gold Rush. By 1851, Jerry had opened his first bar in New York – beneath Barnum's American Saloon – before travelling through the US and Europe. He was a flamboyant man, fond of 'bling' as we might say today. He liked to wear jewellery and, since he could earn $100 a week practising his mixing skills (more than the Vice President of America at the time), he could afford bar equipment made from silver and studded with jewels.

His book, *The Bar-Tender's Guide*, published in 1862, was the first drinks book to be published, preserving for posterity what was once an oral tradition of recipes handed down from barman to barman. It contained recipes for Fizzes, Sours and Flips and later editions featured the Tom Collins and the Martinez.

Did you know?

It's likely that Jerry Thomas was the 'Genuine Yankee Professor' who appeared at the American Bar in London's Cremorne Pleasure Gardens in 1859. He also opened his own American Bar in Leicester Square before returning to New York in the early 1860s.

Harry Johnson, 1845–1933

Harry Johnson's *Bartenders' Manual* was published in 1882 (an earlier version may have been published in the 1860s, but this is the edition that is best-known) and gives a fascinating and very comprehensive picture, not just of what drinks to serve, but also of how to conduct yourself as a bartender, and how to run your bar – right down to how you should dress and how you should collect money from your customers.

In 1869, while working in New Orleans, Harry won a bartending competition by mixing a dozen cocktails using a striking arrangement of a pyramid of glasses. He mixed the cocktails by pouring the ingredients so that they trickled down through the pyramid. Harry went on to run bars in Chicago, Philadelphia and New York – most famously, 'Little Jumbo' in the Bowery, and his bar at Trainor's Hotel.

Harry MacElhone, 1890–1958

A Scotsman from Dundee, Harry MacElhone is credited with the invention of the White Lady and the Monkey Gland cocktails, among others. From 1911–14, he worked at the New York Bar at 5 rue Daunou in Paris, managed by the famous American jockey, Tod Sloan, who had dismantled a mahogany-panelled bar in New York and shipped it over to be reconstructed in its new location.

After serving in the First World War, Harry moved to Ciro's Night Club in London, where he soon became head barman, and a seminal figure in the early years of the

239

Golden Age of Cocktails – publishing *Harry's ABC of Mixing Cocktails* in 1915 and *Barflies and Cocktails* in 1927. It was at Ciro's that Harry is said to have invented the White Lady cocktail (though this early recipe used crème de menthe rather than gin, something which Harry revised in 1929). In 1923, he returned to Paris to take over the New York Bar, which became the legendary Harry's New York Bar.

Scott Fitzgerald and Ernest Hemingway frequented the Bar, and George Gershwin wrote his *An American in Paris* suite on the bar piano. The ownership and management of Harry's Bar was kept on in the family after his death, and it remains a lively landmark of Paris nightlife and a must on the tourist trail.

Ada Coleman, 1875–1966

Ada Coleman worked at the Savoy's American Bar from 1903, not long after the hotel was first built by the D'Oyley Carte family. She was a key figure at the American Bar until 1926 and mentored Harry Craddock when he joined the bar staff. She created special cocktails for Mark Twain, Prince Wilhelm of Sweden and also for the Prince of Wales – the future Edward VIII. 'Coley' as she was affectionately know, also invented the 'Hanky-Panky' – for actor-manager Charles Hawtrey. He said, on tasting this variation of a Martini, which featured Fernet-Branca, an unusual and bitter Italian digestive, 'By Jove! That is the real hanky-panky!' And so the cocktail has been known ever since.

Harry Craddock, 1876–1943

One of the most 'in' places to be seen in the period between the First and Second World Wars was the American Bar at the Savoy Hotel in London. American-born Harry Craddock left the US during Prohibition to become Head Bartender in 1925, and wrote *The Savoy Cocktail Book* which was published in 1930. It contains recipes for 'Rickeys, Daisies, Slings, Shrubs, Smashes, Fizzes, Juleps, Cobblers, Fixes and other Drinks…' This has become an important resource for researching the history of cocktails – and it's fascinating to see just how many different mixed drinks were being made at that time. Harry Craddock played a large part in popularising the Dry Martini throughout the 1920s and 1930s.

David Embury, 1886–1960

David Embury's *The Fine Art of Mixing Drinks* is a classic cocktail manual which enjoyed instant success on its publication in 1948. It's still read today by both professional bartenders and keen amateurs. New Yorker David Embury's influence in the world of cocktails is a little surprising given that he was neither a bartender nor a journalist – but an attorney, and a senior partner in a Manhattan law firm. He said of himself, 'I have always possessed an insatiable curiosity about the whys and wherefores of many things and particularly of food and drinks,' and his rigorous attention to detail, his witty and conversational writing style, as well as his passion for a fine cocktail make *The Fine Art of Mixing Drinks* an essential volume on all cocktail-lovers' shelves.

Alessandro Palazzi, 1958–

Alessandro Palazzi, born near Ancona in Italy, came to London in 1975. He's worked at The Ritz and The Connaught, and is now bar manager at Duke's Hotel in St James's. He's perhaps not strictly famous for being a mixologist, but is renowned for the excellence of his Martinis, which are simple but sublime.

Masterclass

Alessandro Palazzi gives a Martini Masterclass at Dukes Bar at the Dukes Hotel in London. During the masterclass you will learn how to make his speciality Dukes Martini, as well as some other classic variations – and you will also hear Alessandro recount the stories behind each cocktail. After the masterclass, relax with the Martini you made and some canapés.

Martini Masterclasses take place Monday to Friday from 3pm-5pm, subject to availability. Groups of 4–8 people can attend each class at a cost of £95 per person.

For further information and reservations, email bookings@dukeshotel.com or call 020 7491 4840.

Dick Bradsell

Born in the Isle of Wight, and moving to London at the age of 17, Dick Bradsell played a big role banishing the umbrella and the swizzle stick and bringing cocktails back into focus after the lost years of the 1970s. He has been involved in establishing many new bars on the London scene, and has had a huge influence on many current mixologists. His best-known gin cocktail, the Bramble, has become a modern classic.

Salvatore Calabrese

Known to colleagues as 'The Maestro' London bartender Salvatore Calabrese ran the well-known Salvatore bar at FIFTY in St James's, and has written 10 cocktail books, including *Classic Cocktails* which became a bestseller. Salvatore's son, Gerry, now follows in his footsteps at the Hoxton Pony.

Dave Wondrich

American Dave Wondrich started out as an academic, specialising in Shakespearean literature, and also enjoyed a brief career as a jazz critic before finding his true metier – as a drinks' writer and educator. He is the drinks' correspondent for *Esquire* magazine, and is also the author of many books, including *Imbibe!* which was published in 2007. He lectures all over the world on drinks and their history, and is renowned both for his wide knowledge and his ability to entertain.

Gary (Gaz) Regan

Author of the comprehensive guide *The Bartender's Gin Compendium*, Gary Regan is an idiosyncratic and highly erudite figure on the cocktail scene. He's written many articles, columns and books, and is well-known for his informal and engaging style. Gary lectures, maintains *The Worldwide Bartender Database* and has been a major influence on the current mixology culture.

Audrey Saunders

Audrey Saunders, who is based at the Pegu Club in New York has a passion for recreating the flavour of the past. This led her to start a whole new vogue for 'house-made' mixers like bitters and tonic water, when she started using them at the Club in 2005.

The Pegu Club's name was chosen by Audrey as a tribute to a legendary club in Rangoon, which served its signature drink (gin, lime juice, orange Curaçao, Angostura bitters and orange bitters) to British colonial administrators stationed in Burma. Audrey's love of researching and recreating vintage cocktails – with such titles as The Maharajah's Burra-Peg – have earned her wide acclaim. Gin cocktails are her preference, as she believes that the complex aromatics have contributed to the creation of some of the best cocktails in history. If you visit The Pegu Club, you will find more than 20 brands of gin on display.

Tony Abou-Ganim

Tony started out as a bartender in the US in the 1980s, just as the new cocktail scene was about to start up. He's a well-known figure in the cocktails world, having made numerous TV appearance on *Iron Chef America*. He's also created his own line of bar tools, and wrote *The Modern Mixologist – Contemporary Classic Cocktails* – a great reflection of the Twenty-first Century developments and a very good guide for the home mixologist.

Origins of the name

Where the name 'cocktail' originated is shrouded in mystery –and there are many possibilities:

- One of the more obvious explanations is that a tavern keeper in the late-Eighteenth Century used feathers from a fighting cock's tail to decorate glasses
- It's said that the different colours of the mixed liqueurs in a cocktail may have reminded drinkers of the varying hues of a rooster's tail feathers – however, in past years, spirits tended to be rather dull in colour and the vivid brightness of many of today's cocktails is quite recent
- The leftovers of a cask of sprits were once called *cock-tailings* and, if the cock-tailings of various spirits were mixed together and sold at a lower price, this may have led to the name
- The French term for a mixed wine cup was *coquetel*. One Monsieur Peychaud, a bartender of New Orleans who took bitters as a stomach remedy, served them in one of these cups. His customers struggled to pronounce the word and so it morphed into 'cocktail' (*Coquetel* is now the French word for a cocktail)
- *The Savoy Cocktail Book* includes a charming story of a Mexican princess named 'Coctel' (possibly in honour of the Aztec goddess, Xochitl). As the story goes, in the early years of the Nineteenth Century, there was frequent conflict between the Mexicans and the American Army of the Southern States. A truce was called, and the King of Mexico agreed to meet the American general. The King called for drinks, and his daughter, Coctel, brought a golden cup containing a delicious potion of her own mixing. But there was only one cup. Who should drink from it first, the general or the King? A moment of intense embarrassement ensued – and, with great tact, Coctel resolved the situation by draining the cup herself. The general, greatly impressed, asked who she was and, when the King told him, he said: 'I will see that her name is honoured for evermore by my Army.'

Timeline

1806 – The word cocktail first appears in *The Balance,* an American magazine, where it's described as 'a stimulating liquor, composed of spirits of any kind, sugar, water, and bitters…'

Early-1800s – The first cocktail recipes are written down, mostly using Hollands (genever-style gin)

1820s – The British in India start to mix gin with their quinine to protect against malaria

Mid-1800s – Sweeter cocktails are very popular through the mid-part of the Nineteenth Century. Old Tom Gin features frequently as an ingredient in recipes but, towards the latter-half of the century, Dry Gins like Plymouth and Gordon's begin to appear, too

1858 – Tonic water is invented, enabling the creation of the gin and tonic

1860s – Officers of the British Navy are now mixing Angostura bitters with Plymouth Gin, to create the Pink Gin

1880s – The 1882 edition of Harry Johnson's *Bartenders' Manual* gives the first published instance of the name 'Martini' – and, although the recipe isn't what we would recognise today as a Martini cocktail, there are others such as the 'Bradford à la Martini' which come pretty close to the Dry Martini of today

Late-1800s – Old Tom Gin becomes more popular as an ingredient, with Dry Gins like Plymouth and Gordon's beginning to feature as well

1919–33 – Prohibition hits the US and the first trans-Atlantic passenger flights bring many Americans to London for cocktails and cocktail parties

1930 – *The Savoy Cocktail Book* is published in London, where the American Bar at the Savoy Hotel is the 'in' place to drink cocktails

1940s-50s – Cocktail drinking becomes popular with the older, more affluent generation. Small, strong cocktails such as Martinis and Manhattans are all the vogue

1970s–80s – The club culture of these decades sees the introduction of longer cocktails, based around fruit juices

1987 – Spicy, floral gin Bombay Sapphire comes onto the market, re-igniting interest in gin as a base for cocktails

---

Twenty-first Century – With gin coming back into vogue, and new brands constantly appearing, cocktails are re-invented, with new ingredients being brought in to match the new botanicals

2000 – Tanqueray 10 appears with whole fresh citrus fruits and chamomile among the botanicals. A new wave of innovative, unusual premium gins and cocktails catches the imagination of the public

2003 – Hendrick's, with its unusual rose and cucumber botanicals, brings some new, summery notes to the cocktail mixer's repertoire

2009 – Beefeater 24, a high-premium gin with Sencha tea as a botanical, is introduced, adding a new impetus to the creation of Twenty-first-century cocktails

---

Cocktails Today

There are so many wonderful ways to make and serve London Gin cocktails. Bartenders and mixologists all over the world are constantly coming up with new ideas and new ingredients – both reinventing the traditional cocktails which have been around for a hundred years or so, and also coming up with brand new recipes, inspired by the new wave of modern gins.

Gin is the perfect spirit with which to make cocktails – because of the botanicals. Each mixer used will enhance the botanicals; fruit juices picking up the citrus, tonic marrying with the bitterness of juniper, and so forth. The permutations are endlessly fascinating, and endlessly delicious.

Most brand websites will carry some cocktail recipes, inspired by their own products. On many websites, you can watch videos of the cocktails being made. The Gin and Tales website (www.ginandtales.com) is a good place to find videos.

But the best way to discover new cocktails, new flavours and new ingredients is to get out there and visit some of the bars where the latest ideas are being developed. Talk to the bartenders, get them to help you choose the cocktails you will most enjoy. (See *Chapter Eighteen – Where to Drink Gin in London* for ideas of where to go.) You might even like to join up with some like-minded gin lovers in a group such as The Juniper Society, and meet up regularly to share tastings and discussions (See *Chapter Eighteen* for details).

Chapter Sixteen

Mixology: Making Cocktails

WHEN you are putting together a cocktail, taste is very important indeed but it's not the only consideration. If the drink looks good and is beautifully presented in the glass, the drinker's appetite will be whetted.

The delivery really matters, too. If you're shaking a cocktail, do it with panache and really *shake* it. That way, not only will you delight your audience, but the ice will really travel the full length of the shaker, and you'll do a great job of the chilling and mixing.

If you're making cocktails at home, always remember that the most important ingredient is fun. You can be as geeky as you like in terms of what gins and mixers you employ, and what high-tech shakers and other equipment you like to use – but the experience of mixing your gin cocktails and sharing them with friends and loved ones should always be enjoyable.

Having stated the obvious, and advised you to enjoy yourself while shaking, stirring, mixing and muddling the contents of your domestic cocktail cabinet, it's important to have some basic knowledge before you start, so below, you'll find some useful terminology, and also some suggestions as to what you might need to create the perfect cocktail.

Equipment

It's not necessary to have all kinds of high-tech gadgets or esoteric items to make great cocktails. By all means, if you like them, use them. But the basic tools you need are quite simple, and it's your judgement and technique that are most important. Once you've worked on those, success is guaranteed.

Shaker
There are two basic types of cocktail shakers on the market. A simple Boston shaker comes without a strainer; other types have an integral strainer, which can be useful for keeping ice and any muddled leaves in the shaker.

Strainer
A Hawthorne strainer or simple tea-strainer is essential if you are using a Boston shaker, and is also used for double-straining (see *Techniques*).

Measure or jigger

This is essential when measuring out your ingredients. You can buy single and double measures – one measure, or shot, is equivalent to 25ml or 1fl oz. By always using the measure, you will ensure that your cocktail has exactly the right proportions of each liquid.

Bar spoon

This is similar to a teaspoon, but has a much longer handle so that it can reach to the bottom of a tall glass. You'll need a bar spoon for stirring and layering your drinks.

Muddling stick

This is similar to a pestle (which you can also use) but is a little smaller. It's used to crush fruit or herbs.

Pourer

Insert a pourer into the top of your bottles and you will be able to control the flow of the spirit.

Mixing glass

This is used for the initial stirring of a cocktail which needs to be strained before serving. You can, of course, mix in a shaker, but some people prefer to use a glass for this.

Cocktail Glasses

Cocktails come in three sizes – long, short or shot. A long cocktail will generally have more mixer than gin, and is usually served with ice and a straw. A short cocktail (often described as 'on-the-rocks' or 'straight up') will be more about the spirit, with just a small amount of mixer. The 'shot' is made up purely from spirits and liqueurs, providing the maximum hit of alcohol. I sometimes like to enjoy neat gin with an ice cube from a shot glass.

The glasses used should be of an appropriate size and shape to best suit the type of cocktail they will contain. Many recipes specify the glass to be used.

A cocktail glass with a bottle of The Botanist.

Stem Glasses

Martini glass (also known as a cocktail glass)
A Martini glass has a long stem and a cone-shaped bowl. It's not comfortable or easy to cup the bowl in your hand, and this ensures that the contents will stay cool, and won't be warmed by your hot palm and fingers.

Champagne flute
This has a long, narrow bowl on a short stem. The small mouth of the glass helps a cocktail made with Champagne to keep its bubbles for a good length of time.

Champagne coupe or saucer
A Champagne saucer is a wide, shallow bowl on a stem. It isn't very practical for keeping the fizz in a cocktail, since the mouth is so wide, but it can be a nice glass from which to sip a thick, creamy cocktail, or one made with the white of an egg, such as a White Lady.

A White Lady made with No. 209 Gin and served in a Champagne coupe.

Margarita glass
A Margarita glass has an unusual bowl, wide as a Champagne coupe at the top, and narrowing to a smaller bowl underneath. Great for layered or fruit-based cocktails, including the Margarita.

Tumblers

These are stem-less glasses with flat bottoms and straight sides, and come in different heights and widths.

Old-fashioned or rocks glass
Also described as a short tumbler, this is a short glass with a thick bottom, often used to serve an Old-Fashioned cocktail.

Collins glass
A tall, cylindrical glass used to serve long mixed drinks, such as a Tom Collins.

Highball glass

Slightly shorter and wider than a Collins glass, and taller than a rocks glass, this is ideal for serving up gin and tonic, or other drinks where gin and just one mixer feature, including a Gimlet.

Techniques

Practice makes perfect. All of these techniques are simple, but they do require a level of skill and concentration. Once they've become second nature, you can add a little flair to your style.

Building

This is a very straightforward method of making a cocktail, and simply involves putting the ingredients together in the correct order.

First, make sure that you have all the ingredients you need, and that, if required, you have chilled the glass. Measure out each ingredient carefully, and add to the glass in the order stated in the recipe.

A Pomada made with Xoriguer Gin and lemonade, served in a Collins glass.

Layering

In some cocktails, the different spirits are layered one of top of the other and, due to their different densities, they will remain separate, as in a Waterloo Sunset.

- Pour the first ingredient into the glass – But take care that it doesn't touch the sides or some may stick there and spoil the effect
- Place a spoon in the centre of the glass, resting lightly on top of the liquid, with the round end downwards and facing towards you
- Pour the second ingredient along the spoon, so that it floats on top of the first ingredient, making a second layer (rather like pouring cream so it sits on top of coffee)
- If there's a third ingredient, pour this down the spoon in the same way
- Carefully remove the spoon

Muddling

This is a technique whereby you can bring out the flavours of fruits and herbs by crushing them with a 'muddler' or pestle. The Mojito is made using this technique.

- Add fruits, leaves or berries as required to your glass, together with sugar syrup or gomme, if the recipe calls for it

- Holding the glass firmly, push down on the ingredients with the pestle or 'muddler', twisting it to break them up and release the flavours. Continue this for about 30 seconds or so
- To complete the cocktail, add crushed ice up to the top of the glass and pour in the liquid ingredients over the ice. Your 'muddled' cocktail is now ready to drink – just add a garnish, if you wish

Stirring

This technique is used when the cocktail ingredients need to be mixed and chilled. It sounds simple, but requires a degree of precision and accuracy to be done well, since there should be no fragments of ice or air bubbles in the liquid. A classic Martini is made in this way.

- Chill the glass, either in the refrigerator, or by adding a few ice cubes and some cold water. Swirl this around, then discard
- Add the ingredients to the glass in the order and amount stated in the recipe
- Use a bar spoon to stir. Some recipes call for a light stirring, and some state that the stirring should be vigorous
- Some stirred cocktails may be made first in a mixing glass, then poured through a fine strainer into the serving glass, for absolute clarity and perfection
- Add any garnish to the glass before serving

Shaking

Shaking is the best-known cocktail technique, and it's important to get it absolutely right. It's used to mix ingredients quickly and thoroughly, and to ensure that they are properly chilled before serving.

- Half fill your shaker with ice – Cubed, cracked or crushed
- If necessary, chill your glass as for stirring
- Add the ingredients to the shaker
- Take the shaker and, using both hands, one at each end so it doesn't slip, shake until you see a 'frost' form on the outside of the shaker
- Strain the cocktail into the glass and serve

Double straining

If you want to keep all traces of ice and fruit from your serving glass, use a fine mesh strainer in addition to the built-in strainer in your shaker. A Hawthorne strainer, or even a clean tea-strainer (preferably one which you only use for cocktails – make sure that there are no traces of flavours or ingredients from other recipes) will work well.

Blending

For frozen cocktails, add a little crushed ice to the blender, and then whizz the ingredients at high speed until they are of a smooth consistency. Don't add too much ice, or the cocktail will be too dilute.

Last But Not Least – The Garnishes

The finishing touch of decoration, which often adds a vital extra note of flavour to your cocktail, is all important. A garnish doesn't need to be fussy or overstated but, if it's perfectly presented, can make all the difference to how your cocktail looks and tastes.

Slices

Any round fruit, such as apples, kiwis or citrus fruits, can be cut in into halves or quarters, and then finely sliced. Choose the fruit or fruits that are appropriate for your cocktail ingredients, and then either float the slices on the surface of the drink, or sit them on the rim.

Wedges

This is a great way to add citrus fruits to cocktails. The wedge can be squeezed into the drink and then dropped in or rested on the rim. If you make a cut in the flesh of the fruit, the wedge will balance easily.

Twists

This is a great way to impart flavour to a cocktail. Peel a strip of rind from a citrus fruit, making sure that you remove all the pith. Singe the strip in a flame (this will give the zest an extra zing) and then twist it over the drink to release the essential oils. Finally, drop it into the glass.

Spirals

These take a few moments to make, but are well worth the effort as they look fantastic draped over the side of the glass or floating in the cocktail. Use a specialist canelle knife or zester to cut a long, thin strip of rind from a citrus fruit. Wind the strip around a pencil or a straw – any narrow cylinder will do. Press it the strip there for a few seconds until it has set into shape. A tricolour of lemon, orange and lime peel spirals looks wonderful in a fruit-based cocktail.

Fruit sticks

Spear berries on a cocktail stick and rest against the side of the glass. You can use the same fruit, such as raspberries, or different berries, fixing them in descending order of size, from strawberry to blueberry.

Herbs
The leaves and sprigs of herbs can make very attractive, scented decorations draped over the rim of the glass. Be careful not to overdo this, though – the scent and flavour of the herbs must enhance, rather than overwhelm the cocktail.

Flowers
There are some edible flowers which look great floating in a cocktail. Small blue borage flowers are a staple of the summer fruit cup, such as Pimm's No. 1, and a single violet flower would also work well in a light, floral cocktail.

Frosting
Dip the rim of the glass in a saucer of lime or lemon juice. Then, spread the sugar or salt on a plate and rub the rim of the glass over it so that it is coated. Use a lemon or lime wedge to take off any excess frosting from the inside of the glass, so that it won't affect the flavour of the cocktail. If you want to be sure the frosting will stick, use egg white in place of the juice.

Sugar syrup

This ingredient is used as a sweetener in many gin cocktails. In the cold liquid of a chilled cocktail, it will mix in much more quickly than sugar crystals. You can buy this syrup (sometimes called *'gomme'*) in bottles but it's cheaper to make your own simple sugar syrup.

- Add one part caster sugar to one part water (250g sugar to 250ml water will make around 16 servings)
- Boil for around two minutes, stirring occasionally
- Once cooled, your sugar syrup is ready for used. If you keep it in a sterilised bottle, it will last for up to two months in the fridge

---

Classic Gin Cocktails

Please note, throughout the recipes 1 shot = 25ml or just a little less than 1fl oz

It's always best to use mixers such as tonic or soda from a bottle or a can. The 'guns' which can be found on bars utilise a concentrate which often has an inferior flavour, and the fizz isn't always great, either.

The Dry Martini

No cocktail arouses such strong feelings and so much controversy as the Dry Martini. Mixing a perfect Martini is the ultimate test of a bartender's skill, and every mixologist and gin enthusiast you encounter will have his or her theory as to the best way to do this. So, it's impossible to come up with a recipe that will satisfy everyone – although the following suggestions will provide some basic guidelines:

2½ shots of good London Dry Gin (Beefeater or Tanqueray are two different styles that work well)
½ shot dry vermouth
Olive or lemon twist (always a source of controversy as to which is the appropriate garnish – if you opt for the lemon peel, it's probably best just to twist the peel over the drink so that the zest lightly coats the surface)

Fill a mixing glass two-thirds full of ice and pour in all the ingredients. Stir to mix, and then strain into a chilled Martini glass. See notes above as to garnish.

If, like Winston Churchill, you believe the only way to make a Martini is to fill a glass with ice cold gin, the following, very strong alternative recipe may be appealing:

1 shot dry vermouth
4 shots London Dry Gin

Fill a cold metal shaker with cracked ice and pour in the vermouth so that it covers the ice. Strain out the vermouth and discard. Add the gin, stir for around 10 seconds and then strain into a chilled Martini glass.

Despite what you may have heard about James Bond and his preferences, stir, don't shake! Many cocktail experts believe that to shake a Martini will 'bruise' the gin and destroy the integrity of the flavour. A stirred Martini will be just as cold, and far smoother and silkier than one which has been shaken.

Though in this Martini recipe, the vermouth has been discarded, it's surprising how very different the result will taste as opposed to chilled neat gin. Add an olive for garnish.

Gibson

The simple addition of a pickled cocktail onion will transform your Dry Martini into a Gibson cocktail.

Did you know?

The Martini first came on the scene in America in the latter-half of the Nineteenth Century. Bartenders' manuals from the 1880s give recipes for a cocktail called a 'Martinez' typically made with Old Tom Gin, bitters, Italian vermouth and sugar syrup. It's often thought that the Dry Martini is a direct descendent of the Martinez – the 'z' and the sweeter ingredients being lost in translation, so to speak. However, there were other recipes in these manuals, for such cocktails as the Marguerite and the Bradford à la Martini, which come much closer to the Dry Martini we would recognise today. (The Bradford à la Martini in the 1882 edition of Harry Johnson's *Bartenders' Manual* lists one part Old Tom Gin, one part vermouth, four dashes of orange bitters and lemon peel as its ingredients.) So, perhaps the Martinez is more of a 'cousin' than a direct relation.

There's also a story that the Martini-Henry rifle – notorious for its vicious 'kick' when fired – might have inspired the Martini's name. In fact, it's much more likely that the cocktail was named after the Italian vermouth. The exportation of Martini vermouth to America began in the 1860s, and the Martini & Rossi company vied with Noilly Prat to gain control of the US market. They ran intensive advertising campaigns, including one in 1904 which reminded drinkers that a real Martini could only be made with Martini vermouth.

The Vesper Martini

In the Ian Fleming novel, *Casino Royale,* secret agent James Bond ordered a Dry Martini in a deep Champagne goblet. He asked the bartender to make it with three shots of Gordon's Gin, one shot of vodka and half a shot of Kina Lillet. He wanted his Martini shaken, not stirred, and garnished with lemon peel.

This iconic moment has firmly imprinted itself on the mythology of the Martini. But attempts to recreate the Vesper (named for Vesper Lynd, Bond's love interest in the novel) have been disappointing – it comes across as rather soft and low key, and not at all the extra strong and perfectly-made cocktail that 007 was after.

The key to this lies in the changes in the ingredients which have taken place since 1953. American cocktail guru Dave Wondrich has experimented with an export strength (47% ABV) Gordon's, a 50% ABV Stolichnaya Vodka, and also added a pinch of quinine to Lillet Blanc so that it comes closer to the now unavailable Kina Lillet. The results are much more satisfactory. However, guru Dave advises against shaking, as 007 demands. Stirring is best, if you want a smooth and delicious Vesper.

Dirty Martini

A delicious variation on the classic Dry Martini – but go steady with the olive brine, as just a drop too much and you will overpower the drink. This would be an interesting one to try with Gin Mare.

2½ shots gin
½ shot dry vermouth
1 tsp olive brine
1 olive, to garnish

Place the ingredients in a mixing glass with some ice, strain into a chilled cocktail glass and serve with the olive garnish.

Vermouths

Let's talk about some of the different varieties of vermouth – so important in the Martini cocktail. Vermouth is wine which has been infused with herbs, alcohol, sugar, caramel and water. It's a speciality of both Italy and France, and comes in three types – dry, sweet and half-dry. Dry is pale in colour; sweet is red; and half-dry, as you would expect, is somewhere between these two, resembling a rosé wine in colour. It generally has an ABV of around 40%.

For the making of Martinis, it's dry vermouth that's needed. There are several brands on the market, and most have been around for a long time. Sacred Spirits Company have recently introduced a new English Vermouth, and it's likely that other producers will follow suit as the Gin Craze continues.

The name 'vermouth' comes from '*Wermut*', the German name for the bitter herb wormwood, which is used to add flavour to the drink. Fortified wines with wormwood were popular in Germany as early as the 1500s. A hundred years later, similar products were being made in Italy – and, by the mid-Seventeenth Century, vermouth was drunk in England, too.

Martini

Not to be confused with the cocktail of the same name, this is an Italian brand of vermouth first produced by Martini and Rossi in Italy in 1863, at a distillery near Turin. Martini comes in several varieties – Bianco and Rosso are probably the easiest to find and the best known – but the perfect mixer for your Martini cocktail is Martini Extra Dry. This vermouth was launched on New Year's Day, 1900. It's straw-coloured, with a sharp perfume of raspberry, lemon and iris and as the name suggests, it's extremely dry, with just a hint of bitterness.

Noilly Prat

Made in France, this dry blend of white wines, fruits, herbs and spices has been around since 1813, when Joseph Noilly first came up with the recipe. It has a delicate, complex and very dry flavour and is still produced in the South of France. Noilly Prat is often described as 'The Rolls Royce' of vermouths.

Before blending, the white wines are aged in large oak barrels for eight months. They are then transferred to smaller casks which are left outside, exposed to the weather, for a whole year. Through this process, the wines take on a deep amber colour. When the ageing is complete, they are blended with fruit essences and more than 20 herbs and spices.

Noilly Ambre Vermouth has a slightly darker hue, and is a little sweeter.

Dolin de Chambéry

Dolin is another historic brand of vermouth, made in the Alpine hills near Chambéry since 1821. It was awarded an *appellation d'origine* in 1932. Chambéry vermouths were very popular in the 1800s and early-1900s, and Dolin is the last remaining example of the style, which is very light and dry, and less pungent that some of the other vermouths.

The herbs and plants in the locality give a light, fresh quality to the vermouth, which has a subtle, bittersweet palate.

Lillet

Lillet Blanc is the dry version of the Lillet vermouths, which hail from the French village of Pondensac, where they have been made since the end of the Nineteenth Century. The wines for Lillet are aged in oak vats for 12 months, before blending with fruit liqueurs, herbs and spices. It has a warm, golden colour with hints of candied orange peel, honey, lime, mint and pine among the flavours.

Not to be confused with Kina Lillet, which James Bond demanded for his 'Vesper' Martini. Kina Lillet, which was stronger in flavour, is no longer produced.

Sacred Spiced English Vermouth

This new creation from the Sacred Spirits Company in Highgate uses English wine from the winery at Chapel Down in Kent as a base. It has a rich, bitter flavour profile, with hints of cinnamon, chocolate, aniseed and mint and uses organic wormwood and thyme among other herbs and spices.

Fernet-Branca

Some bartenders like to use this bitter Italian digestive when making cocktails. Created in 1845 and still made to the same family recipe, Fernet-Branca is made with grape spirits and 27 botanicals. These include aloes, myrrh, rhubarb and quinine bark.

Did you know?

Queen Elizabeth the Queen Mother is reputed to have been fond of a drink. She is said to have had her own particular favourite cocktail – a gin and Dubonnet. Dubonnet is a wine-based aperitif like vermouth, but much sweeter. The Queen Mother liked to have this mixed with two parts of Dubonnet and one of gin, and would usually have her first of the day around noon. Later in the day, a more traditional Martini with just a sensation of vermouth – à la Winston Churchill – would be her preference – followed by several glasses of Champagne.

More Classic Cocktails

Alexander

You may be more familiar with a Brandy Alexander, but the gin version is delicious, too, and dates back to around 1915.

1½ shots gin
1 shot cream
1 shot crème de cacao (white)
Grated nutmeg or chocolate shavings, to garnish

Put all the liquid ingredients into a shaker with cracked ice. Shake well and strain into a Champagne saucer. Sprinkle with nutmeg or chocolate.

You may also like to try frosting the rim of the Champagne saucer with sugar and lemon juice for this one.

Aviation

1½ shots Dry Gin
½ shot maraschino liqueur
½ shot crème de violette
½ shot fresh lemon juice

Shake with ice and strain into a chilled cocktail glass.

Did you know?

This recipe appeared in America during the First World War, when the early aviators were being praised as heroes for their efforts in dropping grenades over enemy encampments. It was first mixed by bartender Hugo Ensslin at the Hotel Wallick in New York, and was published in his book, *Recipes for Mixed Drinks*, in 1916.

Aviation Gin (see *Chapter Eleven*), one of the first of the new wave of hand-crafted gins, was inspired by this cocktail.

Bramble

This cocktail was created in the mid-1980s by Dave Bradsell. It's perfect for some of the newer floral and spicy gins, and a lovely one to enjoy in autumn, when the blackberries are bejewelling the hedgerows.

2 shots gin
1 shot fresh lemon juice
½ shot sugar syrup / 1 tsp caster sugar
½ shot crème de mure

Put the gin, lemon and sugar syrup or sugar into a shaker with crushed ice. Shake, then strain into a rocks glass filled with crushed ice. Drizzle the crème de mure over the ice very slowly, to create a marbled or 'ripple' effect. Garnish with a lemon slice and some fresh blackberries.

Dog's Nose

1 pint Guinness / stout
2 tsp brown sugar
1–2 shots London Dry Gin, to taste (a robust gin like Bulldog or Beefeater would be ideal)
Grated nutmeg, to garnish

Pour the Guinness or stout into a large, sturdy tumbler. Heat in a microwave for around one minute. Add the sugar and gin, stir gently. Garnish with grated nutmeg. You can experiment with this one – try porter, pale ale or even bitter as as subsitute for the Guinness and see which you prefer.

What the Dickens?

This unusual mixture may sound a little odd, but it works very well indeed, that's why it's still around over 200 years since its creation. Charles Dickens mentions a Dog's Nose in his *Pickwick Papers*.

Gimlet

This very simple, classic cocktail has an interesting history – in the Nineteenth Century it was drunk on board the ships of the British Royal Navy and Merchant Navy as a preventive against scurvy, which is a disease caused by lack of Vitamin C in the diet. The Gimlet's pragmatic origins haven't prevented it from becoming a

---

Did you know?

Rose's Lime Juice Cordial was invented by Lauchlin Rose in 1867, when he discovered a method of preserving fruit juice without using alcohol. In that very same year, a law was introduced requiring all ships of the Royal and Merchant Navies to give a daily ration of lime juice to their crews. Soon, British sailors were known all over the world as 'limeys'.

Ordinary sailors drank rum, but the officers were allowed gin – which would have been Plymouth Gin. British Royal Navy Surgeon General Sir Thomas D. Gimlette, KCB, who served between 1879–1913, is said to have experimented with adding gin to the officers' lime juice ration to make it more palatable – hence the 'Gimlet' cocktail.

popular way to enjoy gin. Philip Marlowe, Raymond Chandler's fictional detective in the 1930s-50s, was very fond of a Gimlet.

1 shot Plymouth Gin
1 shot Rose's Lime Juice Cordial

Fill a mixing glass three-quarters full with ice cubes, and pour the two ingredients over. Stir well, and strain into a chilled Martini glass. Garnish with lime slice or peel.
Don't be tempted to try this one with fresh lime juice, it doesn't work!

Gin Fizz

A 'Gin Fiz' [sic] cocktail first appeared in the 1887 edition of *The Bar-Tender's Guide or How to Mix all Kinds of Plain and Fancy Drinks* by Jerry Thomas. At that time, it would probably have been made with Old Tom or Hollands Gin and, through the early-1900s, became a very popular drink.

2 shots dry gin
½ shot fresh lemon juice
Dash of sugar syrup / ½ tsp caster sugar
Soda water, to top

Shake the gin, lemon juice and sugar syrup/caster sugar with ice. Strain into a Collins glass and top up with soda water. You can use Old Tom Gin for this recipe, too – but you won't need as much sugar syrup.

Ramos Gin Fizz

The Ramos Gin Fizz hails from New Orleans, and was created in 1888 by the bartender, Henry C. Ramos. It's a much more complex drink to make than the ordinary Gin Fizz, and it's crucial to get all the ingredients absolutely right.

2 shots dry gin
1oz double cream
1 egg white
½ shot fresh lemon juice
½ shot fresh lime juice
2 dashes sugar syrup / 1 tsp caster sugar
3 drops of orange flower water
Soda water, to top
Cocktail cherry, to garnish (optional)

Add the ingredients (except the soda water) to a shaker with plenty of ice, then shake hard for two minutes. Strain into a chilled Collins glass and top up with the soda. Garnish with a cocktail cherry, if you wish.

If using Old Tom Gin, reduce the amount of sugar being used.

Gin Rickey

This is another cocktail from the early years of the Twentieth Century, and it's based on a Joe Rickey cocktail – which was made with Bourbon whiskey.

2 shots dry gin or Old Tom Gin
¾ shot fresh lime juice
4oz soda water
Dash of sugar syrup / ½ tsp caster sugar, optional
Lime wedge, to garnish

Pour the liquid ingredients into a chilled Collins glass and lightly stir. Garnish with the lime wedge. If you are using dry gin, you might want to use a dash of sugar syrup and add it with the liquid ingredients.

Hanky-Panky

As created by Ada 'Coley' Coleman of The American Bar at the Savoy, for theatre manager, Charles Hawtrey.

1 shot vermouth
1 shot dry gin
2 dashes of Fernet-Branca
Twist of orange peel, to garnish

Shake well over cracked ice, and strain into a chilled cocktail glass. Twist orange peel over the top. 'The real hanky-panky'!

Long Island Iced Tea

This is a classic of the 1970s – named for the US's longest island in New York State. It doesn't contain any tea, although the taste resembles that of a non-alcoholic iced tea drink – hence the name. Long Island Iced Tea been extremely popular over the last four decades, and has been the inspiration for many other complex mixed drinks.

½ shot gin
½ shot vodka
½ shot rum
½ shot triple sec
1½ shots sweet and sour mix
Splash of Coca Cola
Slice of lemon, to garnish

Mix the ingredients together with some ice in a glass. Pour into a shaker and shake briskly once. Pour into a Collins glass, ensuring that there is a little fizz at the top. Garnish with a slice of lemon.

Did you know?

Sweet and sour mix is a cocktail ingredient which can be bought ready-mixed, but it's very easy to make your own:

225g sugar
225ml water
225ml lime juice
225ml lemon juice

Mix sugar and water until the sugar is completely dissolved. Add the lime and lemon juices and keep in the fridge to use as required.

If you prefer not to use sweet and sour mix in this recipe, you can replace it with:

½ shot fresh orange juice
½ shot lemon juice
1 tsp of sugar syrup

Maiden's Prayer

This has been resorted to by many an ardent young man since the early 1900s, and it's listed in *The Savoy Cocktail Book*.

1½ shots London Dry Gin
½ shot Cointreau
½ shot lemon juice
½ shot orange juice

Pour into a shaker with cracked ice and shake briskly. Strain into a chilled cocktail glass.

Monkey Gland

The Monkey Gland is a creation of Harry MacElhone, of Harry's New York Bar in Paris. It was named after a controversial surgical treatment of the time, intended to give gentlemen's vitality a boost by transplanting tissue from monkey's testicles... a procedure which fairly soon fell into disrepute!

1½ shots gin
1½ shots fresh orange juice
3 dashes absinthe
3 dashes grenadine
1 tsp sugar syrup / 2 tsp caster sugar

Put everything into a shaker with cracked ice. Shake very well for 10 seconds and strain into a chilled cocktail glass. If you are using a sweeter style of gin, you may prefer to dispense with the sugar syrup.

Negroni

1½ shots gin
1½ shots Campari
1½ shots red vermouth (Cinzano or Martini Rosso)
Crushed ice
½ slice orange, to garnish

Stir the liquids gently in a mixing glass filled with ice. Pour everything, including ice, into a cocktail glass and garnish with a slice of orange.

The gin, Campari and vermouth work so well together that, no matter what brands of gin or vermouth you use, you will always get a great result, making it a very good cocktail to experiment with.

Did you know?

The iconic and deliciously simple Negroni cocktail was created in Italy in around 1920. At that time, one of the most popular cocktails there was the Americano, made with Campari, sweet vermouth and soda water. One of the regular drinkers at the Bar Casoni in Florence, a certain Count Camillo Negroni (reputed to have lived for some years in America , where he made his living as a rodeo rider), always ordered an Americano, but asked the barman to replace the soda water with gin. Soon everybody was asking for their Americano to be made 'Negroni-style' – and the Negroni was born.

Old-Fashioned

1 sugar cube, brown or white, as preferred
2 dashes Angostura bitters
1 tsp water
2 shots dry gin or geneva gin

Put the sugar cube in the bottom of a rocks glass with the bitters and the water. Muddle until the sugar has dissolved. Pour the gin into the glass and add two ice cubes. Let the Old-Fashioned rest for a couple of minutes before drinking.

This was one of the most popular American cocktail recipes in the 1880s. The 'Old-fashioned' style of glass is named after it.

Pegu Club

The earliest reference to this cocktail is in Harry MacElhone's *Barflies and Cocktails*. In the 1920s-30s, the Pegu Club in Burma was a popular haunt of colonials. If you visit SoHo, New York, you'll find a bar of the same name, presided over by cocktail guru, Audrey Saunders, which serves great cocktails with 'house-made' bitters and tonic water.

2 shots gin
1 shot Cointreau
½ shot fresh lime juice
1 dash orange bitters
1 dash Angostura bitters

Pour all ingredients in a shaker with crushed ice. Shake well and strain into a cocktail glass.

Pink Gin

This is a very traditional British drink, sometimes known as 'Pinkers'. Like the Gimlet, its origins are naval. Angostura bitters were prescribed as a remedy for

---

Did you know?

Pink Gin or 'Pinkers' gained its name from the reddish-brown dregs of Angostura bitters that remain in the glass after the cocktail has been drunk. Bitters were considered a useful remedy for all types of digestive upset, and were popular in many of the British Colonies. In British Malaysia, Pink Gin was known as 'Gin Pahit' – 'Pahit' being the Malaysian word for 'bitter'.

Did you know?

'Bitters' are alcoholic beverages flavoured with herbal essences. Once very popular as patent medicines, they are now considered as digestifs, rather than remedies. With an ABV of around 45%, they have always been popular as cocktail flavourings. Angostura bitters – made to the same recipe since 1824 – are probably the best known, but there are many other brands and flavours.

The Bitter Truth make an exceptional range of all types of bitters, and even offer a 'Traveller's Set' for enthusiasts. You can view and purchase all of their products on their website – www.the-bitter-truth.com – where you will also find some unusual cocktail recipes which use bitters.

Gerry's of Old Compton Street carry a very wide range of bitters from all over the world.

---

seasickness and, of course, it made perfect sense for the officers to combine their prophylactic dose of bitters with a glass of gin.

1½ shots Plymouth Gin or London Dry Gin
1 dash Angostura bitters

Take a rocks glass, and swirl the bitters around in it. Discard the residue of bitters and add the gin.

Singapore Sling

This deliciously refreshing cocktail was invented around 1915 by Ngiam Tong Boon, one of the bartenders at the famous Raffles Hotel in Singapore. At the time, one of the ingredients would have been fresh pineapple juice from Sarawak pineapples, which added a luscious frothiness to the drink. By the 1980s, this element had been lost, with bottled juice used, and sometimes dispensed with completely. Now that longer cocktails using plenty of fresh juice are back in vogue, it looks like the Singapore Sling can return to its former glory.

1 shot gin
1 shot cherry brandy
1 shot Benedictine
1 shot lime juice
Soda water, to top
Lime peel, spiralled

Stir the shots with ice cubes in a chilled shaker, then pour without straining into a Collins glass and top with chilled soda water. Garnish with a lime peel spiral.

For a more old-style take on the **Singapore Sling,** try something a little closer to the original recipe:

1½ shots gin
½ shot cherry brandy
¼ shot Cointreau
¼ shot Benedictine
4 shots fresh pineapple juice
½ shot fresh lime juice
⅓ shot grenadine
1 dash Angostura bitters

Pour into a cocktail shaker with ice. Shake, then strain into a Collins glass, filled with ice.

Tokyo Tea

There are many different types of 'teas' and one of the most colourful – and alcoholic – is the Tokyo Tea.

2 shots Midori
1 shot London Dry Gin (Tanqueray 10 is a good choice)
1 shot vodka
1 shot rum
1 shot tequila
1 shot triple sec

Pour the ingredients into a shaker filled with ice, shake and strain into a Martini glass.

Tom Collins

On a hot summer day, there are few drinks as refreshing as a classic Tom Collins. A close relation of the Gin Fizz and the Gin Rickey, it's mentioned in the 1876 edition of Jerry Thomas' *The Bar-Tender's Guide.*

2 shots London Dry Gin
1 dash sugar syrup / ½ tsp caster sugar

½ shot fresh lemon juice
Soda water, to top
Lemon slice, to garnish

Mix gin, lemon juice and sugar syrup in a Collins glass which is three-quarters filled with cracked ice. Top up with soda water, garnish with a lemon slice, and serve with a long spoon.

A Twenty-first Century take on this old cocktail is the **Elderflower Collins**.
2 shots gin (one of the modern, floral ones such as Bloom would work well)
2 shots lemon juice
½ shot elderflower cordial
1 tbsp sugar syrup / 1 tbsp caster sugar
Soda water, to top

Mix the shots with cracked ice in a Collins glass. Top up with soda water, stirring as you add.

Waterloo Sunset

A view from Waterloo Bridge as the sun goes down at the cocktail hour, encapsulated in a glass – and a delicious and very beautiful way to celebrate London Dry Gin, The River Thames, and London itself.

¾ shot London Dry Gin
½ shot elderflower cordial
4 shots Champagne
¼ shot crème de framboise
Raspberry fruit stick, to garnish

Stir the gin and the elderflower cordial in a cocktail shaker filled with ice. Strain into a Champagne flute. With a bar spoon, pour the Champagne over this so that it floats on top. Carefully drip the crème de framboise into the glass using a bar spoon so that it sits in a narrow layer above the gin and elderflower cordial. Garnish with a raspberry fruit stick.

It would be great to end this cocktail section as the sun goes down over London. But alphabetically, that won't work. There's one very important cocktail still to come. As you turn away from the glorious sunset over the river, why not continue your evening with a luscious White Lady?

White Lady

The White Lady was created in the 1920s by Harry MacElhone, while working at the legendary Ciro's Club in London before moving to Paris and setting up the legendary Harry's New York Bar.

2 shots London Dry Gin
¾ shot Cointreau
¾ shot freshly-squeezed lemon juice
1 tsp sugar syrup / 1½ tsp sugar
½ egg white
Lemon twist or spiral, to garnish

Shake with plenty of ice and pour into a Martini glass. Serve with a lemon twist or spiral.

This frothy, smooth white cocktail zings with the freshness of lemon and the sweetness of the Cointreau. It's been the inspiration for many other cocktails, too, including the **Boxcar** which substitutes lime juice for lemon juice, adds a dash of Grenadine, and requires the maker to sugar the rim of the glass.

Chapter Seventeen

Nurse Gin

A SIDE from the pleasure and relaxation gained from drinking gin, the spirit has always had a reputation for certain medicinal qualities.

Perhaps the most common claim for the healing properties of gin comes from the many people who recommend a small glass – preferably neat or poured over a lump of ice – to be sipped before a meal. This will soothe and calm the stomach, and act as a perfect apéritif.

Did you know?

Alcohol is one of the first remedies people will turn to when they are feeling low and depressed. It can be a great comfort, and give a nice lift, too, but it isn't always the best option. Alcohol is a depressant and, while relieving symptoms in the short term, in the longer term, if used to excess, it can make the symptoms worse, as well as causing harm to the body.

Childhood Gin Remedies

Until relatively recently, a drop of gin would be given to babies and toddlers to relieve colic and teething pain. There are many people who can remember those days. I heard a friend, now in her 70s, recall that, if she was unwell and fractious as an infant, her grandfather would step in and offer help to her exhausted parents: 'I know what the babby needs,' he'd say. He would pour out a small measure of gin, heat it up with the fireside poker, and then offer it to her to drink.

Another friend tells how, when he was a child, his mother would make hot poultices with gin, and apply them to boils – with great success. He describes the fresh, herbal, clean smell of the poultice, which he found soothing and almost healing it itself. Perhaps it was just the application of heat that helped to draw off the pus from the boil – but alcohol is, of course, a very good disinfectant.

In the Twenty-First Century, gin as folk remedy has made a huge comeback. Gin-soaked raisins as a palliative for the pain and discomfort of arthritis are all the rage. You can find thousands of recipes and testimonials for the remedy on the internet.

Did you know?

In the Seventeenth Century, before the over-indulgences of the Gin Craze, there was a strong link between distilled spirits and medicine. The only mention made of gin in Samuel Pepys' famous diary is in a medicinal context.

On 10th October, 1663, he writes that he was suffering from constipation and pain in making water. Samuel's colleagues recommended 'strong water made of juniper'. In typical, unabashed Seventeenth Century language, the diarist records the results: 'Whether that ... did it, I cannot tell, but I had a couple of stools forced after it and did break a fart or two.'

Gin and Arthritis

US radio icon Paul Harvey first gave the gin-soaked raisins remedy a publicity boost when he mentioned it on his show in the 1990s. In 2004, the remedy entered the political arena, when Teresa Heinz Kerry (wife of the US Democratics Presidential candidate, John Kerry) ended a discussion on health care in Nevada with a mention of a 'highly effective' remedy for arthritis. Her championing of gin-soaked raisins amused her audience and delighted the political bloggers.

But Teresa's words have been echoed many times over by delighted arthritis sufferers who believe they have been cured by this simple homemade remedy.

How to make the gin-and-raisin arthritis remedy

- Take a handful of golden raisins, sometimes called 'white' raisins. (The ordinary black raisins are not suitable)
- Place the raisins in a shallow container or bowl and cover with gin
- Leave the raisins to soak for six weeks until all the gin has evaporated
- Cover the bowl with a piece of cheesecloth or a coffee filter (to protect against dust and flies) and put in a safe place where it will be kept at room temperature
- Finally, eat nine of the gin-soaked raisins every day. (The number nine seems a bit arbitrary, but it crops up in most of the recipes for this cure)

Most arthritis sufferers who have had success using this remedy, report that it took several weeks – or even a couple of months – before the benefits became noticeable.

There haven't been any scientific studies to support the claims for this remedy, but there are a number of theories as to why it might seem to have so much value:

Grapes – from which raisins are made – contain chemicals which are known to be pain-relieving and anti-inflammatory.

Golden or 'white' raisins are treated with sulphides, which help to slow down the natural browning process as the grape becomes a raisin. Before the advent of antibiotics, sulphur-based drugs were commonly used to reduce infection and inflammation.

Gin is made with juniper which is used in herbal medicine as a diuretic, and to reduce inflammation and gas in the stomach. It is also believed to ease joint and muscle pain.

It's important not to forget the **placebo effect**. When people believe strongly that something will help them (and it's very clear that they do believe in the efficacy of gin-soaked raisins from the wealth of testimonials on the internet) their brains release endorphins and these will act as natural pain relievers.

It's important to remember, too, that arthritis is a condition which is subject to flare-ups and remissions. Any improvement, which seems to be the result of eating nine gin-soaked raisins a day, may simply be due to a period of remission which might have happened anyway.

A cautionary note

If you're considering trying the gin-soaked raisin remedy to help with your arthritis, do consult your doctor first. There may be contra-indications if you are receiving other drugs as part of your medical treatment, or if you are experiencing any liver problems or reddening of the joints. It's wise to consider any complementary treatments as an addition to, rather than a replacement for, the medical help your doctor can provide.

The Lady's Friend

In the days before the Abortion Law Reform Act in 1967, an unwanted pregnancy could spell disaster for an unmarried girl, or a wife who was already struggling with a large family. If you didn't know a kind and reliable back-street 'Vera Drake' or didn't have the resources to pay a discreet Harley Street practitioner, you had to turn, frightened and helpless, to the old folk remedy – gin and a hot bath.

You filled the tub with scalding water, and forced yourself to get into it, bottle of gin in hand, ready to drink down as much neat gin as you could manage. If you did undergo a miscarriage as a result of this, it was more like to be as a result of shock – similar to that you'd experience if you tried the other folk remedy for an unwanted pregnancy, throwing yourself down the stairs.

The mostly likely results of taking hot baths with liberal doses of gin would be a bad scalding and then, some months later, a live baby suffering from foetal alcohol syndrome.

Juniper

Juniper, the signature ingredient of London Gin, is still available today as a herbal remedy. It's considered to be a very good natural diuretic, and has also been used for upset stomachs, bloating, kidney and bladder stones, heartburn, loss of appetite, and also joint and muscle pain.

It's not advisable to take juniper in large quantities, or over a long period of time. It can cause kidney problems and seizures, and may also irritate the skin if applied externally.

As with any other complementary remedy, only take juniper after consultation with your doctor. It should not be taken if you are already using diuretics, if you are pregnant or breast-feeding, if you are scheduled for surgery within two weeks, or if you have problems with stomach disorders, blood pressure or diabetes.

Did you know?

Juniper oil has been used to induce abortions. It may be the juniper berries used in the distillation of gin which led to the spirit's use as a remedy for unwanted pregnancies.

Juniper pills – under the name of 'The Lady's Friend' could be found for sale on the small-ads pages of women's magazines, right up until the 1980s.

Please Note: The above mention of juniper as a remedy for unwanted pregnancy is included for historical interest only, not as advice or a recommendation. Under no circumstances would I recommend the use of juniper pills or oil without medical supervision.

Chapter Eighteen

Where to Drink Gin in London

HERE are details of four top London bars – each has a completely different ambience, but all provide a fantastic gin-drinking experience.

Graphic Bar

www.graphicbar.com

4 Golden Square
London, W1F 9HT
020 7287 9241
info@graphicbar.com

Also on Facebook and Twitter

A stone's throw away from Soho, location of some of the Eighteenth Century Gin Craze's most momentous events, the stylish Graphic Bar is right at the heart of today's Gin Craze.

Did you know?

The Juniper Society (www.junipersociety.com) is a great way to learn more about gin, juniper, genever and all related subjects with congenial company in the very pleasant surroundings of the Graphic Bar. It's an informal group which meets for special events at Graphic on the second Monday of every month. Its aim is to bring together people who love juniper – and a typical night will comprise a very mixed bunch of enthusiasts, from complete novices to industry professionals and long-time connoisseurs. A different brand or style of gin or genever is featured at each meeting and, afterwards, there are cut-price gin and tonics and Martinis made with the featured brand. Check the Juniper Society or Graphic Bar websites for further details, or check on the Facebook pages.

Situated in Golden Square, just a couple of minutes walk from Piccadilly Circus or Oxford Circus, Graphic hosts one of the largest collections of gins in the UK. The gin cocktails are elegant and scrumptious, with new recipes a speciality of the experienced and very knowledgeable bar staff and there's a simple but delicious food menu, which perfectly complements the cocktails. As you sip and sup, you can feast your eyes on some stunning contemporary art exhibits, as Graphic regularly showcases the work of well-known urban artists.

It's a perfect place to drop by after work or a shopping expedition – but be prepared to want to stay all evening! In summer, the front windows roll back to open up the bar to the night air, and there's a spill-over area on the pavement outside. It's a bright and welcoming venue in winter, too.

The Hoxton Pony

www.thehoxtonpony.com

104–108 Curtain Road
London, EC2A 3AH
020 7613 2844
info@thehoxtonpony.com

The Hoxton Pony is run by EastEnder Gerry Calabrese, and, as you might expect from the creator of the controversial Hoxton Gin, it makes a strong style statement. It's situated in the trendy Shoreditch area of the East End, and regularly plays host

Bottles of Hoxton Gin line up to start work at the Hoxton Pony.

to well-known faces from the fashion and music worlds. Even if there aren't any celebrities in, the neon blue-and-purple lighting gives a certain glamour to the ambience, making everyone look like a rock star or supercool fashion model.

There's a cocktail bar and lounge at ground level with a club area downstairs. The Hoxton Pony is an ideal venue for younger fans of gin and gin cocktails to enjoy a night out – the latest music is playing, and the bar staff are young and hugely enthusiastic about all the fantastic cocktails available. Whether you are in a group, or turn up solo, you are sure of a welcome.

Check the website for details of The Hoxton Pony's quirky twist on the classic English tea party, with unique cocktails served up in vintage china teacups, accompanied by cupcakes. Look out for 'Birthday' nights, too – when anyone is welcome to drop by and celebrate, whether it's their birthday or not. And – if you want to eat something to balance the cocktail intake – there's a great food menu, featuring satisfying and well-cooked English bar meals.

Portobello Star and The Ginstitute

www.portobellostarbar.co.uk

171 Portobello Road
Notting Hill
London, W11 2DY
020 7229 8016
portobellostar@gmail.com

*The Portobello Star
ground floor bar.*

Portobello Road Market

The popular London market runs on weekdays between 8:00am-6.30pm with a half-day closing at 1.00pm on Thursday. It's also open on Saturday between 8:00am-6:30pm and this is by far the busiest day, when the market can become very crowded.

The Portobello Star – once a traditional Notting Hill pub – has been transformed by bartender and gin guru Jake Burger into a mecca for fans of the cocktail.

The downstairs cocktail bar is long and thin, stretching back from the pavement, but the atmosphere is great and the cocktail menu (based around Jerry Thomas' 1862 *The Bar-Tender's Guide*, one of the very first books on the subject to be published) is a joy. The cocktails are classics, or classics with a modern twist – and the mock-historical descriptions on the menu are almost as delicious as the contents of the glass. (For more of this entertaining retro theme, see the website.)

In the unlikely event that you can't find anything you like on the cocktail menu, chat to the bartenders, and they will work out what will best suit your tastes. This is definitely not a bar where the staff 'know better' and try and impose their ideas on you. They're very knowledgeable indeed, but they're there to help out and make sure you really enjoy your drinks.

The atmosphere is very relaxed and convivial at the Portobello Star. There's usually plenty of old-school classic tunes playing, and sometimes a DJ at weekends. You can lounge on black leather seats, sit outside if it's sunny, or perch on bar stools and chat to the staff.

A word of caution – when the Portobello Road Market is up and running, the bar can get very busy.

The Ginstitute

This little gem of a Gin Museum/snug bar is situated on the floor above the cocktail bar. It's a recreation of a Victorian Gin Palace,

The Ginstitute Snug Bar, upstairs at the Portobello Star.

complete with dark wood and gleaming mirrors. It houses a huge collection of old gin bottles and other artefacts, including lots of advertisements from the Nineteenth and Twentieth Centuries. Pride of place must go to Jerry Thomas' calling card, a memento of one of the pioneers of the cocktail – known as the 'Genuine Yankee Professor'– who visited London in 1859.

It's free to visit the Ginstitute and look at the exhibits, and you can call in during the day and do so. Pre-booking is necessary for evening visits, or if you would like to have cocktails served in the Ginstitute. For further details, see the Portobello Star website.

If you are inspired by your visit to the Portobello Star, you might like to book yourself in for a session with Jake Burger in the Still Room on the top floor, where you can make your very own blend of premium gin under his expert guidance. (See *Chapter Twenty-one – Blend your Own Gin* for more details.)

The antique bar stove at the Ginstitute.

Rules Bar

www.rules.co.uk

35 Maiden Lane
Covent Garden
London, WC2E 7LB
020 7836 5314

Rules Cocktail Bar is situated over the famous restaurant of the same name – one of the best-known eateries in London.

The Cocktail Bar has an old-world, understated, dark wood interior with a timeless, elegant atmosphere and it's a really relaxing place to sit and sip on a beautifully made Martini. The cocktail list is short, only around 10 recipes, and most of them are classics. If you have a special request, though, the bartender will probably make it up for you. There is a superb collection of ingredients behind the bar, with absinthe, eau-de-vie, rare bitters and unusual vermouths featuring, all of which guarantee that your cocktail will – like the bar itself – bring the very best of the classic cocktail age into the Twenty-first Century.

Perfect for drinks before or after dinner – and you don't have to venture far afield if you are hungry. The restaurant downstairs specialises in game, oysters and other traditional British dishes.

Did you know?

Rules Restaurant claims to be the oldest restaurant in London. Established more than 200 years ago it's been owned by three families. The Rule family founded the restaurant then, just before the First World War, Charles Rule swapped it for an eaterie in Paris and Tom Bell (handing over his Alhambra Restaurant to Charles) took over. Tom had to leave the head waiter in charge while he did duty through 1914–18 in the Royal Flying Corps, but Rules survived and stayed open through the Second World War, too – supplementing the statutory 5 shilling rationed meals with liberal servings of rabbit and game, which weren't rationed. Tom Bell's daughter took over, eventually selling Rules to the current owner, John Mayhew, in 1984.

Hotels

Since the Golden Age of cocktails, many famous and influential people have enjoyed a drink in the beautiful bars of London's finest hotels. Again, each of the four I've chosen has a very different ambience; but all are elegant, inspiring, very welcoming and serve superb cocktails.

An important point – don't turn up at one of these hotel bars in jeans and trainers, or sportswear. Smart casual is the dress code, and you may be turned away if you don't observe it. But who'd want to dress down in such sophisticated surroundings?

The Connaught

www.the-connaught.co.uk

16 Carlos Place
Mayfair
London, W1K 2AL
020 7314 3419 (Cocktail Bar)

The décor of the Connaught's Cocktail Bar is inspired by the Cubist Art Movement and by Irish art from the 1920s. It's a shimmering, pastel gem of a place, with gleaming leather chairs to sit in, and walls of platinum silver overlaid with soft pink, pistachio and lilac. Everywhere you look, you'll find many exquisite design details.

The attention to detail extends to the cocktails. If you order a Martini, the waiter will make it at your table, pouring gin and vermouth into your ice-cold glass and offering you the choice of an extensive range of bitters should you care to add a dash to your drink.

You can choose from traditional or newer-style cocktails, and the range of ingredients is outstanding, including many vintage Champagnes. If you are hungry, complementary bar snacks are provided and you can also order from a menu based around the cuisine of South-west France. The Connaught Bar is a perfect place to linger and relax at any time, but its soft pastel hues are especially alluring around dusk – the cocktail hour.

The Dorchester

www.thedorchester.com

Park Lane
Mayfair
London, W1K 1QA
020 7629 8888

The Dorchester celebrated its 80th birthday in 2011, and its luscious, opulent bar maintains a reputation for being one of the capital's most fitting locations in which to 'see and be seen'.

Don't be put off by the name, which has something of reputation for exclusivity. If you visit The Bar, you'll see a very diverse clientele. There will be couples quietly sipping a pre-dinner drink, high-flying business men chatting at the bar, and groups of friends relaxing after a stroll in the Park. The Dorchester Bar is sophisticated, but it's very welcoming, too.

Did you know?

The Dorchester Hotel was built in 1931. During the Second World War, due to the use of thick reinforced-concrete in its construction – a very modern building technology at the time – the Dorchester was thought to be one of the safest places in Blitz-torn London.

The Dorchester Bar's décor is based around tones of aubergine, black and brown, complemented by gleaming mahogany and plenty of mirrors. The bar itself stretches out in a long, inviting curve and houses one of the largest selections of wines and spirits in London – including the Dorchester's own brand of Old Tom Gin. You can choose classic or new cocktails from the menu, and they will be made for you with great expertise and panache by an award-winning team of bartenders.

Duke's

www.dukeshotel.com

35 St James's Place
London, SW1A 1NY
020 7491 4840

Tucked away down a little side-street, Duke's Hotel is one of the hidden gems of London. As you walk into the elegant, timeless hall you'll see a door on the left with 'Cocktail Bar' above it and, if you step through, you will be in for a fabulous cocktail experience.

Did you know?

Ian Fleming, author of the James Bond spy novels, was a frequent visitor to Duke's Bar. Alessandro Palazzi has created a 'Fleming 89' Martini to celebrate the link. The drink was created in partnership with Floris perfumiers, whose '89' Eau de Cologne was a favourite of 007.

The intimate, timeless Duke's Bar specialises in Martinis. Bartender and Martini-legend Alessandro Palazzi is one of the world's best at mixing this classic drink. If you want to know how to do it, just watch him or one of his team mix one for you, and appreciate the simplicity and the total attention to detail that makes for perfection.

The American Bar at the Savoy

www.fairmont.com/savoy-london/

91–92 Strand
London, WC2R 0EU
888 265 0533 (freephone)
savoy@fairmont.com

The Savoy's American Bar has survived the recent multi-million pound revamp of the Hotel relatively untouched – and its blue-and-gold Art Deco environs are still buzzing with the elegance and passion of the 1920s Cocktail Age.

The Bar's legendary figures Ada 'Coley' Coleman and Harry Craddock were famous for their superb cocktails in those golden years. One of the traditions begun by 'Coley' was that of making signature cocktails to celebrate particular people or special events, and the American Bar's current team are continuing with this.

In April 2011, the Bar Manager Daniel Baenreuther created a Royal Tribute Cocktail to celebrate the wedding of Prince William and Kate Middleton. Ingredients included Bombay Sapphire Gin, Martini Rosso, Chartreuse, maraschino and Champagne.

Did you know?

Harry Craddock's work *The Savoy Cocktail Book*, written in the 1930s, is a wonderful record of the recipes of the time. The book is still available today and is frequently consulted by modern mixologists looking both to recreate the tastes of the past, and also seeking inspiration for dazzling new cocktails.

Gin Palaces in the Twenty-first Century

If you want to step back in time to the century before the great Cocktail Age, you can still find and enjoy some of the old Gin Palaces in London's West End. They operate as pubs now, but many retain a substantial amount, if not all, of the original fixtures and fittings. These fittings are usually of a slightly later date than those that Dickens would have seen, since most of them were created in the late-Victorian era, but all boast a glorious glitter of etched and engraved glass, and are agleam with polished mahogany. They immediately evoke the 'light and brilliancy' Dickens describes. Above and beyond this, each of these historical gems offers something special all of its own – an atmosphere and a style that is very distinctive.

Several of these pubs, like The Salisbury, lie close to the heart of London's Theatreland, and are ideally situated for a pre- or post-show gin. The Red Lion is close to the Houses of Parliament – and the location of the some of the slums which gave so much concern to government at the time of the Gin Acts. The Gin Palaces outside central London are also worth a visit.

Central London

The Argyll Arms

18 Argyll Street, London, W1F 7TP
020 7734 6117
www.nicholsonspubs.co.uk/theargyllarmsoxfordcircuslondon/

Within a short stroll from Oxford Circus, this pub was built in 1742, and takes its name from the second Duke of Argyll, who once had a mansion on the site of the London Palladium. The present day building is Victorian, and the interior offers a fascinating insight into the social divide of that time. You can still sit in the 'snug' areas which were designed to separate the upper and lower classes.

Rumour has it that, at one time, a secret tunnel linked the Argyll Arms to a nearby theatre.

The Princess Louise

208–209 High Holborn, London, WC1V 7BW
020 7405 8816

Built in 1872, The Princess Louise is a jewel of a late-Victorian Gin-Palace-style pub, named after Queen Victoria's fourth daughter. The interior has been renovated with outstanding authenticity.

The architect, Arthur Chitty, created the original interior of The Princess Louise in 1891, employing only the top craftsmen of his day and using tiles made by Simpson & Sons and glasswork from Morris & Son.

Similar care has been lavished on the pub's recent restoration. Thanks to the Princess Louise's current owners, Samuel Smith, the Yorkshire brewers, she still has her original Victorian layout. Even the discreet cubicles for private imbibing, which were stripped out several decades ago, have been replaced and the sparkling etched and cut-glass panels are exactly as they would have been in the late-Nineteenth Century.

You really will feel as if you have stepped back in time when you visit The Princess Louise. You'll be surrounded by the finest cut and gilt mirrors, and every inch of available wall space is covered by richly decorated tiles; ornate plasterwork; and gleaming, high-quality joinery. This lavishness extends even to the toilets – which are Grade II* listed in their own right.

The Red Lion

48 Parliament Street, London, SW1 2NH
020 7930 5826
www.redlionwestminster.co.uk/

This classic late-Victorian pub is located halfway between the House of Commons and Downing Street, so it's a perfect oasis for a weary tourist exploring the landmarks of Westminster – though it can get quite busy when Parliament is sitting. With Downing Street so close, it's tempting to imagine the Prime Minister dropping by, but you are more likely to see a less-famous MP. They do call in, as The Red Lion offers TV broadcasts from Parliament, (not intrusive, as they are silent) and also a division bell to call them back to the House when important votes are happening.

The interior retains solid hardwood fittings, broken up by carved wood and insets of decorative glass, with some fabulous cut and etched mirrors. You will also find some amusing political prints on the walls.

The Salisbury

90 St Martin's Lane, London, WC1N 4AP
020 7836 5863
www.taylor-walker.co.uk/pub/salisbury-covent-garden/c3111/

The Salisbury is another outstanding example of a late-Victorian Gin Palace. Situated in the heart of the West End's Theatreland, it's a great place to pop into for some refreshment if you are taking in a show.

Built in 1892 as a restaurant, The Salisbury was subsequently revamped into a pub six years later. Its huge, glittering mirrors, the fantastic cut and etched glass to be found everywhere, and the gleaming mahogany furnishings create a dazzling and extravagant interior, which offers a delightful oasis of 'light and brilliancy' – to quote Dickens – amidst the bustle of St Martin's Lane.

Particularly striking are the Art Nouveau light fittings; the electric lights are supported by beautiful bronze nymph figures holding long-stemmed flowers, with light bulbs at their centre. Victorian customers would have been in no doubt that this was the very latest in luxury and design when they popped in for their dram of gin.

West London

The Prince Alfred
5a Formosa Street, London, W9 1EE
020 7286 3287
www.theprincealfred.com/

The Prince Albert is situated on a quiet street close to the canal at Little Venice and the Paddington Basin Development. Dating from 1863, The Prince Alfred's façade has bowed windows crafted from etched glass. At the time it was built, plate glass was a new invention, and was used to create an impression of wealth and sophistication. The tall front window still makes a spectacular impression as you approach the pub.

Inside, there are five bar compartments, separated by wooden partitions. Each bar has its own access from the street. As at The Argyll Arms, this reflects the Victorian insistence on segregation, not just of gentleman and ladies, but of upper and lower classes also. Special 'snob screens' over the bar counter ensured even

---

Did you know?

Ins and Outs of London by W. O'Daniel, published in 1859, gives an amusing insight into the consumption of gin by females in the mid-Eighteenth Century. Not all of them were lucky enough to enjoy the seclusion of a private 'snug'. And, clearly, some preferred to opt for home consumption.

> *In the gin palaces, bars are always put up for ladies' use. The common girls of the city are by no means admitted to the ladies' bar; they must stand at the common bar among crowds of men ... At a large establishment I once enquired the number of sales averaged at the ladies bar. I accidentally spoke to the proprietor; he handed me a written account, which he had been keeping for his own instruction and amusement. This was an account of sales from two casks. From one of the casks were drawn only the drinks; from the other, all liquor that was to be carried away from the store by respectable women. From the retail cast, or the ladies' drink cask, the small drinks had averaged ... sixty-three gallons – the contents of one cask – every four days. From the other cask, in pints and quarts, had been drawn on an average for the same length of time thirty gallons a day. This was all gin – that being the general drink of the ladies.*

---

more privacy and anonymity. To be seen drinking by your inferiors – or perhaps by your superiors, too – was a definite no-no.

The Prince Alfred who gave his name to this outstanding building was the second son of Queen Victoria. In 1862, aged 18, he became Duke of Edinburgh and was also elected King of Greece. He declined to take up the throne, but ruled as the Duke of Saxe-Coburg and Gotha from 1893–1900.

South London

The King's Head
84 Upper Tooting Road, London, SW17 7PB
020 8767 6708
www.taylor-walker.co.uk/pub/kings-head-tooting/c1215/

This large Victorian building, dating from 1896, resembles a palace more than a pub – complete with an ornate canopied balcony at the front for the reigning monarch to stand upon when waving to his or her subjects. The architect responsible for the extravagant flight of fancy that is The King's Head was W.M. Brutton, and the building reflects the exuberant style for which he was famous.

The cavernous interior retains many original features, though the modern world has taken over to some extent with Sky 3D available on TV screens – but the atmosphere on a non-football day is calm and it's easy to relax in one of the typical private nooks and muse on bygone days, surrounded by gleaming old tiles and the usual abundance of engraved and embossed glass.

Crossbones Graveyard
Redcross Way, London, SW1
www.crossbones.org.uk/

This is one of the most unusual and evocative environments in which to drink a glass of gin in London – and it has a resonant and fascinating connection with the history of the spirit.

Walk along Redcross Way, a tranquil backwater of a street running parallel to Borough High Street at 7pm on the 23rd of any month, and you will encounter an unlikely-looking group of people carrying flowers, musical instruments – and bottles of gin. They will be heading for the iron memorial gates that mark the entry to Crossbones Graveyard.

Crossbones Graveyard was in use from the Sixteenth Century. At that time, it was unconsecrated ground, and was known as a burial place for single women – or, to be more specific, for the prostitutes who frequented the area. These prostitutes were called 'Winchester Geese' because they were licensed by the Bishop of Westminster to work within 'the Liberty of the Clink' – an area outside the jurisdiction of the City of London, where brothels, theatres and such activities as bull-baiting flourished. By the mid-Eighteenth Century the land had been consecrated, and served as a cemetery for the paupers of St Saviour's parish.

In 1853, Crossbones Graveyard became so full that it was no longer usable, and it was closed. The site lay forgotten for many years until, in 1990, the extension of the Jubilee Line brought it to light again. Archaeological excavations revealed a highly overcrowded burial ground, with bodies – mostly those of women and children – piled on top of each other.

A 2010 BBC documentary, *Crossbones Girl*, focussed on a quest to find the identity of one of the bodies found in the graveyard – a young woman who had most likely been a child prostitute.

The future of Crossbones Graveyard looks uncertain – the site is likely to be developed in the near future – but the Friends of Crossbones are fighting to keep at least part of the land, including the memorial gates, for posterity.

In recent years, the gates have been transformed into a communal art-work representing a shrine, and you will always find them decorated with flowers, messages and mementoes – including offerings of bottles of gin.

Since 2004, an informal group has held a 7pm vigil at the Crossbones gates on the 23rd of each month. People gather there to honour the 'outcast' women who are buried in the graveyard. The drinking of gin, and the sprinkling of the spirit over the ground is an important part of the vigil. It's an extraordinary experience to join the group in Redcross Way (one of the most notorious slums in London in the Nineteenth Century, despite its tranquillity today) and to sip your gin as you pay your respects to the dead women – many of whom would have lived out their harsh and precarious lives at the time of the Eighteenth-Century Gin Craze.

Chapter Nineteen

Where to Buy Gin in London

YOU CAN go to any supermarket and pick up a bottle of gin. Most supermarkets offer their own brands, plus some of the traditional favourites, and many, at the time of writing, will also stock the premium gins, too. Sainsbury's sells Sipsmith and Blackwood's Vintage Dry Gin. Waitrose has a very good range, too, including Sipsmith and Hoxton Gin. You can also find additive-free Fever-Tree Tonic in many supermarkets today.

There are also a number of very good online options, if you are looking for unusual gins. **The Whisky Exchange** (www.thewhiskyexchange.com) offers all the classic London Dry Gins, plus some Spanish, American and Celtic varieties. **Gerry's Wines and Spirits** which is based in a wonderful shop on Old Compton Street (see below), has an even greater range, with around 60 gins on its listings (www.gerrys. uk.com). And a lot of the smaller distilleries, such as Sacred Spirits, Sipsmith and also Plymouth have a mail order option available on their websites. (See *Chapters Ten* and *Eleven* for details.)

These options are convenient and quick. But, if you love London Gin, why not treat yourself to a really special experience, and visit one of the retailers in London, where you will find yourself steeped in the history of the spirit? It's well worth taking the time and trouble to go to one of London's specialist shops where you will not only pick up a little of the atmosphere of bygone eras, but will also have the benefit of a superb, friendly service and an outstanding level of knowledge.

Gerry's Wines and Spirits

74 Old Compton Street, Soho, London, W1D 4UW
020 7734 2053/4215
info@gerrys.uk.com
www.gerrys.uk.com

In London's Soho, not far from Frith Street – where, when it was known as Thrift Street, one of the worst Eighteenth-Century gin riots took place – you will find a small shop that has been a legend for alcohol aficionados for more than 25 years.

Gerry's is an Aladdin's Cave – an absolute treasure trove for the lover of distilled spirits. As you venture from vibrant, bustling Old Compton Street into the dim interior, you'll see that the walls are lined with shelves from floor to ceiling, and that

The exterior of Gerry's Wines and Spirits.

every available inch of those shelves is crammed with glinting bottles containing rare and unusual products of the distiller's art. You'll find some familiar labels there, alongside the weird and wonderful, and you can browse at leisure. Gerry's stocks the UK's largest selection of spirits and liqueurs.

There are always several assistants on duty behind the small counter facing the door. They are incredibly welcoming, knowledgeable and enthusiastic. Between them, the staff share more than 45 years of experience in the drinks trade; many of those years spent working at Gerry's. If you're after a particular type of unusual gin, not only will Gerry's probably stock it, and be very familiar with what makes it special and different, but they'll have a couple of similar brands to tempt you as well. Alongside the gin selection, you'll find some interesting Dutch genevers – and again, the staff will answer any questions you may have.

If you want to know what's happening in the world of gin, what new brands are about to emerge – just ask. Gerry's prides itself on being the first to stock the 'next big thing.' They were the first retail outlet to sell the ground-breaking Sacred Gin from Ian Hart's micro-distillery.

Gerry's

Gerry's was opened in 1984 by Greek Cypriot Michael Kyprianou, a landmark figure in the bohemian Soho of the 1960s. Previously, Michael managed Del Monico's, another off-licence (but no longer trading), a few doors away on Old Compton Street, where he started in 1959.

In the 1960s, just like Gerry's today, Del Monico's was famous for carrying a very wide range of spirits. However, some of the unusual bottles on the shelves came from an unconventional source – British Customs. If you came back from your foreign trip with too many bottles of the local spirit, you would have them confiscated. Often, rather than pouring the contents away, the Customs officials would get on the telephone to Michael and let him know what they had. So long as he could drive to the airport and pick them up himself, Michael could buy these confiscated liquors for a nominal sum.

Del Monico's became so notorious for stocking exotic spirits that queues of customers would stretch all down Old Compton Street and police with loud hailers would often turn up to keep them in order. Not perhaps such a frightening scene as back in 1738, when magistrate De Veil had to read the Riot Act just around the corner in Frith (then Thrift) Street – but an interesting echo of the past.

Now retired, Michael still has a very strong connection with Gerry's, and frequently calls in. If you are lucky, you may encounter this legend from the Swinging Sixties when you make your visit.

Gerry's usually have some bottles open for tasting, and they are very happy to share the experience with customers, so you will probably get lucky on your visit. On Friday and Saturday afternoons, there are often more specialised tasting sessions, which are always very interesting. However, the shop can get busy on Friday and Saturday, as connoisseurs hurry in to buy their supplies for the weekend, so, if you want to take your time browsing the shelves and enjoying a detailed chat with the expert and friendly staff, it's probably better to choose a quieter time.

The shop front is quite modest – there are no glaring signs attempting to pull you in off the street – but an incredible number of customers find their way inside. Some of them are almost as interesting as the rows of miniatures that line the shop window. Apart from the regulars and the passing tourists who beat a path through the door, you may also spot a famous performer from a show at one of the nearby West End Theatres dropping by to pick up a bottle, or a barman from one of the local hotels or clubs looking for an exciting ingredient for a new cocktail. If your arms

Leading brands of the current Gin Craze lined up on the shelf at Gerry's.

don't feel quite up to the strain of carrying home all the gins that you want to try, you can always order online later – and, after your visit to the shop, you'll be much better informed about your purchases.

Berry Bros. & Rudd

3 St James's Street, London, SW1A 1EG
0800 280 2440
www.bbr.com

Primarily a wine merchants, Berry Bros. & Rudd of St James's is one of the most remarkable establishments in London. Very little has changed at No. 3 since the business was first opened there, more than 300 years ago, by a lady named the 'Widow Bourne'.

As soon as you step through the door into the calm, wood-panelled interior, you'll notice the antiquity of the steeply slanting wooden floorboards. It's hard not to stand for a moment and just soak up the atmosphere, before you move on to look more closely at some of the Eighteenth Century engraved portraits hanging on the wall. Before too long, a polite and very helpful assistant will be at your side offering help and also directions, if it's gin you are seeking, to the Spirits Room. It isn't just the surroundings that are so redolent of the past – the service at Berry Bros. & Rudd also harks back to a more courteous age.

Did you know?

The Scales at Berry Bros. & Rudd.

One slightly unusual service offered to customers in the past was the opportunity to weigh themselves in the large coffee scales, which still stand near the entrance at Berry Bros. & Rudd. Originally used for weighing coffee, tea and spices, the scales are almost as old as the shop itself. Since bathroom scales are a relatively recent invention, gentlemen – including such celebrities as Lord Byron and the Aga Khan – would hop onto the leather-covered seat when they called in to purchase their wine. The *Register of the Weight of the Customers of this Establishment,* dating back to 1765, is still kept at the shop and fills several ledgers. It makes fascinating reading, with notes such as 'without hat' and 'thin clothes' added next to the pounds and ounces. Some ladies' weights are also logged, but it was mostly gentlemen who called in at the shop.

The shop was founded in 1698 – just a fraction before the run-up to the Gin Craze of the Eighteenth Century. Close to St James's Palace, it provided a handy source of much-needed luxury items such as coffee, tea and spices to the nearby St James's Palace, which was then surrounded by green fields. In the mid-Eighteenth Century, the Berry family, who were wine merchants, married into the business – and the Rudds came on board in the 1920s.

Beneath the shop are two levels of ancient cellars. These house some of the more valuable wines, as well as providing space for the many educational events hosted by Berry Bros. & Rudd. When Napoleon III was exiled from France, he used one of these cellars as the base from which he organised his coup d'état – no doubt availing himself of some of the best vintages during his stay.

Despite the long tradition, and the obvious focus on the past that permeates the shop, Berry Bros. & Rudd have always been at the forefront of new developments. They were the first wine merchants to have a website and to sell online, and have also pioneered a very successful online fine-wine trading platform, BBX or Berry's Broking Exchange, where customers are able to sell their wines that are stored in the company's bonded warehouses. They can set their own prices, but BBX offers a free valuation service.

This spirit of innovation extends to the Berry Bros. & Rudd Spirits Department. In 1923, they developed Cutty Sark whisky and, more recently, Glenrothes single malt whisky and The King's Ginger liqueur have been added to the list. And in July 2010, in response to director Simon Berry's desire for a gin that would deliver a supremely good Martini, Berry Bros. & Rudd launched their premium gin, No. 3.

The Spirits Room has just a few very select gins for sale. They have been carefully chosen so that each offers something special, and there is no overlap between the types. Their own-brand 'Good Ordinary Gin' and the premium No. 3 hold pride of place. You will also find Hayman's Old Tom and Plymouth Navy Strength (57% ABV). From Holland, Bols Geneva is represented, and also, when I visited, a five-year-old genever from the Zuidam Distillery. Though you might find more gins on sale in other outlets, these represent a very good selection of the different types available. And it's well worth chatting to the highly-knowledgeable Spirits staff.

As you leave, follow the narrow passage at the side of the shop leading into Pickering Place – the smallest public square in London. As you walk down, you can see the remains of a Tudor tennis court, still visible in the wall. And the tiny square itself gives a real feel of the courts and alleyways of Eighteenth-Century London. There are two large Victorian era gaslights which are still operational.

Did you know?

Another delight at Berry Bros. & Rudd is a collection of items from a miniature Edwardian wine cellar. It contains tiny bottles of vintage wines and Champagnes, all listed just as in a real cellar – but the entries are written in a dolls' house-sized ledger. There is even a miniature bottle of Berry Bros Finest Sloe Gin, dated 1903. It's almost two-thirds empty now. The angels have taken their share, as they say in the whisky business.

Chapter Twenty

Holding a Gin Tasting

MOST of us have a favourite gin. We love it, it's probably been around in our lives for a long time, and we feel we know it very well. Some of us, myself included will have an everyday staple on the shelf or in the drinks cabinet – but will keep a selection of other brands for special occasions. I also like to keep a stock of the gins that I know are particular favourites of my family and friends.

But have you ever worked out what exactly it is that you like about your favourite? What makes up that quintessential flavour that gives us so much pleasure? And why there are so many new brands emerging, all boasting of their uniqueness and 'premium' quality? A tasting may help to answer some of those questions.

It's one thing to invite some friends round, open a few bottles, and enjoy chatting about the impressions you are getting from what you are drinking. There's nothing wrong with that – it's really good fun. However, if you are prepared to invest a little time preparing and organising the arrangements for your tasting session, you and your friends will gain far more knowledge and satisfaction from the experience.

Have a clear goal. If you are not very experienced and don't know a lot about gin, start with some of the basic brands for your first tasting, as outlined below. As your palate becomes more sophisticated, you can move on to some of the suggestions at the end of the chapter.

Warming up the Palate

To help your guests get the most out of the tasting, introduce them to some of the important botanicals before they start on the gin samples. This will help them to recognise each flavour note in the gins.

A useful selection would be:

- Juniper berries – Indispensible, since they give gin its defining flavour
- Dried orange and lemon peels – A refreshing note of citrus zest
- Coriander seed – Again, very characteristic of many gins
- Cardamom – A slightly stronger spice
- Powdered angelica root – Not such a familiar flavour, but an important one for your guests to get to know
- Powdered orris root – As above

Juniper berries, coriander seed and dried cardamom pods can all be found in the herb-and-spice section of most good supermarkets. Orange and lemon peels can be prepared by gently drying them in a warm oven. Ground angelica root and orris root may be a little harder to come by, but there are many suppliers of herbal products online who stock them. *You should be able to source what you need from www. spice-master.com/ or from www.thespiceshop.co.uk/.*

Arrange the botanicals in small dishes in the middle of the table. They'll add a lovely note of colour and depth to your tasting – a great reminder of the exotic history of gin.

Savouring the Smell

Start with the juniper berries. Invite everyone to pick up a couple and crush them between their fingers, sniffing the volatile oils that are released. Let them really savour the clean, pine freshness of the wrinkled berries.

Take your time with this. It's really worth focussing on the complex aromas. Some whisky experts prefer to use just one nostril when 'nosing' – either the left or right, whichever works best. You may want to experiment with this. What gives you the most intense experience of the juniper, left nostril or right? Or are you happiest when using both?

Did you know?

Our sense of smell and taste are closely linked – and smell dominates. You can prove this by taking some cinnamon-flavoured sugar, and eating it while holding your nose. (Or use a diver's nose clip, if you've got one.) You'll certainly pick up sweet, since it's one of the five flavours our taste buds recognise – (sweet, sour, salt, bitter and umami) – but that's all. Then release your nose and taste again. Bingo – there's the cinnamon.

Next, let your guests twist some of the orange and lemon peels, to catch the zesty brightness of the citrus oils – a great contrast to the juniper.

As you experience each botanical, ask each person to describe the different aromas. Everyone will have a slightly different response. Our sense of smell is very much related to experiences we've had in the past. Most people will associate juniper with the fresh, green ambience of a walk through a conifer wood as they crush the berries. Everybody will recognise the marmalade tang of dried citrus peels. As you move on to the cardamom, anyone who loves Indian food will be reminded of the delicate fragrance of pilau rice. They'll probably be very familiar with the scent of coriander, too.

Did you know?

Another way to get to know the individual botanicals would be to use botanicals which have already been distilled. An Open Sauce Traditional Gin Blending Kit from Sacred Gin (www.sacredspiritscompany.com) contains separate distillates of juniper, coriander, citrus, angelica, liquorice and cardamom. Sampling the delicious aromas and flavours of these isn't such a tactile experience as handling the raw botanicals, but it's a great way to get your palate tuned-in.

Things get more complex with the less familiar smells. Angelica, for instance. It reminds me of my Grandfather. It makes me recall the smell of his coat, which was impregnated with pipe smoke. But, for someone else, angelica might evoke a hayfield in summer, or the interior of an old church, fragrant with incense. Orris root is often said to smell like Parma violets. I'm not sure if I agree – my memory of the childhood tube of little violet sweets is very vivid, and doesn't quite fit with the subtlety of the ground orris. I think it smells – not unpleasantly – like stale tea leaves, but that's a very personal opinion, and is tied to a childhood memory of our kitchen cupboards at home.

Preparation

If you're a newcomer to gin-tasting, don't be too ambitious for your first session. Four or five gins, including some of the well-known varieties, will be plenty. If you're already an expert, you might prefer to use some of the more unusual suggestions at the end of this chapter. But, for an initial session, I would suggest:

- A well-known, popular staple, such as Beefeater London Dry Gin or Gordon's London Dry Gin – These classic gins with a standard range of botanicals are a good place to start
- Something also well-known, but a little different – Bombay Sapphire, and Hendrick's are both very popular, and each has its own very distinctive quality
- Sloane's Gin – It has separately distilled botanicals. How has the distillation process affected the way the botanicals come through? Can you tell the difference?
- One of the new luxury premium gins – Berry Bros. & Rudd No. 3, Beefeater 24, Tanqueray 10 or Sacred Gin would all fit well here
- For a lively contrast, and if you want to be really adventurous – Hoxton Gin, with its strong hit of coconut and grapefruit, or Gin Mare, bringing a breath of olive and herbs from the Mediterranean, will work well

- Another possibility is to offer one of the higher-alcohol gins – Such as Plymouth Navy Strength or Blackwood's Superior Strength Vintage. But keep the portions small!

Did you know?

The samples should be chilled before you try them. You mouth acts almost like a distilling column as you savour a sip of cold gin. First, the light, volatile notes of citrus will come through, followed by juniper and spices. Finally, you will get the deeper and less volatile oils that need more warmth to release – orris and angelica.

For each guest you will need:

- A row of Cognac or wine glasses (see below) containing a small amount of each gin to be tasted. (Make sure *you* can remember which is which, by arranging the glasses and filling them carefully in order)
- Some bottled still mineral water – One bottle for each taster. (Not tap water as the chlorine can deaden the taste buds)
- A small bowl to act as a 'spittoon' for anyone who is driving afterwards

---

Useful tip for tastings

The best type of glass for a tasting is one that concentrates the aromas, while also allowing space between your nose and the surface of the spirit. If your nose is too close, you will experience an 'alcohol burn' in your sinuses. If the glass is short and squat, like a rocks or shot glass, the aromas will dissipate into the air. So a glass around 5fl oz in capacity and quite tall and slender in shape is ideal. Cognac glasses, wine glasses, or Champagne flutes work well. A brandy snifter might seem the obvious choice, but though it concentrates the aromas well, it doesn't allow much room between the nose and the liquid.

The glasses must be completely clean, since any remnants of other drinks will contaminate your sample. You will either need to have a clean glass for each gin, or be prepared to wash up between samples. Plastic 'glasses' will avoid the necessity for this, but you could find that the petroleum products that are used to make the polyurethane will give off a taste that can spoil the subtle aromas and flavours of the gins.

- A piece of paper or notebook to make 'tasting notes' is very useful – It's easy to get confused after trying two or three different samples and your guests will find it helpful to be able to refer back
- Some bread or mild-flavoured crackers to cleanse the palate between samples. (Nothing too salty, as highly-flavoured and salted snacks can blunt the sensitivity of the taste buds)

Blind Tastings

To get the most out of the session, make sure that your guests have no idea which gins are in front of them. A blind tasting takes a bit of organisation, and you will need to take careful note of each round of tasting so you can remember which gin is which. It's well worth the effort, though, to preserve the anonymity of the gins. Your tasters won't have any preconceptions as they try the different samples and there may be some interesting surprises in store for them.

It's best to conduct the tasting around a table, rather than relaxing in comfy chairs. Then, you can keep track of exactly what's happening, and your guests will find it much easier to focus on the experience.

Before your guests arrive, lay out the glasses or plastic cups in a line in front of each guest's chair, and fill from left to right, starting with the staple old favourite, and moving through to the more unusual gins. You may want to make a note of which gin is in which glass in the line-up, so you don't get confused when things get going.

Useful tip: size matters

Think 'small' when embarking on a gin tasting. It's about tasting, rather than drinking. It's all too easy to get extremely tipsy in a very short time, which may be fun, but rather defeats the object. Use just enough spirit to swirl around in the bottom of the glass. And sip, rather than gulp.

A Cautionary Note – If anyone taking part in the tasting is driving, it's advisable for them not to swallow the gins, but to spit them out, as at a wine tasting. Do make this point very clear – it's easy to lose track of how many sips you may have had during the tasting. It doesn't take many to push you over the limit.

The Tasting

Once you've acquainted yourself with the botanicals, it's time to start tasting the gin. Some experts like to try gin neat. It's up to each individual whether or not they want to do this. If they are happy to, that's fine, but a lot of people are not used to the strong burn that neat alcohol causes in the mouth, and may find this a problem. It's a good idea to add around the same amount of water as you have gin in the glass. This will dilute the ABV down to around 20% and will bring out the aromas and tastes inherent in the gin.

With each sample, 'nose' it first. Invite your tasters to discuss what aromas everyone is picking up. Is the sample spicy? Citrusy? Or does is resonate with the bitter, piny tang of juniper, which the tasters will all recognise from the berries you have just crushed? Make sure you write down your initial impressions. This will help you to focus, and will act as a very useful record. By the fifth sample, you'll probably have completely forgotten whether it was the second or the third that smelled strongly of citrus!

Then, taste the sample (with or without water) at room temperature:

• What are the flavours that are coming through for all of you?
• Which do you recognise?
• Can you detect any of the botanicals you have just been sniffing?

When everyone has had a chance to speak, ask them to warm their glasses in the palms of their hands. After a couple of minutes, taste the gin again. How has it changed? It can take time for all the different botanicals to come through, and heat can affect this process. Temperature has a very great effect on the flavour – gin taken straight from the freezer has a much longer 'taste profile' than gin which hasn't been chilled.

Go through the same process with all of the gin samples. How do the flavours differ? What about the textures? Are some gins more 'oily' than others? Do some have a quality which seems to be all their own – where the botanicals are combining to almost create a new flavour? Make sure to keep up your written notes.

When you have tried all the gins and compared your impressions, you can bring out the bottles, and show your guests what they've been sampling. They may be quite shocked at the new viewpoint they've gained on an old favourite, and also at how much they may have enjoyed (or possibly disliked) a gin they would never have thought of trying without your encouragement.

At this stage, you may also like to bring in the tonic and try it with the different brands, to see how the botanicals work with the bitterness of the quinine. How does the tonic change things? Which gins hold their own most strongly? Do some of the ones that you didn't like neat work better with tonic? Or vice versa?

When you've finished your session, and are relaxing with your guests – probably with a proper drink in your hand at last – you might like to refer to some of the tasting notes in the Directory of Gins which you read earlier in the book. How do your results compare with the experts, and with what the producers say about their gins?

You may well find, as the tasting session draws to a close, that you have now started your very own Gin-tasting Circle, and that you and your friends will be keen to meet up again to carry on your researches. What will you want to try next? More traditional London Dry Gins, alongside some of the new American 'artisan' gins? A selection of Scottish Gins with their unusual northern British botanicals? Dutch genevers, enjoying a long-overdue comeback after 300 years of obscurity? Sweet, old-fashioned Old Tom Gins such as Dickens might have enjoyed? There's a whole wonderful world of taste experience out there – and more exciting premium gins are emerging onto the market every year. Enjoy!

Useful tip: using a tasting chart

There's a lot happening taste-wise and sensation-wise as you sample each brand of gin. Which of the familiar botanicals can you identify? Is there anything unusual in the flavour profile? Which flavour comes through first, and which flavour are you left with at the end of the profile? How does the gin feel in your mouth? By the time you get to the end of the tasting, you may have forgotten all but the most overriding impression of each gin. Having a chart where you can note everything down can be very helpful.

On the last page of the book, I've drawn up just such a chart for you to use, or, if you prefer, you can design one of your own.

Chapter Twenty-one

Blend your Own Gin

WHILE making gin from scratch in your home by distilling neutral alcohol from a wash is illegal and highly dangerous, it's perfectly possible to create a signature gin for yourself by blending distillates. There's no risk involved, and you will be delighted with the results.

Did you know?

Making vodka by distilling grain spirit – which is the first part of the gin process – is something that shouldn't be attempted without a licence from HMRC and the proper, safe equipment. It took the Sipsmith company two years to gain their licence, which gives some indication of the complexity of the process. And it simply isn't safe to try and make vodka without adhering exactly to the regulations.

In recent years, there have been several incidents of major explosions and injuries caused by illegal stills being run. The most serious of these explosions occurred on an industrial estate in Boston, Lincolnshire in July 2011. Five men were instantly killed when a massive blast destroyed one of the units on the estate. Police investigations had already uncovered illegal and potentially lethal vodka on sale in shops in the town, and evidence was discovered in the burnt-out remains of the unit indicating that this was probably where the vodka was made. Six fire engines and 30 firefighters were deployed to the scene of the explosion, which took place only 600ft from a nearby block of flats.

Open Sauce Gin Blending Kits

www.sacredspiritscompany.com

The Open Sauce trademark belongs to the Sacred Spirits Company. Ian Hart, creator of Sacred Gin, has developed two collections of individual botanical distillates so that gin enthusiasts can experiment with making their own signature gin.

The two collections of six 20cl bottles come as boxed sets, and are available through Gerry's of Old Compton Street, or by mail order from Sacred Spirits.

Open Sauce Traditional Collection

Angelica
Cardamom
Coriander
Juniper
Liquorice
Triple citrus (lemon, lime, orange)

Blending your own gin from scratch is a fascinating challenge, and everything you need is here, with six separate botanical distillates, at ABV 40% each.

The Traditional Collection contains the essential juniper, and also the balancing, fixative angelica and spicy coriander, which are the signature notes of the classic gin flavour. Ian has created a blend of three different fruits for the citrus element, and added an extra spice with the cardamom. If you like the Old Tom style of gin, there's also liquorice, which will add sweetness and softness.

All the distillates are delicious in their own right. Each individual aroma and flavour can be savoured, and this is the perfect way to get acquainted with the traditional gin botanicals. A little ice as you sip will bring out the flavour. You can try adding your favourite distillate to Sacred Gin, to modify the taste profile, and a swirl of distillate over a gin and tonic will bring an extra flourish of your favourite flavour.

Open Sauce Contemporary Collection

Cassia
Juniper
Nutmeg
Orris root
Pink grapefruit
Star anise

Here are the distillates which you can use to create a more modern gin, in line with the Twenty-first Century Gin Craze.

There's essential juniper, of course, but Ian's replaced angelica with orris root, which has a very light, earthy scent, rather like Parma violets. Nutmeg brings the spice element, pink grapefuit the citrus, and star anise adds a delicate, fennel-like sweetness. Cassia, similar to cinnamon but lighter in quality, is particularly delicious served atop your favourite gin and tonic.

Sacred Spirits Separate Distillates – 70cl

Once you've got addicted to blending your own gin, you may find that the 20cl bottles empty very quickly. Some of the distillates are now available in a larger, 70cl size:

Angelica
Cardamom
Cassia
Juniper
Liquorice
Pink grapefuit

If you're a Martini fan, it's worth knowing that the Sacred Spirits Company also now makes a Spiced English Vermouth.

The Still Room at Portobello Star

www.thestillroom.com

Portobello Star
171 Portobello Road
London, W11 2DY
020 7229 8016

If you'd like to be guided through the 'blend your own gin' experience and have a lot of fun in the process, you can book a session with Ginstitute Curator and Master Distiller Jake Burger at the Portobello Star, 171 Portobello Road – and create your Own Recipe Gin with his help.

Ascending from the Portobello Star bar on the ground floor, you'll peep in at the delectable Ginstitute Gin Museum and small Snug Bar on the first floor, before carrying on up to the Still Room on the top floor. Here, a small copper still named Copernicus is to be found, quietly bubbling away

Botanicals in the Still Room at Portobello Star.

Distillates and bottles at the Still Room – let the blending begin. (Copernicus is just visible through the porthole.)

in his own little area. There's a large table, big enough for four or five friends to sit around, and the pristine white walls are lined with bottles and flasks of distillate.

Jake will offer you a wide selection of distillates to nose and sample – both old-style and very contemporary – and, when you've had a good chance to acquaint yourself with your favourites, he'll help you to blend a unique gin for yourself. You can take your Own Recipe bottle home with you, labelled and signed – and Jake will keep a record of your recipe so that, if you and your family and friends love

Gins of the past line the walls of the Ginsititute Museum and Snug Bar.

your personal gin, you can order another bottle at any time.

My own gin recipe's there on file – a very contemporary one, Jake advised me – but aside from saying that it was deliciously light, fragrant and zinging with notes of black pepper, I'm keeping the details a trade secret!

If you're visiting the Still Room, make sure you have enough time to take in the Ginstitute Museum as well. It's free to visit and is open between 2–6pm Tuesday to Saturday, and the small bar there operates between 9pm-12am. You can also book this lovely, evocative space for your own private party.

The Gin Blending Experience at Portobello Star is only available by prior arrangement – though it might be possible, if you are visiting Portobello Road Market on a Saturday, to drop in as soon as you arrive and arrange an ad-hoc session for later that day.

For further information, call 020 7229 8016 or look on their website.

Chapter Twenty-two

Afterword

I F YOU would like to discover more about London Gin and the other brands which are making their mark as the new Gin Craze takes off, there are a number of ways to do this.

All the gin brands have great websites to look at, and most will offer information about the gin, plus recipes and new updates. You can follow some of your favourite brands on Facebook and Twitter, too.

There are also lots of websites for gin enthusiasts, which are well worth keeping an eye on. Or, if you prefer to meet up with some fellow fanatics, why not link up with a group like the Juniper Society?

The Juniper Society

www.graphicbar.com/juniper-society.php

The Juniper Society exists to bring together all those who love spirits made with juniper. Every other Monday, the Society meets at Graphic Bar in London. Gins and genevers of all types and brands come under scrutiny, and different brand specialists from all over the world visit to share their expertise.

For more information, call 020 7287 9241, email info@graphicbar.com or visit the Graphic Bar Facebook page.

Websites for Gin Enthusiasts

www.barchick.com
Aimed at the younger female drinker, this is a fantastic site for finding out what's going on in the world of bars and clubs – and great for finding a venue. Lots of in-depth information and some great graphics.

www.drinkaware.com
Alphabetically, this one comes near the top of the list – and perhaps that's just as well, as all responsible drinkers should know about this one. Well worth looking at to keep yourself in the picture about all the health and other issues around alcohol consumption.

www.ginandtales.com
The Gin and Tales Website is run by Beefeater and Plymouth Gins. It features lots of recipes, and a Bar School where you can watch videos of mixologists making cocktails. Great for picking up hints for how to shake and stir with panache.

www.ginvodka.org
This is the industry's own website. Lots of information here; history, fact sheets and recipes.

www.gintime.com
This is a great place to find articles about everything in the world of gin, from bar reviews to gin events to the latest cocktails. Its editor is the author and acclaimed gin expert, Geraldine Coates. Recent articles have featured gin packaging, preserves made with gin, and the juniper harvest in Tuscany. There's a bar finder, too, on the site and Gintime regularly hosts events. A really interesting and informative site, and very easy to use.

www.mixellany.com
This colourful, beautifully designed and also very erudite website is a fantastic resource not just for current happenings in the world of gin, but also for online research into the history of drinks and cocktails. It's run by Jared Brown (Master Distiller at Sipsmith) and his partner, Anistatia Miller, who between them have written more than 30 books on the subject, including the two-volume *Spirituous Journey: A History of Drink*, published in 2009 and 2011. The website includes a free online library of classic texts – both contemporary and historical, a video library, a wonderful blog and a news page, plus details of the masterclasses run by Jared and Anistatia.

www.summerfruitcup.com
Summerfruit Cup is run by gin aficionado David Smith, who is a regular at The Juniper Society's fortnightly meetings. It's a wonderful medley of reviews, recipes and experiments. The site is regularly updated – every week there are new posts featuring unusual and rare gins and cocktails.

David has a project called 'World of Gin' and is attempting to try out every gin in the world and share his findings via the website. He also has a section entitled 'Raiders of the Lost Cocktail Cabinet'. You will find all sorts of oddities and delights on this website, including vintage bar equipment – an extraordinary gadget for assessing the dryness of a Martini is my particular favourite.

Bibliography

Anonymous pamphlet, *Low-life, or How One Half of the World Knows Not How the Other Half Live* (1764)

Brown, Jared and Miller, Anistatia, *Spirituous Journey – A History of Drink*, Vols 1 & 2 (2009)

Coates, Geraldine, *The Mixellany Guide to Gin* (Mixellany Ltd, 2009)

Cooper, Ambrose, *The Complete Distiller* (1757)

Craddock, Harry, *The Savoy Cocktail Book* (1930)

Culpepper, Nicholas, *The Complete Herbal* (1653)

Defoe, Daniel, *Brief Case of the Distillers* (1726)

Defoe, Daniel, *Everybody's Business is Nobody's Business* (1725)

Dillon, Patrick, *The Much-lamented Death of Madam Geneva* (REVIEW, Hodder Headline, 2002)

Ensslin, Hugo, *Recipes for Mixed Drinks* (Fox Printing House, New York, 1916)

Mabey, Richard, *Flora Britannica* (Sinclair-Stevenson, London, 1996)

Meade, Marian, *Bobbed Hair and Bathtub Gin* (Harcourt Books, Orlando, 2004)

Miller, Martin, *Born of Love, Desire and Some Degree of Madness – The Story of Martin Miller's Gin* (London, 2008)

Picard, Liza, *Dr Johnson's London* (Weidenfeld & Nicolson, 2000)

Regan, Gaz, *The Bartender's Gin Compendium* (Xlibris, Indiana, 2008)

Solmonson, Lesley Jacobs, *Gin: A Global History* (Reaktion Books Ltd, 2012)

Thomas, Jerry, *The Bar-Tender's Guide* (Dick & Fitzgerald, New York, 1862)

Walpole, Horace, *Letters of Horace Walpole to Horace Mann*

Warner, Jessica, *Craze: Gin and Debauchery in the Age of Reason* (Profile Books, 2003)

Watney, John, *Mother's Ruin* (Peter Owen, 1976)

Acknowledgements

MY THANKS to all those from the world of Gin who've been so welcoming to me and so generous both with their time and their knowledge:

Luigi Barzini, Jake Burger, Michael Eaves, Sam Galsworthy, Gerry's Wines and Spirits, Fairfax Hall, Sean Harrison, Ian Hart, James Hayman, Charles Maxwell, Sarah Mitchell, Desmond Payne, Pippa Robinson, David Smith, Adam Smithson, Myles Thomas, Hilary Whitney – and the many other people who have assisted me along the way.

Thanks also to my panel of tasters:

Susan Bentley, Francesca Chetwin, Martha Close, Julie Geraghty, Pippa Griffiths, Jenny and Tony Harpur, Anna Hope, Helen Hunt, Keith Jarrett, Olja Knesevic, Cynthia Medford Langley, Philip Macatrewicz, Janice McKenzie, Josh Raymond, Wolfgang Walter, Matthew Weait, Ginevra White

Last but not least, I must thank my editor Fiona Shoop and my agent Caroline Montgomery for their wonderful support throughout.

Index of Gins

Index